Emission Baselines

ESTIMATING
THE UNKNOWN

OECD

ORGANISATION FOR ECONOMIC CO-OPERATION AND DEVELOPMENT

INTERNATIONAL ENERGY AGENCY

ORGANISATION FOR ECONOMIC CO-OPERATION AND DEVELOPMENT

Pursuant to Article 1 of the Convention signed in Paris on 14th December 1960, and which came into force on 30th September 1961, the Organisation for Economic Co-operation and Development (OECD) shall promote policies designed:

- To achieve the highest sustainable economic growth and employment and a rising standard of living in Member countries, while maintaining financial stability, and thus to contribute to the development of the world economy;
- To contribute to sound economic expansion in Member as well as non-member countries in the process of economic development; and
- To contribute to the expansion of world trade on a multilateral, non-discriminatory basis in accordance with international obligations.

The original Member countries of the OECD are Austria, Belgium, Canada, Denmark, France, Germany, Greece, Iceland, Ireland, Italy, Luxembourg, the Netherlands, Norway, Portugal, Spain, Sweden, Switzerland, Turkey, the United Kingdom and the United States. The following countries became Members subsequently through accession at the dates indicated hereafter: Japan (28th April 1964), Finland (28th January 1969), Australia (7th June 1971), New Zealand (29th May 1973), Mexico (18th May 1994), the Czech Republic (21st December 1995), Hungary (7th May 1996), Poland (22nd November 1996) and the Republic of Korea (12th December 1996). The Commission of the European Communities takes part in the work of the OECD (Article 13 of the OECD Convention).

INTERNATIONAL ENERGY AGENCY
9, rue de la Fédération, 75739 Paris cedex 15, France

The International Energy Agency (IEA) is an autonomous body which was established in November 1974 within the framework of the Organisation for Economic Co-operation and Development (OECD) to implement an international energy programme.

It carries out a comprehensive programme of energy co-operation among twenty-four* of the OECD's twenty-nine Member countries. The basic aims of the IEA are:

- To maintain and improve systems for coping with oil supply disruptions;
- To promote rational energy policies in a global context through co-operative relations with non-member countries, industry and international organisations;
- To operate a permanent information system on the international oil market;
- To improve the world's energy supply and demand structure by developing alternative energy sources and increasing the efficiency of energy use;
- To assist in the integration of environmental and energy policies.

IEA Member countries: Australia, Austria, Belgium, Canada, Denmark, Finland, France, Germany, Greece, Hungary, Ireland, Italy, Japan, Luxembourg, the Netherlands, New Zealand, Norway, Portugal, Spain, Sweden, Switzerland, Turkey, the United Kingdom, the United States. The European Commission also takes part in the work of the IEA.

PREFACE

Climate change is one of the most significant challenges facing the international community as it seeks a path to sustainable development. The threat to our climate is broader than a simple "environmental" problem. It covers international trade, energy supply and demand, the development of new technologies and new management styles in power generation, transport, industry, agriculture, forestry and waste disposal. Ultimately it affects the way in which we conduct our everyday lives.

At the Davos meeting of the World Economic Forum in February 2000, leading government officials, industrialists and representatives of civil society voted the climate issue the most important. The G-8 meeting in Okinawa, in July 2000, focused on climate change as a key international challenge and called for concrete action to promote the ratification of the Kyoto Protocol and the mitigation of climate change.

This broad level of political, industry and academic concern has given rise to many new and innovative responses. National laboratories and private research programmes are working on breakthrough technologies such as fuel cells, new materials and unconventional energy sources. In the political arena, the focus is on the equities (and inequities) of the distribution of energy and wealth.

Two of the most innovative policies grow out of the United Nations Framework Convention on Climate Change (FCCC) and its Kyoto Protocol. The Clean Development Mechanism (CDM) combines technology transfer, sustainable development and climate change mitigation through specific projects in developing countries. It allows greenhouse gas (GHG) mitigation projects to produce "emission credits" for sale on an international market. Joint Implementation uses a similar approach, but applies only among developed countries (listed in Annex I of the FCCC). Both mechanisms use the market to create an asset from greenhouse gas emission reduction.

CDM and JI could result in enormous cost savings in meeting national emission reduction targets for investing countries, while transferring technology and resources to developing countries and countries with economies in transition. However, the mechanisms are new, untested and, as yet, unregulated. To make them operational, details must be worked out, including who will participate, how projects will be evaluated, how "credits" for reductions are to be transferred and how to ensure real environmental benefits.

Analyses (including those by the OECD and the IEA) suggest that if the mechanisms work "perfectly" they could generate revenues of US$10 billion per year or more and reduce emissions by up to 100 million tons of carbon. They could reshape investment and new infrastructure in the developing world and in economies in transition. The interest is equally strong from the developed country perspective. The Kyoto Protocol calls for significant emissions reductions, the costs of which will ultimately fall on private industry and consumers. Therefore, any mechanism that can reduce costs is to be encouraged. These project-based mechanisms, if fully and efficiently implemented, could reduce costs significantly - by close to 50% in some estimates.

As so often, the "devil is in the details". Ways of structuring the mechanisms that provide environmental benefits while meeting market requirements for simplicity of use are still under discussion. This book aims to facilitate that discussion and to focus attention on one key aspect of the project-based mechanisms: the emission baselines that are used for evaluating credits.

The Protocol mechanisms - some background

The FCCC commits all Parties, both developed and developing countries, to implement policies and measures that mitigate climate change. However, developing countries are not bound by any quantitative limits on greenhouse gas emissions under the Kyoto Protocol and countries with economies in transition (EITs) were given special dispensations on some commitments. The FCCC describes this as a system of "differentiated responsibilities". In general, developing countries (non-Annex I countries) have resisted adopting any emission limits until Annex I countries demonstrate real emissions reductions themselves. Annex I countries in turn have agreed to take the lead.

At the same time, developing countries are experiencing extremely rapid growth in their emissions of greenhouse gases. The increases in these emissions are tightly tied to economic growth and economic development continues to be those countries' highest priority. Finding a way to provide low cost emissions offsets for the developed countries while simultaneously providing development opportunities to developing countries was a key aim of the Kyoto process. For the transition economies, the Kyoto process also recognised the need for investments to help them get off the energy intensive growth path they had followed until their economic collapse.

The CDM will allow project developers from the developed world, both governmental and private, to enter into co-operative projects to reduce emissions in the developing world. Among the most likely projects are construction of environmentally sound power plants. The investors will be able to reduce emissions abroad at lower costs than they could do at home. Developing countries will receive the kind of technology, processes or infrastructure that will help them grow more sustainably.

The CDM (outlined in Article 12 of the Protocol) is the first mechanism to become operational under the Protocol (although it seems unlikely this will be in 2000 as originally proposed). Work on the institutional and technical aspects of implementing, monitoring and verifying projects is a priority.

Joint Implementation is only briefly outlined in the Kyoto Protocol (in Article 6). Unlike the CDM, it focuses explicitly on emissions reduction and emissions sequestration through carbon sinks. It does not, like the CDM, refer specifically to sustainable development.

Many believe that the most cost-effective emission reduction opportunities for Annex I Parties lie in upgrading or retrofitting the inefficient plants and factories of the former Soviet Union and Eastern Europe. They believe, too, that JI will not only allow least cost reductions to be taken on a global scale, but can also provide assistance to the transition economies in improving their energy efficiency. However, while the bulk of the projects in the Activities Implemented Jointly (AIJ, the pilot phase of Joint Implementation) were indeed with EITs, some projects have now been proposed between OECD countries (between the Netherlands and the US State of New Jersey or between the US and Canada). It is likely that very diverse projects would continue to be developed under the JI regime.

The current texts of the Kyoto Protocol's Article 6 (on JI) and Article 12 (on CDM) contain only an outline of how the mechanisms should operate, but AIJ has provided some insight into the operation of project-based mechanisms. Analyses of options, including those in this book, benefit greatly from experience with those early projects.

The devil is in the details

One critical difficulty lies in determining how to count the emissions reductions that accrue from projects. Kyoto called for no new commitments for developing countries. This means in practice that there is no national "cap" on emissions against which reductions might be measured. CDM was to count reductions project by project only. In the case of JI, a national cap exists for both participating Parties. But emission reductions from JI projects may be transferred without host countries necessarily adjusting their national emissions balances appropriately. The key question is: how can we know that a project will produce "reductions in emissions that are additional to any that would have occurred in the absence of the certified project activity" (Article 12)?

It is tempting to suggest that as long as the sums are invested in "good" projects, we need not worry whether the reductions are "real" or not. Unfortunately, such an approach would be deeply flawed. If rules are not carefully designed, CDM could provide Annex I countries with a potentially limitless pool of lower-cost reduction opportunities, rendering their own emission limits virtually meaningless. While this issue does not arise with JI, a different problem may emerge there. Depending on how liability rules are established, the purchase or sale of "bad" emission credits could drive a country out of compliance and so would not deliver the expected environmental benefits.

One solution is to develop emission baselines for projects. Emission baselines for JI and the CDM are required to assess the potential environmental performance of a project. Inasmuch as reductions under the mechanism are supposed to be additional to what would have happened without action, the "no-action" case needs to be quantified. The "no action" case, or "what would have happened anyway" therefore represents the project's emissions baseline. Of course, emission baselines are difficult to validate. Yet they form the basis for determining emission reductions or credits. The difference between actual emissions and this hypothetical case would determine the emissions credit from the project.

The Protocol text that establishes these mechanisms does not include the word "baseline". However, the fact that projects have to result in *measurable* environmental benefits implies the need for a quantitative reference or baseline against which to measure their performance. There is currently no internationally agreed methodology on how to calculate emission baselines for either CDM or JI projects.

For the potential investor or project developer, participation in the mechanisms could become hopelessly complicated. Any individual project has to have its own baseline. The entire result would have to be judged for acceptability by government representatives of at least two countries and possibly an international organisation, such as the Executive Board set up to supervise CDM projects. The situation might be further complicated if a project was developed unilaterally by a non-Annex I country, in which case separate rules might apply - for example it might "only" need approval of the Executive Board and not necessarily by the investor country. Such a situation is fraught with difficulties. It is likely to discourage any potential investor, no matter how environmentally inclined. Unless ways can be found to streamline the process of project development and to create standards, few projects will ever be inaugurated.

The aim of this book is to help in developing such standards. A project developer, armed with this information, could then evaluate whether its proposal might qualify as a potential JI/CDM project. This approach seems to work relatively well in some sectors. In the cement sector, new plants tend toward a comparable (and relatively efficient) global standard. It seems reasonable that only those projects that do better than this standard might qualify as being an improvement over business as usual and thus be credited under one of the Kyoto mechanisms. The cement sector is explored in considerable detail in chapter 2 of this book. Similarly, in the iron and steel sectors, there is considerable global convergence in new plant standards - allowing for the development of a fairly robust international standard - explored in chapter 5 of this book.

Project standards, however, will not be universally applicable. In the energy sector, global averages mask considerable diversity in national and regional performance. Fuel mixes, as well as differences in fuel costs and costs for the transport of energy, are not comparable. Here one could look at national or regional averages for comparative purposes. Alternatively, one could set arbitrary restrictions (a particular category of generating plant could be excluded, no matter how efficient it might be) or inclusions (all small renewable projects could generate emission credits). This set of issues is explored in depth in chapter 3.

Similarly, energy efficiency is a variable phenomenon. This book looks at efficiencies in lighting and motors in chapter 4. It concludes that there are essentially three options, or levels, for the standardisation of energy use baselines for energy efficiency projects. These are (a) standardising baseline calculation methods; (b) standardising operating and performance parameters; and (c) standardising energy-use indices. Unfortunately this book does not conclude that a single, simple value might be applied to all energy-efficiency projects, but suggests that in this area at least, multiple bases will need to be developed to assess project credit-worthiness.

Where to from here?

JI and CDM could play a significant role in lowering the overall cost of meeting GHG targets. By providing financial and technical support to developing countries and to countries with economies in transition, projects under the mechanisms can move us towards more sustainable development. Since the primary investors in these projects will come from the private sector, the potential size of the JI and CDM market will depend largely on the attractiveness of the mechanisms to project developers and investors. Transparency and a reduction of transaction costs while maintaining environmental protection are critical in this regard.

The case studies presented here are part of a larger analytical project undertaken by the Annex I Expert Group to evaluate emissions baselines in a variety of sectors. Additional work in these and other sectors will go further into the issues raised in this work. One critical area for future analysis is that of "sinks". The question is whether and, if so, how projects which seek to capture and store greenhouse gases in forests or other locations might be credited. Other sectors face very daunting questions. Do agriculture projects qualify? Can we develop CDM or JI projects in the transport sector? How can we assess distributed emissions of gases we do not accurately monitor, such as nitrous oxides? These questions, if answered, could provide significant new opportunities for reducing emissions at lower costs, while promoting new development around the world.

The authors hope that this work will move the climate change negotiations to more efficient and robust solutions to protect the global environment for present and future generations. Estimating the unknown, whether it is the structure of a hypothetical emission baseline or the value of a project credit using that hypothetical baseline, is never easy. If we can help to avoid the equally unknown and potentially much more dangerous consequence of global climate change, this work will not have been in vain.

ACKNOWLEDGEMENTS

The analysis in this book was undertaken at the request of - and with considerable input from - the OECD/IEA Annex I Experts Group on the United Nations Framework Convention on Climate Change. The Annex I Expert Group oversees development of analytical papers for the purpose of providing useful and timely input to the climate change negotiations - work that may also be useful to national policy makers and other decision makers. In a collaborative effort, authors work with the Annex I Expert Group to develop the analysis. However, the final product does not necessarily represent the views of the OECD or the IEA, nor are they intended to prejudge the views of countries participating in the Annex I Expert Group. Rather, they are Secretariat information papers intended to inform Member countries, as well as the UNFCCC audience.

The Annex I Parties or countries referred to in this document refer are those listed in Annex I to the UNFCCC (as amended at the 3rd Conference of the Parties in December 1997): Australia, Austria, Belarus, Belgium, Bulgaria, Canada, Croatia, Czech Republic, Denmark, the European Community, Estonia, Finland, France, Germany, Greece, Hungary, Iceland, Ireland, Italy, Japan, Latvia, Liechtenstein, Lithuania, Luxembourg, Monaco, Netherlands, New Zealand, Norway, Poland, Portugal, Romania, Russian Federation, Slovakia, Slovenia, Spain, Sweden, Switzerland, Turkey, Ukraine, United Kingdom of Great Britain and Northern Ireland, and United States of America. Where this document refers to "countries" or "governments" it is also intended to include "regional economic organisations", if appropriate.

Producing this book involved many people in different capacities. Jane Ellis (OECD) and Martina Bosi (IEA) were the main authors and co-ordinated the inputs from Hagler Bailly Services Inc., Summit Blue Ventures and Ecofys. All chapters of this book benefited from the insightful comments and useful guidance of Jonathan Pershing (IEA) and Jan Corfee Morlot (OECD). The book also benefited from the peer review of many OECD and IEA colleagues, of delegates to the Annex I Expert Group and from other experts. Carolyn Sturgeon was in charge of assembling the publication in its final format. She was assisted by Jenny Gell.

TABLE OF CONTENTS

LIST OF FIGURES

LIST OF TABLES

1. INTRODUCTION AND OVERVIEW

1. INTRODUCTION AND OVERVIEW

1.1 Context: brief history of the policy-making exercise

International co-operation will be necessary to respond effectively to the challenge of climate change. Governments around the world recognise this and have already begun to act through the 1992 United Nations Framework Convention on Climate Change (UNFCCC)[1] and its subsequent Kyoto Protocol[2].

The ultimate objective of the UNFCCC, as set out in Article 2, is the "stabilisation of greenhouse gas concentrations in the atmosphere at a level that would prevent dangerous anthropogenic interference with the climate system". As a first step towards meeting this objective, developed countries and countries with economies in transition (collectively referred to as the "Annex I Parties"[3]) agreed to adopt policies and measures with the aim of returning GHG emissions to their 1990 levels by the year 2000.

The UNFCCC also includes a provision whereby Parties (both the Annex I Parties and the non-Annex I Parties[4]) can mitigate emissions jointly through projects undertaken in any country. This provision is an explicit recognition of the fact that the environmental effect of GHG emissions does not vary with the origin of the emission, but that mitigation costs do (OECD 1999a). At the First Conference of the Parties (COP 1) to the UNFCCC in 1995, an international pilot phase of Joint Implementation was launched to gain experience with such international joint projects: the pilot phase is called Activities Implemented Jointly (AIJ).

---

[1] By August 2000, 184 Parties had ratified the UNFCCC.

[2] By August 2000, 84 countries had signed and 23 had ratified the Kyoto Protocol.

[3] These are: Australia, Austria, Belarus, Belgium, Bulgaria, Canada, Croatia, Czech Republic, Denmark, the European Community, Estonia, Finland, France, Germany, Greece, Hungary, Iceland, Ireland, Italy, Japan, Latvia, Liechtenstein, Lithuania, Luxembourg, Monaco, Netherlands, New Zealand, Norway, Poland, Portugal, Romania, Russian Federation, Slovakia, Slovenia, Spain, Sweden, Switzerland, Turkey, Ukraine, United Kingdom of Great Britain and Northern Ireland, and United States of America.

[4] Developing countries are known in the UNFCCC as non-Annex I Parties.

A growing scientific consensus about the nature of the climate change problem, its causes and impacts has stimulated the development of international policy under the Convention. The effect of human activity on the global climate was further confirmed by the Intergovernmental Panel on Climate Change (IPCC) in its 1996 Second Assessment Report. Partly in response to the IPCC's findings and motivated by a desire to act more aggressively on the climate change issue, the international community took additional steps to deal with climate change, adopting the Kyoto Protocol to the UNFCCC in December 1997.

The Protocol establishes specific obligations on Annex I Parties to reduce their emissions of six greenhouse gases, "with a view to reducing their overall emissions of such gases by at least 5% below 1990 levels in the commitment period 2008-2012". The Kyoto Protocol recognises Parties' different national circumstances, such as their natural resource endowments, possibilities and costs of mitigating GHGs. In the Kyoto Protocol, each Annex I Party has been allocated an "assigned amount" for the 5-year commitment period. This "assigned amount" is the level of a Party's emission commitment. These emission commitments are "differentiated", ranging from an emission reduction target of eight percent below 1990 levels for the European Union[5] and a seven percent reduction for the United States, to an eight percent increase *above* 1990 levels for Australia and a ten percent increase for Iceland. Compared to "business-as-usual" emission projections for the dates of the commitment period, these emission commitments will require significant reductions for most Annex I Parties, in particular those that are OECD Member countries.

Among the most innovative features of the Kyoto Protocol are its provisions for international "market" mechanisms. These enable Parties to minimise the economic cost of meeting their GHG commitments by providing flexibility as to the location of the GHG mitigation activities. The rationale is that Annex I Parties facing relatively high domestic mitigation costs could count emission reductions (or emission sequestration through sink enhancements) achieved in other countries, where mitigation costs are lower, against their own emission commitments. These mechanisms should help Annex I Parties meet their emission commitments in the most economically-efficient way.

The Protocol includes three such mechanisms: international emissions trading, Joint Implementation (JI) and the Clean Development Mechanism (CDM)[6]. The rules, modalities and guidelines establishing how these mechanisms will work in practice, have yet to be developed and agreed upon through the formal Convention negotiating process.

---

[5] The European Union subsequently agreed to divide its overall commitment among its member countries through emission targets differentiated among themselves.

[6] Article 4 of the Kyoto Protocol also contains another mechanism whereby a group of countries can formally agree to meet their overall emissions target "jointly". European Union countries have agreed to redistribute their Kyoto Protocol emission targets under this "bubble".

International emission trading, which allows for emission units to be transferred and acquired by Annex I Parties, is based on each Annex I Party's target or assigned amount for the commitment period (Mullins and Baron, 1997; and Mullins, 1999). JI and the CDM, on which this book is focused, are based on actual mitigation or sequestration projects and are referred to as "project-based" mechanisms. JI and the CDM build on the concept of mitigating emissions "jointly" elaborated in the UNFCCC and AIJ. Projects undertaken under these two project-based mechanisms can generate "emission credits" if they result in emission levels lower than would otherwise be the case (without the projects).

JI involves projects to be undertaken in Annex I countries. The "emission credits" generated by each project can be deducted from the Annex I host country's assigned amount and added to an investing Annex I country's assigned amount, with the overall assigned amount for Annex I remaining unaffected by such transactions. The benefits of hosting the JI project include reduced local pollution and increased access to and know how on climate-friendly technologies. The Kyoto Protocol also explicitly allows for private entities in Annex I countries to participate in such projects and emission transactions.

The CDM refers to projects undertaken in non-Annex I Parties. The Kyoto Protocol specifies that the CDM is to meet two objectives: 1) assisting Annex I Parties in meeting their emissions commitments; and 2) assisting non-Annex I Parties in achieving sustainable development[7]. Emission credits resulting from CDM projects in non-Annex I countries can thus be acquired by Annex I Parties and added to their assigned amount. (Although it is widely expected that private entities will participate in the development and investment of CDM projects, this is not explicitly stated in the Kyoto Protocol and is likely to be one of the elements of the CDM decisions taken in the UNFCCC negotiations.)

The general objectives and some elements of the frameworks for these "Kyoto mechanisms" are included in the Kyoto Protocol. The biggest challenge now is to develop the rules, modalities and guidelines that will enable them to operate in a credible and efficient manner. For JI and the CDM, the development of rules and guidelines for emission baselines, in order to define "what would occur otherwise", is one of the key elements needed to put theory into practice.

1.2   Why do we need baselines?

To determine the number of greenhouse gas "emissions credits" that could be generated by an individual JI or CDM project, an indication is needed of the volume of greenhouse

---

[7] The Kyoto Protocol does not specify a similar sustainable development objective in Article 6 on Joint Implementation.

gas emissions (or sequestration) in the absence of that project. The amount of GHG emitted in the hypothetical "what would have happened otherwise" case is referred to as a project's baseline. A baseline attempts to quantify this hypothetical emission (or sequestration) level and, through this, the greenhouse gas "additionality" of an individual project (see box). Actual, monitored greenhouse gas emissions (or sequestration) levels of the JI or CDM project are compared with the agreed baseline and the difference between the two is the mitigative effect of the project, or the total credit amount. This book examines baselines for potential emission-reducing projects in four sectors and uses the term "baseline" and "emissions baseline" interchangeably.

A note on environmental additionality

Only projects that result in "additional" GHG emission reductions can generate emissions credits. Project-specific assessments of the benefits of AIJ projects have raised questions about the additionality of some of these projects. However, determining a standardised procedure to assess the environmental additionality of a potential JI or CDM project is not straightforward. A project may be inherently climate friendly, such as generating electricity from wind power, or increasing the energy efficiency of an industrial process. But this climate-friendly project may have gone ahead in the absence of JI and CDM and in this case would not in principle be eligible for crediting. At the other extreme, a JI or CDM project may generate more greenhouse gases than another similar existing activity, but may still result in greenhouse gas emissions being lower with the project than they would have become in the absence of the project. Such a project would be considered "additional" and eligible to generate emissions credits under JI or CDM.

The comparison of actual emissions to the estimation of what would have occurred otherwise, determines the environmental additionality of any given project and of any credits generated. Given the hypothetical nature of such a comparison, some suggest that it may be valuable to establish simple "rules of thumb" *e.g.* all project types of a particular variety are assumed to be additional. Such rules could significantly speed up the project preparation and approval cycle for JI and/or CDM. Yet it is possible to imagine a project type that is considered additional, *e.g.* an energy efficiency project, where non-additional credits are generated because the baseline is unrealistically lax. Thus ensuring the environmental additionality of project credits requires establishing a baseline at a realistic level of stringency.

Determining the range of possible values that a standardised baseline could have is inextricably linked to the stringency of that baseline, including how it is set up (which aggregation, timeline, boundary *etc.* are used). These factors are discussed individually in section 1.4.

1.2.1   What is the experience to date with emission baselines?

Much of the experience with project-level emission baselines has been gained during the AIJ pilot phase. Many countries also have experience in estimating the energy and/or greenhouse impacts of particular climate change policies - a task which is related to that of determining the mitigation effects of individual projects.

An examination of approximately 45 AIJ projects (OECD, 1999) reveals that the methodologies and assumptions used to calculate emission baselines were not necessarily consistent, comparable or transparent. This is not surprising given that no quantitative, agreed guidance was readily available to developers of AIJ projects. More surprising is that justification of the data and assumptions used in estimating the emission baseline was also frequently absent from project reports. This could also be explained by the limited instructions given to those reporting projects. Although some national reporting requirements were fairly rigorous, international requirements were vague: asking developers to provide quantitative estimations of greenhouse gas emissions in a with and without project scenario. Project developers were not specifically prompted to provide references or justifications for methods, data or assumptions used in developing these scenarios.

Most of the emission baselines used to determine the environmental benefits of AIJ projects have been project-specific. The baseline was drawn up on a case-by-case basis and all key parameters used in the baseline construction were measured or estimated for a particular project. However, emission baselines for projects could be drawn up using other approaches. These include "multi-project" baselines[8] where standardised baseline value(s) and/or methodology(ies) are drawn up for several different potential projects. A "hybrid" baseline approach might also be used, where the values of some components of an emissions baseline are standardised, while others are project-specific. Some of the more recent AIJ projects, such as those initiated in 1999 between Estonia and Sweden, included baselines that could be used for several similar projects (UNFCCC, 1999). Each approach to calculating emission baselines has its advantages and disadvantages.

Project-specific baselines are the least aggregated type and can be tailored specifically to one project. The individual nature of project-specific baselines also makes them relatively difficult and time-consuming to review (unless accompanied with significant background documentation). Although it might be assumed that project-specific baselines result in low uncertainty, some research (Begg *et. al.,* 1999) has indicated that uncertainties of project-specific baselines from simple, refurbishment-type energy sector projects can be in the order of $\pm$ 80%. Project-specific baselines may also rely heavily on expert judgement to determine some key parameters, which may mean that their environmental credibility may be compromised if these experts artificially inflate the baseline level. Another disadvantage of project-specific baselines - particularly to potential project

---

[8] Also referred to as "benchmarks".

23

investors - is that there may be relatively high transaction costs. In addition, the cost of establishing a project-specific baseline will fall on the project developer. Interest in multi-project baselines has developed in part as a reaction to some of the shortcomings identified from experience with project specific baselines.

Multi-project baselines are more aggregated emission baselines and can be used for several projects. These baselines would indicate either a standardised emission level associated with certain activities, or a standardised methodology that could be used to calculate an emissions level for those activities. Actual emissions from individual JI or CDM projects are then compared to the multi-project baseline to determine whether or not the projects could generate emissions credits.

1.2.2 How can we build on lessons learned from this experience?

The advantages and disadvantages of multi-project baselines are different from those of project-specific baselines. Studies indicate that standardisation of baselines, methodologies or individual parameters would help to ensure consistency in the treatment of similar projects. Standardisation would provide a high degree of transparency in baseline determination and could also, if developed by independent experts, limit the level of gaming and free riders (examined in section 1.3.1 below). It could also reduce the overall costs of baseline setting, compared to a project-specific approach, through economies of scale, as it could apply to several projects. Using already established multi-project emission baselines could also facilitate and accelerate the required governmental acceptance and approval procedures for proposed projects in potential host countries, particularly those with limited administrative capacity and/or experience in baseline-setting. In addition, developing a value and/or methodology for a multi-project baseline could help increase data collection and/or availability at a national level, which could create positive synergies with a country's other requirements under the Convention and its Protocol.

Nevertheless, as with project-specific baselines, there appear to be several important disadvantages of multi-project baselines. Multi-project baselines would allow some projects that would have gone ahead anyway to generate emission credits. In the abstract, it is difficult to assess the environmental effects of such "free riders". This will depend upon the volume of projects generated under both a multi-project and project-specific baseline approach and the relative level of the baseline under each (see also below).

Establishing credible multi-project baselines or assumptions is also likely to be a complex, highly technical and time-consuming process. Analysis presented in chapters 2 - 5 indicates that the parameters that need to be taken into account when establishing multi-project baselines vary from sector to sector. For example, an electricity generation baseline could be set as a standardised value in terms of GHG/kWh for individual countries or for regions within a country. For other sectors, like cement, it may only be desirable or possible to standardise some key parameters, such as direct fuel use per ton of clinker produced. The need for different guidelines for different sectors and project types has significant implications on the amount of work and time that is needed to set up comprehensive guidelines to project developers.

The potential advantages of multi-project baselines, or of hybrid approaches that standardise baseline calculation methods or parameters, would appear to outweigh the disadvantages for project categories in which many JI or CDM projects with similar characteristics are expected to be initiated. A careful consideration of issues specific to different project categories is undertaken in the following chapters for potential projects in cement production, electricity generation, increased energy efficiency and iron and steel production.

1.3   Finding the environmental and economic "balance"

In practical terms, the success of the project-based mechanisms depends on their overall contribution towards achieving the commitments adopted under the Kyoto Protocol. The issues surrounding emission baselines (*e.g.* development, design and approval) are likely to be key factors influencing the overall success of the project-based mechanisms. It is thus critical that baselines be developed in a way that maximises investment in and development of "additional" GHG mitigation projects.

Baselines must seek to strike a balance, remaining conservative to be environmentally credible while at the same time providing incentives to potential project developers to invest in emission reduction projects. As an emission baseline quantifies a hypothetical scenario, it is subject to uncertainty through inaccuracies, such as in the emission factor used or the assumption about what technology would have been used without the project. Project proponents could exploit these uncertainties to artificially inflate the baseline in order to increase the resulting number of credits ("gaming"). In contrast, overly conservative or stringent baselines could deter investment and render the project mechanism under the Protocol meaningless, or at best, ineffective.

An ideal baseline would strike a balance among these concerns. It would be (Ellis and Bosi, 1999):

- environmentally credible;
- transparent and verifiable by a third party;
- simple and inexpensive to draw up; and
- provide a reasonable level of crediting certainty to investors.

25

Baseline approaches

Three main baseline approaches: project-specific, multi-project and hybrid, are distinct in theory, but can be difficult to label in practice. For example, if 9 of 10 key parameters of a baseline are drawn up for a particular project, the baseline may be labelled as "project-specific". But how many of the parameters would have to be standardised before the baseline became labelled as "hybrid"?

The distinction between a multi-project baseline set up in terms of a standardised emission value, a methodology set up to apply to many projects and a "hybrid" baseline in which only some of the baseline parameters have standardised values is equally blurred. While none of these baseline approaches is inherently "better" than another, each type of baseline does have distinct characteristics, advantages and disadvantages.

1.3.1   Environmental effectiveness of projects

Ensuring environmental effectiveness means that the emission baseline needs to be a credible reflection of the business-as-usual scenario. The environmental effectiveness of the project-based mechanisms[9] will largely depend on whether the emission credits that they generate reflect real emission reductions. Environmental credibility is needed to ensure that participating in JI projects does not increase the difficulty for host countries to reach their domestic targets and that participating in CDM projects does not result in increased global greenhouse gas emissions, compared to what would have occurred without the projects.

Clearly, there is no perfect "test" for determining the environmental effectiveness of baselines, as baselines, by definition, seek to represent an emission scenario that will not occur. However, there are some factors that can provide indications on the environmental effectiveness (or credibility) of the emission baseline. In fact, an assessment of the potential for free-riders, gaming and leakage can be a useful exercise in this context.

Free riding means that some projects generate emission credits even though they would have gone ahead in the absence of the project-based mechanisms. The "additionality" of the emission credits resulting from the emission reduction (or sink enhancement) effect of these projects would thus be questionable, at best. Overly lax baselines could allow "free

---

[9] Unlike the CDM, JI is a zero-sum process in which transfers and acquisitions of emission credits will not affect the overall emissions assigned to Annex I, as determined by the Kyoto Protocol. The implications on overall environmental effectiveness (in terms of GHG emissions) are thus different for JI and the CDM.

rider" projects to qualify for credits and would therefore inflate the estimated environmental benefits and emission credits arising from JI and CDM.

The number of free-rider projects could be limited if projects used a very stringent baseline and an extremely rigorous "additionality" evaluation in order to determine the number of credits that a project is eligible to generate. However, this could restrict the number of projects initiated and severely limit resulting emission reductions (and thus emission credits). It might also render some truly additional projects ineligible for JI/CDM status.

Standardising all or parts of the baseline-setting process could facilitate greater scrutiny of what a credible business-as-usual scenario is and thus limit the likelihood of free-riders. However, the baseline standardisation process will need to take into account that different countries (or regions within countries) have different circumstances, which may limit the scope of baseline standardisation for some types of projects. Different sectoral characteristics will also be a determining factor in the scope and type of the standardisation that is appropriate. Emission baselines should therefore aim to reduce the likelihood of free-riding, while taking into account different national (regional or local, as appropriate) circumstances.

Gaming artificially inflates the level of an individual baseline and consequently the amount of emission credits associated with a given JI or CDM project. In fact, the relatively high potential for gaming is a significant drawback noted in the project-specific baselines, which were the main approach used under the AIJ pilot phase.

Increased transparency and standardisation of baselines, or baseline components, helps reduce the likelihood of gaming. However, gaming may also be possible when using standardised, multi-project baselines if the standardisation process is systematically biased to a higher baseline level. Nonetheless, the potential for gaming can be expected to be lower if standardised baseline assumptions are developed through a process engaging independent experts.

Leakage occurs if a given JI or CDM project leads to increases in emissions that are not taken into account in the baseline, *i.e.* emissions that occur outside the project boundary and the evaluation of the project's performance. If significant, leakage could obviously undermine the environmental effectiveness of the emission reductions achieved through the project-based mechanisms. However, the case studies in this volume note that seeking to include a comprehensive coverage of all direct and indirect emissions that could be associated with a given project could be very burdensome when setting baselines, whether standardised or project-specific. In addition, accounting for indirect emission reductions over which the project has no direct authority or control (such as the fuel mix used for grid electricity generation), may lead to "double-counting" of emission reductions if these reductions are also accounted for by another, separate, project.

Clear rules to balance the need to minimise leakage, the need to avoid double-counting of emissions and the need to streamline the baseline-setting process, will help increase the baselines' environmental effectiveness. Standardised methods or baselines could be part of such rules.

1.3.2 Transparency

Emission baselines should be transparent enough to allow a third party to understand the key features of the project, the "no-project" scenario and any credits generated by the project. Transparent baseline reports need to include information stating clearly what the situation was before the project, how this level was determined, what the expected crediting lifetime of a project is and how (if at all) the level of the emissions baseline is expected to vary over the crediting lifetime. Such transparency can enhance the credibility of the baseline. Third-party verification of credits is also mandatory for CDM projects.

Transparency in how an emissions baseline is calculated can help to facilitate approval and acceptance of the project by the different parties and entities involved in it and can therefore contribute to a shorter delay between proposing and initiating a project. A short start-up time is of particular significance for CDM projects, where credits can, in theory, start accruing from the year 2000.

Multi-project baselines or some degree of standardisation in baseline construction could greatly enhance transparency and ease of review. Publicly available guidance for baseline calculation and reporting could be an important tool, covering calculation methodology, parameters in the calculation and data requirements for different types of JI and CDM projects. Such guidance could simplify and accelerate the project preparation and review process by providing a reference for project developers as well as for third-party reviewers. Standard reporting guidance is essential to improve the transparency of baseline proposals.

1.3.3 Baseline development cost and crediting risks

The term "transaction costs", common in financial and economics literature, is used in this paper to describe additional expenditures specifically related to the development and implementation of CDM and JI projects. Such costs include variables such as the amount of additional preparation time projects might require - which relates to the complexity of the rules and the review/approval process, as well as information flows about where/what possible projects and investors are. However, transaction costs diminish the relative economic feasibility, or profitability, of commercial activities and thus have to be minimised in order to minimise barriers to investment. Of course, fixed transaction costs have a proportionally larger negative impact on smaller projects than larger projects.

The absolute costs of developing an emission baseline are likely to be significant, whether project-specific or standardised. As illustrated in the following chapters, developing multi-project baselines or standardised components of a baseline can be a difficult and time-consuming task. Through standardisation, however, economies of scale can be achieved which would reduce the relative cost of baseline development and approval for each project. Moreover, while project developers would pay for the development of project-specific baselines, others (*e.g.* investing country governments) would meet the cost of developing standardised baselines.

For investors, an ability to foresee with certainty the number of credits likely to be generated by a particular project, at least in the first few years of it's life, is also likely to boost both confidence and investment in the mechanisms. Increasing the degree of certainty in generating credits will therefore increase both the number of projects initiated and the total mitigation effect of the mechanism. Standardisation of baselines or baseline methodologies would help provide potential investors with more certainty about the baseline level.

1.3.4   Finding the balance

In summary, maximising the potential environmental effectiveness of an individual JI or CDM project through the baseline-setting process requires limiting gaming, free-riding and the magnitude of leakage. However, maximising the overall environmental effectiveness of project-based mechanisms needs to incorporate other elements that work to encourage participation in JI and CDM, notably increasing transparency and minimising the baseline development costs. Thus it will be necessary to find a balance and decisions on the specific technical aspects of baselines methods and assumptions, standardised or not, will influence these outcomes. Standardisation of some elements for baseline construction, leading to multi-project or hybrid forms of baselines, is likely to simplify baseline construction and the review process, which in turn can contribute to lower project development costs. A key question is whether standardisation of baseline and baseline development can be done without compromising such environmental criteria as limiting free-riders. These issues are examined, drawing on the case study results, in section 1.4 below.

1.4   Key steps/issues in standardising baselines and baseline development

The Kyoto Protocol language on the CDM (and to a lesser extent, the text on JI) presumes a level of international co-ordination on the issues related to evaluating projects. With respect to baseline standardisation, this suggests the need to develop a handbook or "reference manual" as a logical next step. The aim of such a manual would be to increase transparency and consistency by making publicly available standard or multi-project baselines (or components thereof) in a centralised format. Clearly, such analyses will need to address the critical question of whether standardisation is appropriate for a particular sector; which baseline parameters should be standardised; and how such standardisation should be carried out.

This analysis summarises four areas as starting points: cement, iron and steel, power generation and appliance energy efficiency. In the analysis, we sought first to understand the key characteristics of the sector in order to estimate what possible paths future developments within the sector could take. For example, the relative importance of modernisation ("refurbishment") projects versus new production facilities is likely to be higher in sectors that are highly capital-intensive, such as cement manufacture, than in sectors where equipment is relatively cheap, such as lighting. Future developments in a sector, such as a shift in fuel mixes or technologies, need to be taken into consideration when constructing a baseline.

The cost of equipment is also likely to have an effect on the length of time that the equipment is in use and will therefore affect the number of years for which emission credits can appropriately be accrued. The length of time that equipment is used can also vary depending on the growth of activity in a sector. For example, a high-growth sector such as electricity generation is likely to maintain existing capacity for as long as possible, particularly in countries with little access to capital, even if old plants do not operate at their maximum efficiency.

The ownership, structure and diversity of players within the sector can also influence baseline levels. For example, a sector made up of mainly large-scale multi-national companies, or whose product is internationally traded, may have relatively easy access to investment capital and to newer, more efficient technologies. In contrast, sectors whose players are publicly owned and/or mainly small-scale who produce a product for local/national consumers may have limited access to investment capital and new technologies.

Examining recent trends and the types of projects already underway in a potential JI/CDM project sector provides useful indications of what would happen in the absence of a project. This information can be used to help decide whether or not a proposed project is indeed "additional" and if so, by how much. Projects recently initiated as part of business-as-usual practice in a particular sector may be significantly different (either more or less climate-friendly) than the "average" project in that sector. If this is the case, it indicates that the average performance of all existing operating facilities may not be a good indicator of "what would have happened otherwise". In such a case, emission baselines could therefore more appropriately be based on the characteristics of recent capacity additions, even if these data are more difficult to obtain. In addition to gathering this general type of information, it is important to examine the difference in sectoral performance and trends among (and within) countries to assess the importance of national circumstances in decisions about baseline levels.

More specific information is also needed in order to determine at which level a standardised project baseline could be set. Analysis of the sectoral information presented later in this publication indicates that the most important aspects to consider when assessing if and how to standardise emission baselines for a particular project type are:

- whether standardisation should be in terms of baseline levels, *i.e.* a numerical value, methodologies, or both;

- an appropriate level of baseline aggregation;

- the length of time over which a project can generate emissions credits;

- which project boundary is appropriate (*i.e.* which gases and sources should be included in the baseline);

- which data assumptions are appropriate and the availability of this data; and

- the units in which baselines should be expressed.

The underlying factor in many of these points is the variability across different projects that might be assessed under a single baseline or baseline assumption. Baseline levels will vary between project types, but also to a certain extent within project types. Any baseline reference manual will need to determine what level of variation in project types and project performances is acceptable under any one baseline.

1.4.1   *How can baselines be standardised?*

Once it has been established that standardisation of a baseline for a certain project category is appropriate, it has to be determined what form the standardisation takes. Forms could include standardising:

- absolute baseline levels, or "values";

- methodologies that would apply to a group of projects; and/or

- parameters that could be used in so-called hybrid baselines (baselines that have both project-specific and standardised components).

Determining which of these levels is most appropriate for a particular project category is strongly linked with the issue of baseline aggregation. If it has been decided that a baseline can be applied to a particular project category irrespective of where in the world a project takes place, a standardised level, or value, could be set up that would apply to all projects of this particular category. Setting a standardised baseline value is therefore appropriate for baselines that are based solely on the performance of an individual technology, such as the production of a particular type of steel by a particular technology.

However, if the value of the baseline is influenced by country or region-specific factors, such as the GHG-intensity of energy input, a better approach may be to standardise the baseline methodology and indicate where country or region-specific information should be input into that methodology. For example, a standardised methodology for grid-connected electricity generation could be determined to be the average GHG-intensity of all recently installed capacity. Any reference manual would therefore include this methodology and may also specify how it should be calculated and where suitable data sources can be found. However, country or region-specific data would be used in order to determine the baseline values for individual projects. While this process involves slightly more work for the project developer than using a standardised baseline value, it is much cheaper and less time-intensive than determining how to calculate an emission baseline from scratch.

Standardising individual parameters can help to reduce the cost and increase the comparability of baselines for projects where it has been judged that a project-specific component is needed. For example, the mitigation effect of electricity-efficient equipment depends on the GHG-intensity of electricity displaced and the number of hours the new equipment is used. While the extent to which the equipment is used may need to be measured or estimated, a standardised parameter could be set up that indicates the electricity expected to be saved by installing certain energy-efficient equipment. "Translation" of kWh saved to GHG mitigated would also need to be done using country or region-specific data.

1.4.2   *Baseline aggregation*

A single, standardised baseline value or methodology is likely to be most appropriately used when applied to a set of projects that are similar in nature. For example, a baseline that can be applied to certain projects in the cement sector will need to take different parameters into account (*e.g.* growth in construction) than a baseline in another sector, such as lighting (*e.g.* floor space of households). Indeed, more than one baseline value or methodology may be appropriate for different project types within a particular sector. For example, grid-based and off-grid electricity projects are likely to be of different scales and influenced by different factors, even though they occur in the same sector. Thus, while a standardised baseline will apply to a group of similar projects, many such baselines may need to be set up to take into account the diversity of possible projects that could be undertaken. "Baseline aggregation" assesses which project types in which areas can be reasonably assessed using a single baseline.

There are two different types of aggregation that are important in baseline setting. These are:

- the geographic aggregation, *i.e.* over what geographical area should a particular baseline apply; and

- activity-based aggregation, *i.e.* to which sector, sub-sector *etc.* a baseline should be valid for.

When a project activity has very similar characteristics in different world regions in terms of homogeneity of inputs/outputs or production processes, a baseline can be aggregated at the global performance of the sub-sector, technology or process level. This recommendation follows from the case studies in the cement and iron and steel sectors. However, when a project activity differs substantially between (and/or within) countries in terms of inputs, outputs, processes and levels of performance, a baseline may be more appropriately based on more geographically disaggregated data, such as country or region-specific. For example, the variation in GHG intensity of electricity generation within a country that has distinct electricity grids and substantial differences between those grids in fuel mix and technology *etc.* may be as large or larger than the variation in GHG intensity of electricity generation between different countries. So for electricity generation projects, national or regional (*i.e.* sub-country or a group of countries) baselines may be appropriate, depending on the circumstances of a particular country.

The activity-based aggregation, *i.e.* which project activities a baseline can be used for, also needs to be determined. For example, should a baseline apply to all possible JI/CDM projects within a particular sector even if the projects are of different types? Insights from the cement sector indicate that different project types should have different baselines, *e.g.* baselines for projects that change the cement manufacturing process should be different from baselines used for projects that change the fuel inputs to cement manufacture. A certain degree of sub-sectoral disaggregation is also recommended in the iron and steel sector: baselines should be adjusted to take into account the different energy (and GHG) intensity of the steel products manufactured. Activity-based aggregation is also an issue in the electricity sector. Even though the output is homogeneous the inputs and the context in which electricity is generated is not. Relevant questions are: should projects be treated identically if they affect only peak-load or only baseload generation? Should potential JI/CDM coal-fired projects be compared to the performance of coal-fired equipment already in place, or should they be compared to the average of recent fossil fuel, or total capacity additions?

The four sectors examined in chapters 2 - 5 indicate the difficulty of setting out general rules for standardising baselines. However, one rule of thumb that can be set is that the lower the homogeneity in the inputs, processes and outputs within a sector, the more disaggregated the baseline will need to be. This inevitably leaves room for interpretation about what can be considered homogeneous in each sector (or project category). It may be difficult to ensure a consistent interpretation across sectors about what level of homogeneity should be required for determining (sectoral) aggregation.

Determining the appropriate activity-level aggregation for a baseline may have large implications in terms of the incentives given to project activities within a sector. Selecting the "wrong" aggregation level might lead to over-crediting of projects or acceptance of projects that are not additional or, alternatively, under-crediting or rejection of projects that are additional. For example, a gas-fired electricity generation project may generate credits when compared to recent gas-fired additions, but not when compared to the average of all capacity additions (if the share of *e.g.* nuclear and/or hydro electricity is significant in the overall power mix). Thus, the level of aggregation can affect whether or not a particular project will generate emission credits and how much. Given the scale of some potential projects, this could make a substantial difference to the economic viability of a project. For example, a gas-fired power station in India could generate almost US$300,000 worth of credits a year (assuming a relatively low carbon value of US$5/t CO_2) if compared to recently constructed capacity (all generating sources), but significantly less if compared to recently constructed gas plants. It is therefore important for project developers to provide a clear justification for selecting a specific level of aggregation.

1.4.3   Baseline lifetime

The number of credits that a potential JI/CDM project could generate also depends in part on the number of years that the project can generate credits for. Because of this influence on the total number of credits obtained by a project, the baseline lifetime can play an important role in ensuring that incentives to and credits from comparable JI/CDM projects are consistent and comparable. However, objectively determining the baseline lifetime is difficult, particularly for projects that refurbish or modernise existing equipment, as JI/CDM investment may be used to hasten improvements that would have been made anyway in the long run. Large variations in baseline lifetimes were noted in similar AIJ projects (OECD, 1999b). The baseline lifetime also influences the likelihood of the project going ahead, through the certainty or otherwise it gives to investors regarding the level of crediting over the project's life.

Baseline revisions, *i.e.* changes made to the baseline for a particular project during its lifetime, are also closely linked to both environmental additionality and investor certainty. Technology performance and business-as-usual practices can change substantially within a relatively short space of time. Therefore a baseline set up for a project with a relatively long crediting lifetime (*e.g.* 10-15y) may need to be revised during the course of that crediting lifetime in order to ensure that credits generated by the project are truly environmentally additional. Of course, any change in the baseline will affect the credits obtained by a project and so will increase investor uncertainty. Baseline updates are also likely to be needed at periodic intervals, *i.e.* reviewing whether the standardised baseline value or methodology initially set up is appropriate for future projects.

The recommendations for baseline lifetimes made in the sectoral case studies are based on expert judgement. These recommendations attempt to balance considerations relating to the technical/economic lifetime of equipment installed and replaced, the payback time for the investor and the period in which a project may be considered as additional. The different case studies suggest two main options for standardised baseline lifetimes:

1. the entire crediting lifetime is fixed at a relatively short level from the start of the project (*i.e.* the project developer can use the agreed baseline for the whole crediting lifetime of the project); or

2. that baseline revisions should be undertaken at certain time intervals during the course of the project.

In practice, it is possible to think of these two options in combination with each other, where project developers could be guaranteed a certain number of years for crediting at the outset and allowed to apply for extension of project lifetime. The latter would be granted if the project/credits are still considered "additional" at that point in time. As both project lifetimes and the stringency of the baseline determine the volume of credits to be generated from a project, both should be considered in setting baseline standards.

1.4.4 Project boundaries

Particular project types may affect the direct and indirect emissions or sequestration of different greenhouse gases from more than one source (*e.g.* fuel combustion, process emissions). A standardised baseline methodology should specify which sources and which gases are to be included in the baseline.

While in theory a baseline should include all the greenhouse gas impacts of a project, some emissions may be so small that their inclusion in the baseline would not significantly affect either its level or its accuracy. For example, although CH_4 is emitted in cement manufacture by the direct combustion of fuels used, it makes up less than 0.5% of GWP-weighted emissions from direct fuel combustion and so could reasonably be omitted from the baseline for the sake of simplicity. Gases could also be omitted from the project boundary (*i.e.* both the baseline and estimated project emissions) if they are not expected to change following project implementation. For example, a project could reduce the energy-related greenhouse gas emissions associated with manufacturing a particular product, but not alter the process emissions. In this case, the process emissions would not need to be estimated, as to calculate emission reductions from the project the process emissions would need to be included in both the baseline and the project emissions and so would cancel each other out[10].

A standardised baseline methodology should also indicate how to handle indirect sources of emissions associated with a project. Direct sources of emissions are those that occur at the project site. However, a JI or CDM project could significantly affect indirect (*e.g.* off-site) emissions. Perhaps the most extreme example is an energy efficiency project that

---

[10] In this case, the emission reduction of the project would be (fuel-related emissions before the project - fuel-related emissions after project implementation) + (process emissions before the project - process emissions after project implementation). Since the process emissions are equal before and after the project, they cancel each other out and so do not need to be calculated.

reduces electricity consumption: while such a project could unquestionably result in lower electricity consumption on-site, the main GHG mitigation effect of the project is felt "up-stream" in electricity production. Other examples of where indirect effects may be significant can be found in the cement sector. In this sector, increasing the proportion of additives blended with clinker, the main component of cement, can greatly reduce the GHG intensity of cement. However, the production, transport and use of such additives may also result in GHG emissions, albeit at lower levels and an assessment of these impacts would need to be included in a realistic overall assessment of a project's total GHG mitigation effect.

Deciding which indirect GHG effects to include may have to be done by examining each sector individually. The sectoral studies presented here exclude all indirect emissions that occur off-site, other than those associated with electricity generation. Thus, in the example above, the production and transport of cement additives would not be included in the project's baseline, but the GHG impact of energy used on-site to grind the additives would. Indirect emissions associated with the GHG-intensity of construction materials have been excluded here for simplicity and also because their GHG emissions will have been accounted for at the production site.

1.4.5 Data assumptions and availability

Once decisions on what to standardise have been made, data needs to be collected (or assumptions made). Standardisation can assist here by outlining the baseline parameters for which data need to be collected and what the possible data sources or data collection methods are.

The sectoral studies presented here suggest that, at least for new (greenfield) installations, using data on the performance of recently installed plants is a reasonable proxy for BAU behaviour. Moreover, data on what has been installed are more readily available than information on the relative economics of installed plants and alternative investment options[11]. Once a data set of "recently installed" plants has been obtained, a baseline could be based either on an average performance of new plants, or on the average performance of the most common type of new installation. The former may be most suitable in a sector where there are several common ways of producing an output with varying GHG-intensity, but no industry standard to produce the same output (such as in electricity generation). The average performance of the most common technology type may be more appropriate in a sector where one technology or process dominates and/or is the standard technology for new installations (such as cement kilns).

---

[11] Determining a suitable sample size for "recently installed" plants is likely to depend on the number and size of recent plants installed and of all plants operating in that project category and is therefore likely to vary by both sector and country.

New equipment is generally more energy-efficient and less GHG-intensive than older equipment. However, older equipment is not taken out of use just because it is no longer state of the art - it is frequently used to the end of its economic (or technical) life. Thus, the level of a baseline based on "recent" plants will generally be lower than a baseline based on the average performance of plants operating within a sector, as the average will include some older and more inefficient plants. However, most recent capacity additions can also be more GHG intensive than the average of existing plants: this is the case for electricity in Brazil, where fossil fuel plants are increasing their share in the fuel mix. Whether recent capacity is more or less GHG-intensive than "average" capacity is irrelevant, however, as they should still be a better proxy for "what would have happened otherwise" than an average performance of existing plants/equipment.

Trends, such as in technology performance or patterns of use, may also need to be taken into account when developing a standardised (or project-specific) baseline. For example, autonomous energy efficiency improvements may need to be "built into" an energy efficiency baseline to take into account that the performance of recently installed equipment is continuing to improve.

Determining an appropriate data set for JI or CDM projects that refurbish or modernise existing plants may be more complex. For example, it may be that a refurbished plant could never achieve the performance of a new plant, although it could considerably improve its past performance. In such a case, a different baseline for refurbishment projects and greenfield projects may be appropriate- even if they are the same type of project in the same sector[12]. However, if different baselines apply to refurbishment and greenfield projects it is important that these baselines do not preferentially promote one investment type over another.

If a baseline methodology, rather than baseline level, is standardised, the project developer will need to calculate a baseline from the methodology given. by incorporating country or region-specific values for variables in the standardised methodology. The availability of these data will vary according to which data source is used (*e.g.* sub-national, national or international) and on the data sample required (*e.g.* all recent additions or a representative plant type). For example, information on the relative proportion of different cement production processes may be easily available at a national level, but less available in an international collection of statistics.

1.4.6   Baseline units

Standardising the units in which a baseline, or its different components, should be expressed, could help increase the comparability, transparency and verifiability of the

---

[12] However, there are not necessarily clear distinctions between large-scale "refurbishment" projects and greenfield projects.

baseline. While the baseline units may be obvious for some project categories (like measuring the mitigation per kWh produced for electricity generation projects), it may be less obvious for others. For example, the standardised component of a baseline for JI or CDM projects in cement or steel manufacture (where many different products are produced from a single intermediate product) may more appropriately be the intermediate product. For cement projects this could mean that the emission baseline is expressed in terms of emissions/ton of clinker produced rather than emissions/ton of cement.

The numerator of a standardised baseline component is also important and appropriate standardised numerators can vary. For example where a project boundary includes multiple gases, for the sake of transparency, project developers are likely to need to report each gas included in the baseline in terms of mass and CO_2 equivalent, *e.g.* CO_2/kWh + CH_4/kWh. However, the numerator of a standardised baseline component could also be a unit of energy. Both the cement and iron and steel studies suggest standardised baseline methodologies or components based on energy inputs, *e.g.* GJ fuel/ton clinker produced (for cement products).

1.5   Conclusions and next steps

1.5.1   Maximise environmental effectiveness of the mechanisms

Maximising the potential environmental effectiveness of an individual JI and CDM project, through the baseline-setting process, clearly needs to minimise the impacts of gaming, free-riding and leakage. However, maximising the overall environmental effectiveness of the project-based mechanisms needs to incorporate other elements that work to encourage participation in JI and CDM, notably increasing transparency and minimising the baseline development costs.

In practice, drawing up a baseline will involve a trade-off between environmental credibility at the project level, transparency, baseline development costs and investor certainty (Figure 1-1). Ensuring environmental effectiveness and encouraging participation in the project-based mechanisms need not be contradictory aims, yet there is some tension between the two.

Figure 1-1

Possible effect of baseline stringency and complexity
on project numbers and a project's environmental additionality

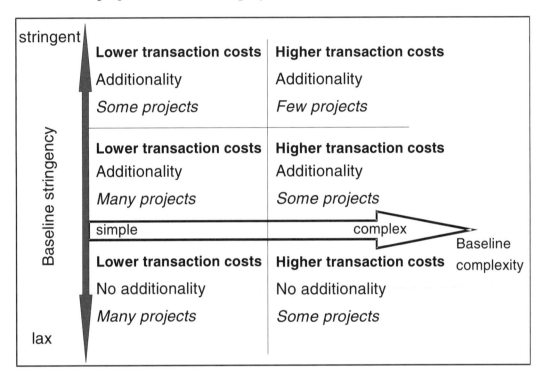

Source: Ellis and Bosi (1999)

Elaborating the project-based mechanisms in such a way that only a few JI and CDM projects are implemented is not likely to be viewed by many as a satisfactory contribution towards achieving either net GHG reductions or sustainable development. Simplifying the baseline-setting process, *e.g.* by establishing standardised baselines or baseline methodologies, should reduce the transaction costs of baseline and project preparation and facilitate the review (and approval) of a JI or CDM project. However, any guidance on baseline standardisation will need to balance the certainty about the environmental effectiveness of individual projects and the desire for simple, low-cost procedures which are needed to encourage a large volume of projects. Moreover, the project-based mechanisms will need to deliver emission credits at a reasonable price in order to limit compliance costs. A failure to do so may increase the difficulty of some Parties to meet the Kyoto commitments, or even, in some cases, to ratify the Protocol.

Standardised approaches to setting baselines could lead to a higher number of good projects being undertaken compared to a lower number of individually better projects, that may (or not) have been initiated using different baseline approaches. The global

39

environmental benefits of a higher number of good projects should be greater than that of a lower number of individually better projects. The rules and modalities that will guide the development and approval of emission baselines can help achieve this "balance" between baseline stringency and baseline complexity.

1.5.2   Learning by doing

As the development of emission baselines is truly an exercise of "estimating the unknown", it is perhaps a better strategy to learn-by-doing than to seek to develop the "perfect" system from the outset. COP6 will need to aim for an initial set of guidance that moves the process forward. The lessons learned from early experiences should be used to refine guidance over time and the guidance will gradually evolve and improve.

The learning-by-doing process should be built on a solid foundation to ensure that the project-based mechanisms are successful in delivering lower cost emission reduction and contributing to sustainable development (in the case of the CDM). The credibility and workability of emission baselines will be key. In fact the baseline development process will need to seek to balance the criteria of environmental effectiveness, low development cost, transparency and a reasonable level of crediting certainty. Focusing on only one of these four criteria, at the expense of the others, is likely to lead to a less than satisfactory outcome for the project-based mechanisms.

However, there is no simple recipe for achieving the appropriate balance. A sector by sector consideration of these issues is needed to provide insight into the way forward to provide guidance to project developers and host countries.

1.5.3   Consider sector characteristics and opportunities for standardisation

The remainder of this volume presents analyses of how baseline values and/or methodologies could be standardised for potential JI or CDM projects in the following sectors: cement, electricity generation, energy efficiency (lighting and motors) and iron and steel. These sectors were chosen because they are all significant sources of energy-related GHG emissions and also because of their perceived potential for baseline standardisation. Our analysis therefore focuses on if and how baselines for these sectors could be standardised. While the studies do not set out to assess how project-specific baselines could be drawn up in these sectors, conclusions from the studies about baseline construction and assumptions are relevant to both approaches.

Each sectoral analysis examines the key issues relating to baseline standardisation (presented above in sections 1.3 and 1.4) in detail and suggests whether baseline standardisation is feasible for particular project types. While each of the sectors examined appears to be amenable to standardisation to some degree, this degree varies substantially between - and even within - sectors. Where standardisation is found to be feasible, suggestions are given as to appropriate standardised baseline levels (*e.g.* cement), methodologies (*e.g.* electricity generation) or parameters (*e.g.* energy efficiency) that would be consistent with the objective of environmental effectiveness.

There are different potential uses for the sector analyses contained in this book. Potential CDM or JI project developers in one of the four sectors analysed could use the methodologies or values presented here as a starting point for their baseline calculations. Negotiators involved in the UNFCCC process could use the structure of the analysis to help them decide which factors a CDM reference manual, or handbook, should address and in what detail, if agreement is reached that such a manual should be elaborated. Analysts and researchers can use the results as a starting point to continue further work to widen the underlying data, or to bring the methodological suggestions a step further.

Some of the general results presented here, such as the need to focus standardisation efforts on intermediates rather than final products and on energy intensity, rather than GHG intensity, may be applicable to potential JI/CDM projects in energy or industry sectors not examined here. However, more detailed insights, such as an appropriate level of aggregation, or an appropriate boundary for a standardised baseline, could only be obtained after an analysis of these other sectors. This report should therefore not be interpreted to suggest that baseline standardisation is feasible for all project categories.

Working towards standardising the baseline-development process in a transparent and environmentally credible way will help move in the right direction. The case studies examined in this book are aimed at helping develop that process. Using this work and other material available on the development of baselines combined with real-world project experience, the baseline standardisation process will improve over time. Achieving and maintaining a balanced baseline process that will contribute to the overall success of JI and the CDM will require ongoing review, building on lessons learned over time.

There are many yet-to-be-answered questions surrounding the issue of how JI and CDM projects can work in practice. Baselines are at the root of many of these questions and any answers will need to include technical, economic and policy elements. This publication provides a first step in gathering the necessary elements and illustrating how they might be used to standardise emission baselines.

1.6   References

Begg, Katie, Stuart Parkinson, Tim Jackson, Poul-Erik Morthorst, Peter Bailey, 1999, *Overall Issues for Accounting for the Emissions Reductions of JI Projects*, presented at Workshop on Baselines for CDM, Tokyo, February 25 and 26, 1999, www.gispri.or.jp/

Ellis, Jane and Martina Bosi, 1999, *Options for Project Emission Baselines*, OECD and IEA Information Paper, Paris, www.oecd.org/env/cc/freedocs.html

IPCC (1996a), *Impacts, Adaptations and Mitigation of Climate Change: Scientific Technical Analysis.* Contribution of Working Group II to the Second Assessment Report of the IPCC. Edited by R.T. Watson, M.C. Zinyowera and R.H. Moss, Cambridge University Press.

Mullins, Fiona and Richard Baron, 1997, *International Greenhouse Gas Emission Trading*, Working Paper No. 9 prepared for the Annex I Expert Group on the United Nations Framework Convention on Climate Change, OECD, Paris, www.oecd.org/env/cc/freedocs.html

Mullins, Fiona, 1999, *International Emissions Trading under the Kyoto Protocol*, OECD Information Paper, Paris, www.oecd.org/env/cc/freedocs.html

OECD, 1999a, *Action Against Climate Change,* Paris.

OECD, 1999b, *Experience with Emission Baselines under the AIJ Pilot Phase,* OECD Information Paper, Paris.

Tellus Institute, Stockholm Environment Institute and Status Consulting, 1999, *Evaluation of Benchmarking as an Approach for Establishing Clean Development Mechanism Baselines,* prepared for US EPA, Boston.

2. CEMENT CASE STUDY

2. CEMENT CASE STUDY[13]

2.1   Executive summary

Cement is produced in more than 80 countries. Its manufacture is very energy intensive and results in significant energy-related and process emissions of greenhouse gases, mainly CO_2. There are a number of ways in which the greenhouse gas "intensity" of cement could be reduced. Thus, cement manufacture could potentially be an object for joint implementation (JI) or Clean Development Mechanism (CDM) projects. This case study explores if and how emission baselines for different types of JI or CDM projects in the cement sector could be standardised.

There are three main steps in cement manufacture: 1) preparing the raw materials; 2) producing an intermediate "clinker"; and 3) grinding and blending clinker with other products to make cement. Clinker production is the most energy intensive of these steps and is also the source of process CO_2 emissions. Process emissions can account for half or more of emissions from cement manufacture.

Clinker can be produced by a number of different manufacturing processes. The "dry" process is much more energy-efficient than the "wet" process (which is gradually being phased out). Which process is used to manufacture cement thus influences the greenhouse gas (GHG) intensity of cement. Other factors that affect the energy and/or GHG intensity of cement production include:

- which fuels are used in the manufacturing process (*e.g.* coal, oil or solid waste);

- which exact technologies are used (*e.g.* which type of cement grinder, exact kiln specifications *etc.*);

- the type of cement that is produced (not all cement types are suitable for all applications and some cement types are more energy-intensive to produce than others);

---

[13] This paper was written by Jane Ellis, OECD. The author would like to thank Jan Corfee-Morlot (OECD) and Jonathan Pershing (IEA) for their comments and oversight and Shigemoto Kajihara (Japan), Shari Friedman (United States), Gene McGlynn, Thomas Martinsen, Stéphane Willems (OECD), Martina Bosi, Kristi Varangu, Cédric Philibert (IEA), Michel Picard (Lafarge) and Jan-Willem Bode (Ecofys) for their advice and comments.

- the physical and chemical properties of the raw materials used;
- the GHG intensity of electricity used in cement manufacture; and
- the proportion of clinker, the most GHG-intensive component, in cement.

Cement manufacturers have different degrees of influence over these different factors. For example, they generally cannot choose electricity of a particular GHG intensity - they use what is available to them.

Potential JI/CDM project types in the cement sector can be divided into two broad categories: energy-related and non-energy related. Energy-related GHG emissions from clinker manufacture could be reduced by:

- increasing the energy efficiency of cement production, *e.g.* by optimising heat recovery or installing an efficient pre-heater,
- changes in the production process, *e.g.* by changing the process by which raw materials are ground, mixed and fed into the kilns from wet to dry, or
- changing the input fuel, *e.g.* by using an increased proportion of waste fuels.

In addition, process CO_2 emissions could be significantly reduced per ton of cement produced by blending (mixing) clinker with an increased proportion of other products ("additives") in cement. This can be done in some cases without incurring significant incremental costs. Potential GHG reductions from cement blending may outstrip those from energy efficiency projects by a significant margin.

Some elements of emission baselines for potential JI/CDM projects in the cement sector could be standardised. Which elements depend on the type of project that is being undertaken (see below). Changes at an individual plant could make it eligible for one or more of these project types.

For energy-efficiency projects, standard energy values for different manufacturing steps could be established, such as x GJ fuel per ton clinker produced. These values would be based on the energy intensity of new technology installed at present, which is a good indication of "what would have happened otherwise". A project that produces cement at a lower energy intensity than the standard threshold value could generate emission credits. These standardised energy values could apply internationally to both existing and new plants. Basing a standardised energy value on technology-specific data has the advantage that such data are readily available (and could be easily updated, if necessary).

Emission baselines need to be expressed in terms of emissions. However, a standardised value for CO_2 emissions/ton clinker cannot be drawn up across countries without effectively prescribing which fuels are used (and for electricity, how efficiently it is generated). Nevertheless, standardised "energy baselines" could be drawn up and then "translated" to GHG emissions. The information needed for "translation" could be default, country-specific or project-specific data, such as multi-project electricity baselines, IPCC emission inventory methodologies and default or site-specific emission factors.

Standardised energy values could also be drawn up for production process change projects. These values would need to reflect both the technology in place and its rate of conversion to efficient technology under BAU conditions and may therefore need to be drawn up at the national level.

For JI or CDM projects that change the fuel used in cement manufacture, the most difficult part of setting a baseline is assessing the quantity of waste fuels that would have otherwise been used, as this can vary significantly over time as well as from site to site. This difficulty is compounded for new plants, where historical "alternative fuel" use data is not available. Thus, no standardised values for the amount of baseline alternative fuel use can be drawn up. Nevertheless, once this amount, the fuel's emission factor and what it is displacing has been established, a standard methodology to "translate" this activity into GHG equivalent is available in the IPCC inventory guidelines.

For all energy-related projects in the cement sector, baselines should be expressed in terms of energy use per ton clinker produced for each of the three main process steps. Since the characteristics of "cement" can vary widely, expressing standardised baselines in terms of tons of cement would not lead to comparable values across projects. An internationally standardised baseline value for the energy required to manufacture cement should be set towards the upper end of the best practice range for energy-efficiency type projects, such as 3.1 GJ/t clinker direct fuel use for the pyro-processing step. This value compares to estimated best practice of 2.9 - 3.2 GJ/t clinker and performance of 2.93 - 3.10 GJ/t clinker in new, best practice cement plants. A lower value would result in fewer "free riders", but could also result in some additional projects not generating any emission credits. It may be more appropriate to set a less stringent baseline (*i.e.* at a higher level) for process change projects, in order to encourage conversion from highly inefficient plant types. The large volumes of cement produced means that the number of credits generated by a particular project is highly sensitive to the baseline level: credits could more than double with a 0.1 GJ/t increase in baseline levels.

Setting standardised values for electricity consumption for each of the main process steps is also possible in theory, although more difficult in practice, as significant variations ($\pm$ 15%) in technology performance are found from site to site. Moreover, more than one standardised energy value would be needed for cement grinding, to reflect the different energy consumption requirements of producing different quality cements (different quality cements are needed for different applications: one cement cannot always be substituted for another). Information on total fuel and electricity use from the three process steps should be included when calculating the emission reductions and related emission credits generated by a project, as projects could reduce the energy requirement in one step but increase it in another.

The energy-related emissions of CH_4 and N_2O combined typically represent less than 0.5% of total energy-related emissions, so could be omitted from emission baselines without having a significant impact on either the stringency of the emissions baseline or on the uncertainty of credits. Thus baselines for energy-related projects in cement manufacture could be simplified to include energy-related CO_2 emissions only. Since process-related CO_2 emissions are not impacted by energy-related projects, they would also not need to be included in the emissions baseline for energy-related projects.

For blending projects, it would be difficult to set either international or national standards for the clinker content of cement produced because the clinker content of cement varies significantly within and between countries, cement plants and cement types and can change significantly from year to year. Moreover, for plants already in operation, data on clinker and cement production before and during a project are likely to be both easily available at the project level and more accurate (and available) at this level than at the country level. However, using a project-specific and potentially highly variable number, increases the opportunity for gaming. This is exacerbated for greenfield plants, which by definition do not have any historical data on which to base emission baselines. Emission baselines for any blending-type projects should include components related to both energy-related and process CO_2 emissions. These components should be separated for transparency and verification purposes. Baselines for blending projects in cement manufacture should be reported in terms of energy-related and process CO_2 emissions per ton cement produced.

This study recommends quantifying the major emission sources that are influenced by a project. For energy projects, the major emission sources are the three major process steps: raw materials preparation, pyro-processing and cement grinding. Process CO_2 emissions are unchanged by energy-related projects and so could be omitted from the project baseline for simplicity. For blending projects, process emissions, emissions from additive preparation as well as energy-related emissions should be included in the project boundary. Emissions from other activities related to cement manufacture (such as transport of raw materials, bagging and transport of finished cement) could be addressed by applying a constant multiplier, *i.e.* as a percentage of baseline or project emissions, to the quantified emission sources. Using this method to quantify small emission sources addresses both simplicity and leakage concerns, but could be contentious because any multiplier used will necessarily be approximate.

Determining the crediting lifetime of potential JI/CDM projects in the cement sector is difficult, because there are no general standards (across different countries and companies) for the technical lifetime of equipment or for how long it is used before being refurbished. For example, although cement plants can have a 50y life, some companies/plants may replace major pieces of equipment, such as kilns, after 25y. Other companies/plants will continue operation using old and inefficient technology until the supply of raw materials is exhausted. Refurbishment (or not) of existing plants will also depend on the competitiveness of the cement supply market. Thus, some plant refurbishments will be business-as-usual activity, while others could be "additional".

It may be possible to set up rough "rules of thumb" to help determine the crediting lifetime of energy efficiency and process change projects. However, great care would need to be taken in order to avoid creating either non-additional credits or perverse incentives that would, for example, reward installing inefficient technology. The best way of doing this may be to opt for either relatively short crediting lifetimes for energy efficiency and process change projects (*e.g.* 5-10y) or baselines that are revised relatively frequently (*e.g.* every 5y) for all project types.

Determining whether a project is truly "additional" may be as difficult as determining for how long an "additional" project should receive credits. Therefore, it may be appropriate to include some qualitative additionality checks as well as the quantitative baseline "test" when determining whether a project should be eligible to generate emissions credits.

2.2   Broad overview of the cement sector

Cement is the key component of concrete, used in the construction of, for example, buildings. The raw materials needed for cement production (limestone, chalk, clay and sand) are widely available and cheap, but expensive to transport over long distances. This has led to cement being produced in over 80 countries. Cement production is highly energy-intensive, leading to significant energy-related and process CO_2 emissions. Energy costs represent 30-40% of the costs of cement production (Cembureau 1997).

Global cement production in 1995 was estimated at 1.45 billion tons (IEA GHG R&D 1999). Total (energy-related and process) emissions from global cement production in 1994 were estimated at 1.1 billion tons CO_2 (Marland *et. al.* 1998), or 5% of global energy-related CO_2 emissions in the same year. Cement production accounted for an estimated 1-2% of global primary energy consumption (WEC 1995, quoted in IEA GHG R&D 1999). There is one AIJ project in the cement sector (between the Czech Republic and France). In addition, Japan has initiated feasibility studies for potential JI or CDM projects in China and Russia and other countries.

There are three main steps to cement production (see Figure 2-1):

- preparing the raw materials;
- producing clinker, an intermediate; and
- grinding and blending clinker with other products to make cement.

The raw materials obtained from the quarry are crushed, ground and mixed (either as a powder or as a slurry). This mixture may then be fed into a pre-calciner and/or pre-heater before being fed into the kiln, for "pyro-processing" (clinker formation). The kiln can reach temperatures greater than 1450°C. The clinker nodules produced and any additives are then ground to the desired fineness in the cement grinder.

Figure 2-1

Process steps in cement manufacture

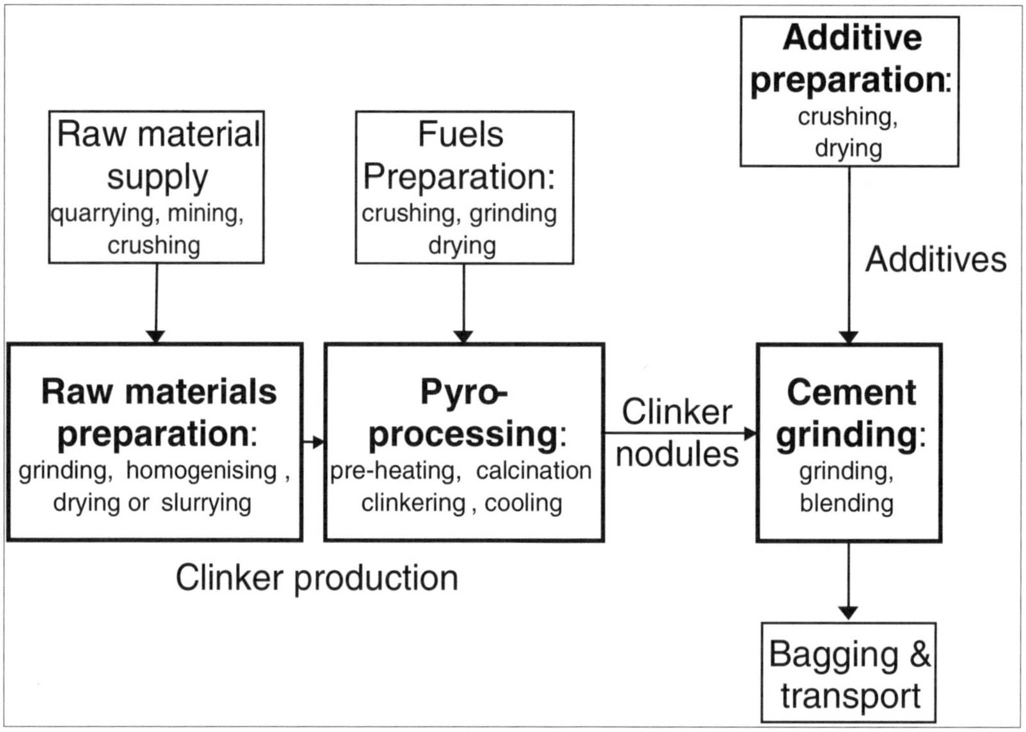

Source: adapted from Ruth *et. al.* (2000)

The second step, pyro-processing, is the most energy intensive (see Figure 2-2) and requires up to 80% of the total energy consumed for cement production (the exact amount will vary depending on the proportion and type of additives in the final cement mix). The majority of fuel inputs, typically coal or fuel oil, are used in the pyro-processing step, whereas electricity is mainly used in crushing/grinding. Pyro-processing also results in process CO_2 emissions from the decarbonisation of limestone. Per ton of clinker produced, approximately half emissions are process-related and the other half are energy-related (fuel combustion and, to a much lesser extent, electricity use)[14].

Clinker can be produced by two main processes: dry or wet. Two other processes, intermediate (semi-dry or semi-wet) and shaft, are also used in some countries. The name of the process refers to how the raw materials are mixed. The dry process is much less

---

[14] The relative proportion of process and energy-related CO_2 emissions can vary significantly depending on the emission factors of the fuel (and electricity) used in cement manufacture.

energy-intensive than the wet process and typically requires energy input of 3.3 MJ/kg clinker, whereas the wet process needs 5.7 MJ/kg clinker (IEA GHG R&D 1999). The wet process is being phased out in many developing countries (Price *et. al.* 1999) and is rarely used for new plants.

Figure 2-2

Energy use of different steps within "best practice" cement manufacture

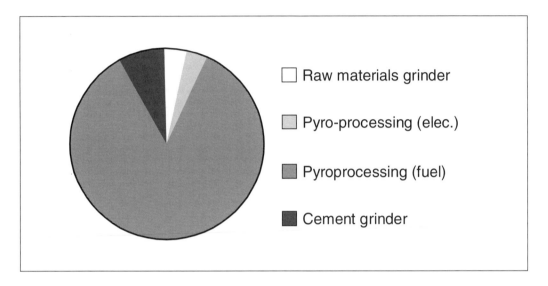

Source: based on figures from Cembureau, (1997) and IEA GHG R&D (1999)

Many different types of cement are produced, varying in, for example, strength and setting (hardening) time. Differing proportions of clinker and other additives in the final product cause these variations. The most common type of cement, Portland cement, contains 95% clinker. Other types of cement (such as composite, pozzolanic, blastfurnace or Portland composite cements) can contain between 20-94% clinker (Cembureau 1991, quoted in IEA GHG R&D 1999). Since clinker is the most GHG-intensive component of cement, it is important to know the proportion of clinker in the cement being manufactured when determining the emissions from cement production.

There has been a sharp increase in cement demand in many developing countries since the mid 1980s (IEA GHG R&D, 1999). This growth in demand is met by either extending the manufacturing capacity of existing plants or by building new cement plants. Cement demand is influenced by the demand for construction and is consequently linked to the economic growth of countries.

Cement plants are highly capital intensive. Thus, when looking to extend production capabilities, refurbishing an existing site can be considerably cheaper than building a new plant. New plants are generally designed to operate continuously, although if demand drops (*e.g.* in winter) and stockage capacities are limited they may temporarily shut. Although cement manufacture uses significant quantities of electricity, most cement plants do not include facilities for on-site electricity generation. However, there are some exceptions. These are found where, for example, the cement plant is in a remote area far from the electricity grid, or where grid-supplied electricity is unreliable (*i.e.* in an area of brown/blackouts).

Outside the Chinese market, cement production is dominated by a handful of multinational companies. These companies often own a majority stake in local cement producers: international trade in cement is limited because of the relatively high cost of transporting a bulky and relatively low-cost product.

There are a number of potential JI/CDM project types in the cement sector. These can be divided into two broad categories: energy-related and non-energy-related. Energy-related GHG emissions from clinker manufacture could be reduced by:

- increasing the energy efficiency of clinker production (*e.g.* by optimising heat recovery or installing an efficient pre-heater);

- changing the manufacturing process (*e.g.* by converting wet process plants to dry process plants); or

- changing the input fuel (*e.g.* by using an increased proportion of waste fuels).

Limiting non energy-related emissions, *i.e.* process CO_2 emissions from clinker production, would be difficult as these emissions are an inherent part of the decarbonisation of limestone ($CaCO_3$) to lime (CaO) during the formation of clinker[15]. However, process CO_2 emissions could be significantly reduced per ton of cement produced by blending clinker with an increased proportion of additives (such as fly-ash, blast furnace slag, pozzolana) in cement, *i.e.* by reducing the proportion of clinker in cement.

This report examines the cement sector in three countries in more detail. The choice of case study countries and the information presented in the remainder of section 2.2 was limited by the information available. In particular, information on the costs and benefits of plant refurbishments was difficult to find. Section 2.3 explores how potential baselines could be constructed and section 2.4 assesses what baseline assumptions could be made. Section 2.5 examines the different options for the potential stringency of baselines and section 2.6 outlines conclusions of the study.

---

[15] Capture of the CO_2 emitted through calcination is possible in theory but not carried out in practice.

Table 2-1

Summary of factors that determine GHG emissions from cement manufacture

Factor	Ability by manu-facturers to influence this factor	Comments
Fuel inputs	High	Coal, coke or oil are usually used as fuel inputs. The high temperatures of a cement kiln make it a suitable place to safely dispose of rubber/plastics or other waste types (*e.g.* hazardous waste). The use of these "alternative fuels" can have positive environmental impacts, as well as positive economic impacts for the cement manufacturer. However, the greenhouse gas impacts of using alternative fuels depends on what would have happened to these alternative fuels otherwise.
Process used (*i.e.* wet, dry or other)	High or low, depending on site layout	A potential process change only applies to plants already in operation, as new plants are almost always based on the dry process. The layout of some wet-process plants precludes their conversion.
Tech-nologies used for individual process steps	High	Within each process, a number of different technologies are available. The choice of one technology in one part of the cement production chain does not necessarily affect choices for the next part. However, the technologies used can influence the capacity of a plant (*e.g.* adding a precalciner can increase production capacity).
Properties of raw material inputs	None (unless raw material source changed)	The chemical and physical properties of the limestone used in cement manufacture can impact the GHG-intensity of clinker production to a certain extent. High moisture content limestone may lead to a choice of using wet or semi-dry processes. High silica content needs a higher kiln temperature for clinker formation and thus higher energy requirements.
GHG-intensity of electricity inputs	None	This can only be altered if the cement manufacturer installs on-site generation, which is not common practice.
Type of cement produced (*e.g.* fineness)	High to medium	The extent to which a manufacturer can change the type of cement produced will depend on the demand for cement and if/how such demand could be met with alternative cement specifications (strength, hardening time, *etc.*).
Proportion of clinker in cement	High to low	This is linked to the point above. There is a significant variation within and between countries and companies on blending regulations and practices. Increased use of additives may be precluded by national legislation and is also affected by the nearby availability (or not) of such additives. Blending is already used by some companies/countries as a means to reduce the GHG impact of cement manufacture. Increased blending is likely to increase the amount of cement produced by a given plant.

2.2.1   India case study

This section is based on information in Schumacher and Sathaye (1999) unless otherwise indicated.

India is the fourth largest cement producer in the world. India manufactures 13 different types of cement, with Portland cement (one of the most common cement types and containing 95% clinker) accounting for 70% of the total.

Cement is manufactured using the dry, semi-dry and wet processes (Sathaye and Gadgil 1999), although the share of kilns operating by the wet process has dropped substantially from 62% in the mid 1970s (Price *et. al.* 1999) to 12% in 1997. The importance of the wet process is expected to fall further as total production capacity increases and through conversion to the dry process.

Growth is variable, but averaged 8.7% p.a. 1973-1993. Production capacity almost tripled between 1982-1996, when it stood at 105.2 Mt and production more than tripled in the same time period. Cement demand is projected to continue growing and is expected to be at 200 Mt/y in 2011 compared to 105 Mt/y in 2001.

Sathye and Gadgil (1999) indicate that if all 61 kilns in India that use the wet process to produce cement convert to the dry process, 1.2 Mt of coal could be saved per year. However, the same source also indicates that only about a quarter of these wet kilns are amenable to conversion (*e.g.* because of current plant layout).

India has substantial reserves of coal and coal is used for the pyro-processing stage of cement manufacture. Coal also generates approximately 70% of India's electricity. India also produces some natural gas (15.6 Mtoe in 1995), but all this is used in the chemical industry (for fertiliser production) and in electricity production (IEA 1997). Schumacher and Sathaye (1999) indicate that reducing GHG emissions from the cement industry by using natural gas instead of coal for the pyro-processing step is unlikely.

India has a significant number of small cement plants. In 1995-96, approximately 9% of cement capacity were "small plants" and they produced just over 7% of cement. These small cement plants were set up throughout the country, in order to promote regional development and to reduce the strain on transport infrastructure. Smaller plants are often less efficient than larger plants, because energy efficiency equipment such as waste heat recovery systems are not economic to install given the small volume of cement manufactured.

However, the cement industry in India is modernising, as well as expanding. The share of dry kilns was more than 70% of the total in 1994 (Price *et. al.*1999) and many more modern kilns include technologies aimed at increasing energy efficiency, such as multi-stage suspension preheaters and precalciners. The modern, dry, process plants are therefore relatively energy efficient.

Table 2-2

Energy Intensity of Cement Production, India

Plant type	Specific Energy Consumption (GJp/t cement*) *(clinker in brackets)*		
	Electricity	**Fuel**	**Total**
Dry process (1993 performance)	1.21	3.00	4.21
Average over all plant types (1993 performance)	1.27	3.58	4.85
Best practice dry process	1.06 *(1.21)*	2.71 *(3.08)*	3.77 *(4.29)*
Best practice dry process with structural change**	0.32	2.14	2.46

Source: Adapted from Schumacher and Sathaye, 1999

To note: GHG emissions depend on electricity and fuel sources.

*Assumes a clinker/cement ratio of 0.88. "Best practice" is defined here as a dry process short kiln with a 4-stage pre-heater.

** Structural change would change the relative proportion of the different type of cements produced. Increasing the production of Portland Slag Cement and reducing that of Ordinary Portland Cement would increase use of blast furnace slag from India's iron & steel industry and could reduce the clinker/cement ratio from 88% to 68%. Combined with potential savings for energy efficiency, this could result in cumulative energy savings of 38% per ton of cement at current production levels. It would also reduce process CO_2 emissions.

There is a large variation in emissions performance between the different type of plants used in India, reflecting the different plant sizes and processes used. Moreover, the average performance of different plant types can fluctuate from year to year. Schumacher and Sathaye (1999) indicate that while the use of "best technology" could reduce emissions from dry process plants by 10-15%, it could improve the performance of an "average" plant by 24-35%. Ruth *et. al.* (2000) give a similar figure: 28% of CO_2 emissions from the Indian cement sector (21 Mt CO_2) could have been mitigated by use of best practice technologies.

Nevertheless, a number of energy conservation options are open to the Indian cement industry, often at little or no cost. However, many of these options have not been taken up, partly because of capital constraints, partly for other technical or technology-related reasons. For example, the adoption of more efficient mills (*e.g.* roller press) is inhibited by the high quartz content of raw materials which leads to increased abrasion of the rolling surfaces and therefore to a shorter lifetime for the mill.

2.2.2   Czech case study

Czech cement is manufactured in five cement plants. Czech production exceeds demand and the country exports some of its cement (to Germany)[16]. Many different types of cement are produced. In the late 1980s and early 1990s, some western European companies (German, Danish and French) invested in refurbishing existing cement plants to modernise and increase their capacity. For example, a German company (Dyckerhoff) modernised the Hranice plant between 1987-1991 to convert it from a wet to a dry plant and to increase production capacity (Cement Hranice 2000). The capacity changes and technology upgrades in another manufacturing plant, Cízkovice, have been approved as an AIJ project by the French and Czech governments.

Table 2-3

Energy Intensity of Cement Production, Czech Republic

Plant type	Specific Energy Consumption (GJp/t clinker)		
	Electricity	**Fuel**	**Total**
Best practice (Cembureau 1997)	0.79	2.9	3.69
National average over all plant types (1996 performance)	n/a	3.58	n/a
Cizkovice (approximately equal to the best national plant, 1996 performance)	0.97*	3.22	4.19

Source: Cembureau 1997 and calculated from figures presented in French/Czech AIJ project report (UNFCCC 1998) and assuming electricity efficiency at 33%.

* Including electricity needed for cement grinding.

This project at Cízkovice is the only AIJ project to date in the cement sector, although Japan has also initiated feasibility studies for different potential projects in a number of countries (such as Vietnam and China) under their "joint implementation feasibility study" programme. The Czech/France AIJ project involved refurbishing an existing cement plant by adding a 5-stage pre-heater and increasing the output from the plant by 150%. Energy consumption from the AIJ plant is planned at 3.385 GJ/t clinker (of which 3.22 GJ is in the pyro-processing step), compared to a national average (excluding the AIJ project) of 3.582 GJ/t clinker. The energy consumption of the AIJ project is essentially the same as that of the best technology operating in the Czech republic (excluding the AIJ project), which is 3.580 GJ/t clinker (Table 2-3).

---

[16] No information on the recent growth rates and type of cement produced nationally was available to the author.

The emissions performance of cement production in the Czech republic is rapidly improving: average thermal energy requirements for the plants excluding the AIJ project dropped from 3.76 GJ/t clinker in 1993 to 3.58 GJ/t cli in 1996 (UNFCCC 1998). Moreover, emissions from electricity production dropped from 865 g CO_2/kWh in 1993 to 707 g CO_2/kWh[17] in 1996, which helped to reduce the GHG-intensity of cement produced (UNFCCC 1998).

2.2.3   China case study

China is the world's largest cement producer, accounting for approximately a third of global cement production. Cement production in China has been growing rapidly and production reached 512 Mt in 1997, compared to 210 Mt in 1990 and 37.3 Mt in 1973 (LBNL 1999). The majority of production is Portland cement (approximately 71% of total production in 1997) (LBNL 1999). Other cement production includes blast furnace cement (approximately 26% of the total in 1997), with small amounts of fly ash and white cement (LBNL 1999).

The cement sector in China is very heterogeneous, with many small and a few large production facilities (using both the wet and dry process). Approximately 80% of cement is produced in small, mechanised shaft kilns (NEDO 1998a). These kilns can have relatively low fuel and electricity intensities, but result in significant emissions of particulates and produce poor quality cement[18]. The electricity intensity of cement production in China is rising as more electrically-run process and environmental controls are being used. The total number of cement kilns in operation in China is unknown, but estimates of total numbers are in the order of 6000-8000[19].

The technology of recently constructed plants in China is different from that elsewhere: some new wet process kilns have been built in the 1990s (although are being phased out in other countries) and many new shaft kilns were also constructed. The advantage of shaft kilns is that they are smaller and relatively quick to construct and could therefore satisfy the rapid growth in demand noted above. However, widespread use of shaft kilns is limited to China and, to a much lesser extent, India. The energy efficiency of shaft kilns can vary significantly, with estimated fuel intensities of 3.2-6.6 GJ/t clinker (IEA GHG R&D 1999).

---

[17] These figures refer to average national emissions per kWh.

[18] Jonathan Sinton, LBNL, personal communication, 22.12.1999

[19] Jonathan Sinton, LBNL, personal communication, 22.12.1999

Table 2-4

**Effect of a process change on the energy intensity
of clinker production in two cement plants in China**

	Tianjin cement plant	Huaxin cement plant
Production capacity (kt/y):		
• pre-project	144	140
• post-project	217	186
Fuel consumption in kiln (GJ/t cli):		
• pre-project	5.12	4.1
• post-project	3.14	3.14
Electricity consumption in kiln (kWh/t cli):		
• pre-project	23.5	23
• post-project	40	40
Total CO_2 (t CO_2/t cli):		
• pre-project	0.518	0.420
• post-project	0.345	0.345

Source: NEDO, 2000 (assuming anthracite is used both for direct fuel use and for electricity generation at 32.5% efficiency).

* These figures are not directly comparable to those in the previous two tables, as the figures in this table do not include the energy required for cement grinding.

The primary energy intensity of cement production in China has been estimated at 5.8 GJ/t (Price *et. al.* 1999). This high value reflects the use of wet process plants and the predominance of (small-scale) shaft kilns. The same analysis indicates significant technical potential to reduce the energy consumption of cement manufacture in China. The theoretical CO_2 impact of using best practice cement manufacture for all Chinese cement production has been estimated (Price *et. al.* 1999) at 2.0 GJ/t cement produced. This is equivalent to a reduction of 96.3 Mt CO_2 (approximately equivalent to the total energy-related CO_2 emissions of Sweden and Norway in 1990) if China's 1995 production of cement had been manufactured using best practice rather than current technology[20].

The Chinese cement industry is undergoing a period of change, with the government's policy of "making large larger and small smaller" (NEDO 1998b). For shaft kiln facilities this could mean either closure of existing facilities or refurbishment with capacity increases.

---

[20] Of course, for technical, financial and policy reasons, this maximum theoretical impact will not be met.

China and Japan have carried out feasibility studies on projects converting two shaft kilns to fluidised bed cement kiln systems[21] (NEDO 1998a). These projects would increase the production capacity and decrease the GHG impact of clinker production in two plants (Table 2-4). The GHG-intensity of the whole process is reduced, although the electricity intensity increases.

2.3 Baseline construction

Emissions from the manufacture of clinker can be expressed by the following equation:

Equation 1:

*Total emissions = Process emissions + emissions from fuel combustion + (indirect) emissions
for clinker prodn.   from electricity consumed*

However, an emissions baseline for energy efficiency and process change projects in cement manufacture may only need to take the energy-related emissions into account. This is because, while the fuel and electricity-related GHG emissions may vary between the baseline and the JI/CDM project, it is unlikely that the process emissions would be significantly different per ton clinker produced[22]. Thus, focusing baselines on the GHG-intensity of clinker production would enable analysis to focus on differences in the fuel and electricity-related emissions between a CDM/JI project and a non-CDM/JI project.

These two components can be disaggregated further:

Equation 2:

*Emissions from fuel   = Quantity of fuel(s) used (GJ) * Fuel emission factor(s) (t CO_2/GJ)
combustion*

*Emissions from   = Quantity of electricity used (MWh) * Electricity emission factor
electricity use   (t CO_2[23]/MWh)*

---

[21] This technology is still under development - and therefore not widespread - and is assessed as suitable only for small plants producing under 360,000t/y (IEA GHG R&D 1999).

[22] Process-related emissions can vary with the proportion of the clinker lime content. However, since trade in cement is limited, demand for any cement not produced by a CDM/JI project is likely to be produced by a local plant using raw materials of similar characteristics. Thus, process emissions from a potential CDM/JI project and from an alternative non-CDM/JI supplier are likely to be very similar.

[23] Emissions of other GHG are also likely to be produced from the combustion of fuels to produce electricity, but their relative GWP-weighted emissions are small compared to those of CO_2. Since electricity-related emissions are only a small proportion of total emissions from clinker production, non-CO_2 emissions from electricity production are likely to represent less than 0.5% of total GWP-

For blending-type projects, an estimation of the process emissions is needed. According to the 1996 IPCC guidelines, process CO_2 emissions should be calculated by estimating the CaO and clinker fraction of cement and then applying a clinker-based emission factor (IPCC 1996).

Equation 3:

Process emissions = Emissions from clinker production + emissions from additional lime used in masonry cement

*Emissions from clinker production = 0.5071 t CO_2/t cli * tons clinker produced*

Most cement types do not include additional lime. Therefore, equation 3 can be simplified in most cases as process emissions = emissions from clinker production.

Blending projects would also need to take into account the GHG intensity of additive preparation. This will vary according to which additive is used (and is discussed further in section 2.3.2).

Thus, emissions from the manufacture of cement can be expressed as following:

Equation 4:

Total emissions for cement production	*= Process emissions*
	+ emissions from fuel combustion
	+ (indirect) emissions from electricity consumed
	+ emissions from any additional lime used
	+ emissions associated with additive preparation

The indirect emissions from electricity include those from electricity consumed at all stages of the cement manufacturing process (such as raw material preparation and cement grinding).

2.3.1 Key underlying assumptions

The key underlying assumptions of emission baselines in cement manufacture relate for the most part to the energy used in the different manufacturing processes. The amount of energy used (*i.e.* fuel use per ton clinker produced, electricity use per ton clinker produced) is determined predominantly by which technology is used for a particular process. Which technology is used is in part determined by the chemical/moisture characteristics of the raw materials.

---

weighted energy-related emissions and may therefore be omitted without significantly affecting the emissions baseline.

Cement has been produced since 1824, with technology evolving steadily. Recent improvements (1970s) have included introducing precalciners[24], which improve energy efficiency and also help to increase the productivity of kilns. The introduction of precalciners has helped to reduce the energy intensity of clinker production in Europe from approximately 4.7 GJ/t clinker in 1973 to 3.7 GJ/t clinker in 1995 (Cembureau 1999).

New cement plants installed under business-as-usual conditions are often state-of-the-art equipment comprising a dry process kiln with a 5-stage preheater/calciner. Such plants have been constructed all over the world during the 1990s, including in Asia and Africa (*e.g.* IFC projects 4955 and 7717 in China and project 8657 in Senegal (IFC 1999) and by Holderbank in Viet Nam (Holderbank 1999)). Plants of this type are considered standard for ordinary new plants in Europe (Cembureau 1997) and are also the most common choice for new plants constructed elsewhere (see example, Ruth *et. al.* 2000, Picard 2000[25]).

Dry kilns with a 5 stage pre-heater/calciner could therefore be considered as business as usual technology for new plants who use raw materials with a relatively low water content[26]. It would therefore be difficult to argue that plants of this type should be eligible for JI/CDM status as credible emission baselines for new cement plants are likely to be based on this technology in most cases. Such plants could nevertheless be eligible for JI/CDM status, for example, by using waste fuels instead of fossil fuels in the pyro-processing step, or if they are towards the lower end of best practice energy use for this plant type.

Wet, semi-wet or semi-dry process plants are rarely constructed nowadays and are only used when the raw material inputs have an extremely high water content. However, given the relatively long lifetime of a cement plant (up to 50y), some wet process plants and many semi-wet and semi-dry plants are still in operation in some countries (including China, US, India and UK).

Given the relative importance of energy costs in cement manufacture, there is a strong economic incentive to increase the energy-efficiency of cement production. Thus, many wet process plants are being phased out under BAU conditions through conversion to

---

[24] Pre-calciners are situated between the pre-heater and the kiln. They are equipped with a burner that enables partial (80-95%) decarbonisation of limestone to lime (IEA GHG R&D 1999). Having a precalciner enables a shorter and, therefore, more energy-efficient kiln to be installed, thereby reducing the energy (and GHG) intensity of clinker production.

[25] M. Picard, Lafarge, personal communication, 10.1.00.

[26] Pre-heaters contain 2-6 stages. Some state-of-the-art plants have been installed using a 6-stage pre-heater, although this is not common practice and is only possible if raw materials have a low moisture content. Plants using raw materials with a relatively higher moisture content may opt for a 3 or 4-stage pre-heater, or for a semi-set or semi-dry process instead of a dry process.

other process types, (such as in China, India, Brazil (Price *et. al.* 1999 and Shumacher and Sathaye 1999) and the Czech Republic (Cement Hranice 2000)). However, not all wet process plants are amenable to conversion because *e.g.* of the plant layout.

Refurbishment of dry process plants also occurs, *e.g.* installing a 5-stage preheater/ precalciner at existing facilities in Italy and Slovenia (Ruth *et. al.* 2000). However, since wet process plants are still in operation in some countries, converting a wet process plant to a dry process plant, or making other energy efficiency improvements be considered as "additional" in some cases, even though conversion also takes place in other cases under BAU conditions. Standardising a methodology to determine when plant conversions are additional or not would be difficult. Nevertheless, some qualitative and quantitative criteria (such as whether similar plants were converted and at what rate) could be developed that may be useful in this regard.

No generalised assumptions about which fuels are used and what the GHG-intensity of electricity used are possible between different countries as there are significant variations, particularly in the GHG-intensity of electricity. Similarly, it is difficult to generalise "key underlying assumptions" for either the amount or type of waste fuels used, or the amount and type of extenders added to clinker, because these vary significantly from plant to plant and country to country. Thus, while production process technologies and their performance could be standardised to a greater or lesser extent across countries/regions, information on which fuels are used may need to be drawn up at a more disaggregated level (possibly even plant-specific).

2.3.2   *Aggregation*

The level of aggregation of an emissions baseline needs to include an assessment of and decisions on:

- the type of projects to which an emissions baseline can apply (*i.e.* all projects within the sector, all comparable processes *etc.*);

- whether each source of emissions (*e.g.* direct and indirect energy-related emissions) and each gas should be estimated individually or for the entire manufacturing process; and

- geographic levels of aggregation (*i.e.* international, country, sub-country).

There are three major components to emissions from cement manufacture. These are:

- on-site fuel combustion (producing CO_2, CH_4 and N_2O);

- process CO_2 emissions; and

- emissions from electricity used in cement manufacture (also producing CO_2, CH_4 and N_2O, but off-site).

Potential projects could impact the energy use and GHG intensity of one or more of the discrete cement manufacturing steps. Thus a standardised value could be set for the energy use of 1) the entire manufacturing process (*i.e.* from limestone to cement), 2) for the major process steps (*e.g.* raw material preparation), or 3) for a step within each major process step (*e.g.* clinker cooling). A standardised GHG value could not be set for any of these aggregation levels (*e.g.* entire manufacturing process, major process steps). This is because a standardised GHG value would need to incorporate assumptions (or prescriptions) across countries on technology use, fuel use for pyro-processing and GHG intensity of electricity generation. The technologies and fuels used can vary from site to site and the GHG intensity of electricity generation can also vary within a country.

However, setting one standardised value for the energy use of the entire cement manufacture process, rather than at a more disaggregated level, may not be appropriate for two reasons. Firstly, a standardised "energy" (rather than fuel and electricity) standard would need to incorporate an assumption about the efficiency of electricity generation, which can vary significantly within and between countries. Secondly, one standardised value could allow credits to be generated by changing the quality of cement manufactured (*e.g.* coarser cement requires less energy to grind, although the consequent GHG reductions are not the result of any "additional" GHG reduction activities)[27].

Setting standardised energy values for sub-process steps (at the international or national level, depending on the project type) may also not be appropriate, as the energy use for one sub-process step may be influenced by the mode of operation of the previous sub-step. For example, optimising heat recovery in the clinker cooler will reduce the amount of energy needed in the kiln and pre-calciner (IEA GHG R&D 1999). Moreover, the number of potential sub-process steps is by definition greater than that of the number of process steps, so disaggregating a baseline to this level of detail would require more data and would be more time-consuming.

As a compromise between the two suggestions above, standardised values for the amount of fuel and electricity (rather than "energy") used in each of the three main process steps could be drawn up, *i.e.*:

- raw material preparation (including crushing, grinding, homogenising);
- pyro-processing (including pre-heating, calcining, cooling); and
- cement grinding (excluding additive preparation).

In addition, information on the preparation of additives would be needed for blending projects. It should be feasible to standardise this energy use (*e.g.* x kWh/t blast furnace slag, y kWh/t pozzolana).

---

[27] It is not always possible to substitute finer cement (higher strength) with coarser cement (lower strength).

Information on each of these steps would need to include information on which energy source(s) were used, their emission factors, emission factors for the electricity used and information on the process-related emissions. Default emission factors for GHG emissions from fuel combustion and for process emissions are available (IPCC 1996). However, significant variations in emission factors for electricity production occur between countries due to national/sub-national variations in the fuel mix, technologies used and efficiencies of those technologies. Thus, a baseline would be more realistic (and credible) if it distinguished electricity intensities between (and possibly even within) different countries. This is examined further in the Electricity Case Study.

The advantage of aggregating emission baselines by major process step would be that plant refurbishments (the majority of capacity extensions[28]) would still be able to generate emissions credits by improving the performance of a process step. In some old plants, the layout may preclude the installation of a more efficient calcining process (Schumacher and Sathaye 1999) or grinding process (Cembureau 1997).

Recommendations

➔ Baseline values for fuel and electricity use should be standardised at the major process step level (raw material preparation, pyro-processing, cement grinding). These values can be applied worldwide for energy-efficiency type projects, with the possible exception of China, which uses a cement manufacturing process not widely used elsewhere. The values for cement grinding may need to be further disaggregated to include, for example, information on the fineness of cement and type and proportion of additives used. This distinction is needed in order to account for the effect of these variables on grinding energy use.

➔ For projects that change the production process technology, a national component in the baseline energy value may need to be taken into account. However, a wet process plant should not be considered as an appropriate technology on which to base an emissions baseline. (For some plants using raw materials with a high moisture content, a baseline based on *e.g.* a semi-dry plant could be more appropriate).

➔ To increase transparency, separate emission baselines should be calculated for the energy-related and process-related emissions involved and then summed to obtain a baseline expressed in terms of CO_2-equivalent emissions.

---

[28] Michel Picard, 20.3.2000, personal communication.

Units for emission baselines

Which units to use for emission baselines is a potentially complicated issue for projects in the cement industry. A credible standardised emissions baseline is one that can be applied to a number of similar projects with homogeneous output. However, as noted in section 2.2, the clinker content of cement can vary by almost a factor of five, in theory and variation in clinker content by a factor of two is common (Cembureau 1997). Since clinker is by far the most GHG-intensive component of cement, the GHG-intensity of cement can also vary by up to a factor of five.

The properties (strength, hardening time, *etc.*) of cements with different clinker contents vary to some extent. Properties of cement with the same clinker proportion can also vary (depending on the fineness to which the clinker is ground, whether the particle size is more or less homogeneous and depending on which other additives are present in the cement). Some cement types are best for certain applications and other cement types for other applications - for example, cement for building bridges needs to be relatively strong. Thus, "cement" is not a homogeneous product, although there is an area of overlap where cements of different types can be used[29]. "Clinker" is more homogeneous and could therefore be used as the basis on which to determine the emission mitigation impacts of projects in the cement sector[30].

However, if emission benefits from energy-related cement projects were expressed in t CO_2/t clinker, projects that aimed to reduce GHG emissions by reducing the clinker component of cement would not be eligible. Thus, if blending-type projects were approved as eligible projects, the GHG benefit resulting from blending would need to be reported in terms of changes in t GHG/t cement.

---

[29] Stronger cements are generally those that are more finely ground and, therefore, more energy and GHG-intensive. The extent of overlap between different cement types will depend on their relative costs and availabilities, which may vary from site to site. The impact of this potential overlap on the implications for setting standardised energy values for emission baselines in the cement sector could benefit from further examination.

[30] The most homogeneous unit is likely to be clinker nodules (from pyro-processing). However, projects in the cement grinding step would not be able to use this as a unit.

2.3.3 System boundaries and data issues

System boundaries

There are several steps involved in the manufacture of cement. A JI/CDM project could impact the fuel and/or electricity use of one or more of these steps and thus influence the direct and indirect energy-related emissions of cement manufacture. A project could potentially also influence process emissions through increased blending of clinker with other additives. This could impact the project boundaries used for different project types (see Figure 2-3).

"Boundary 1" includes the energy-related emissions and potentially the process-related emissions, arising from the three most GHG-intensive steps of cement production. It is a reflection of Equation 1 (outlined in section 2.3). Using this boundary would capture the majority of energy and process-related emissions from a cement plant and may be considered appropriate for greenfield cement projects or refurbishment projects that involve a process-change or that influence both the fuel and electricity intensity of cement production.

Figure 2-3

Potential project boundaries for JI/CDM projects in cement manufacture

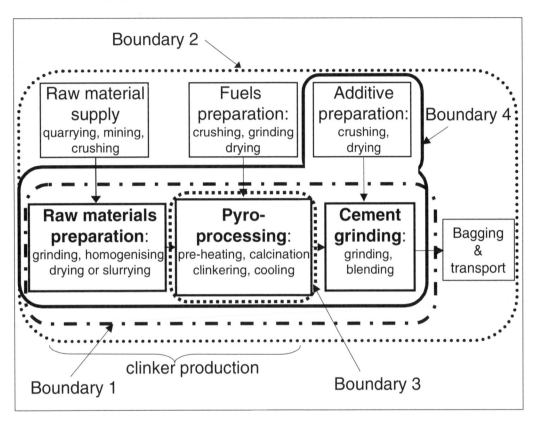

Source: adapted from Ruth *et. al.*2000.

"Boundary 2" includes all energy and process emissions arising from all steps associated directly or indirectly with cement production (but excludes emissions embodied in the materials used for cement manufacture). This boundary is more comprehensive than "Boundary 1", but would be significantly more data and time-intensive to construct and would not be substantially different from "Boundary 1". Given that the majority of emissions associated with cement manufacture would be accounted for in "Boundary 1", it may be considered that "Boundary 2" would not need to be constructed. A further reason for not using "Boundary 2" is that emissions from some steps (such as from the transport of additives to the cement plant) may be off-site and difficult for the project participants to control and/or monitor.

However, a compromise between boundaries 1 and 2 is also possible. Recognising that boundary 2 is more complete than boundary 1, a constant multiplier (such as "boundary

1" * 1.02[31]) could be applied to boundary 1 in order to capture some of the effects included in boundary 2. This would in effect estimate the impact of the identified but non-quantified emissions and thus reduce the level of leakage associated with boundary 1. Such a compromise would have to be applied to both the estimation of the baseline and the monitoring of project emissions in order to be consistent[32]. As for boundary 1, this type of boundary could be applied to refurbishment or greenfield projects.

For boundaries 1, 2 and the compromise boundary, process emissions may not need to be included if it is assumed that the cement produced by a JI/CDM plant would have been produced by a nearby plant in the absence of the JI/CDM project. This is because the process emissions from clinker production at one plant will be almost identical (per ton clinker produced) to process emissions from clinker production at another plant. Small differences can occur due to differences in chemical composition of the raw materials. However, since raw materials are expensive to transport over long distances, nearby cement plants are likely to have raw materials from the same (or similar) source.

"Boundary 3" includes the energy (and potentially the process emissions) from a single process step in either clinker or cement manufacture. This boundary could be appropriate for a refurbishment project that changes only one part of an existing installation, such as cement grinding, while leaving the remainder of the installation (including total capacity) unchanged. However, in order to use this more restricted boundary type, a developer would presumably have to prove that their project did not adversely affect emissions from another part of the cement manufacturing process. If such "proof" is quantitative, it essentially means that a larger boundary has to be constructed anyway, it would essentially mean constructing Boundary 1. For example, changing the way in which raw materials are mixed and the moisture content of this mixture, will affect both the energy used in raw materials preparation and in pyro-processing.

"Boundary 4" includes the energy and process emissions for cement manufacture. This is equivalent to equation 4 in section 2.3. Process emissions would definitely need to be included in a blending-type project as this type of project creates GHG benefits by reducing process CO_2 emissions per ton cement produced. Including the (energy-related) emissions associated with additive preparation would also be needed in any project that claims emission credits for changing the proportion of clinker in the cement produced because some of the clinker additives used can have significant GHG impacts (*e.g.* blast-

---

[31] The primary energy equivalent of the approximately 2kWh electricity needed for raw material crushing (from Table 2-5) and for conveyor belts for the cement produced (IEA GHG R&D 1999) represents under 1% of best practice energy consumption in cement manufacture. However, cement packing has been estimated to account for up to 5% of total power use (IEA GHG R&D 1999), or up to 4% of best practice energy use. This amount will vary according to the proportion of cement shipped in bags.

[32] The "constant multiplier" will have a slightly different effect on the baseline and the project emissions if it is based on a percentage of these emissions.

furnace slag). Not including the energy and emissions needed to grind these additives, which would be done on-site, could lead to a significant over-estimation of a project's GHG benefits (the actual effect depends on which additive is used).

Which gases to include in any project boundary and baseline will also have to be chosen. Process emissions are of CO_2 only, while energy-related emissions are of CO_2, CH_4 and N_2O. Energy-related emissions could be calculated by using the IPCC default emission factors for fuel use in cement kilns. These default emission factors are available for coal, oil and gas but for CO_2 and CH_4 only. However, the GWP-weighted emissions of methane from cement kilns are only approximately 0.02 kg CO_2-equ./GJ fuel input, compared to CO_2 emission factors of approximately 56, 77 and 95 kg CO_2/GJ fuel input for gas, oil and coal respectively. The IPCC guidelines also supply default N_2O emission factors for "manufacturing industries", which would indicate N_2O emissions of approximately 0.4 kg CO_2-equ/GJ coal input (other fuels would produce lower N_2O emissions). Emissions of both methane and nitrous oxide could therefore be excluded from an emissions baseline without significantly altering its accuracy or environmental effectiveness.

Recommendations

→ The "compromise" boundary between 1 and 2, *i.e.* emissions from the three major process step times a multiplier, should be used for estimating an energy-related CO_2 emissions baseline for energy-efficiency, production process-related or input fuel-related greenfield projects. This boundary should also be used for refurbishment projects that significantly increase manufacturing capacity and/or affect more than one process step. This "compromise" boundary would not need to include process CO_2 emissions.

→ Boundary 4, *i.e.* including emissions from additive preparation, should be used for projects that claim credit for changing the clinker proportion of cement. This emissions baseline could include process CO_2 emissions only (if the only aspect of the project was increased blending) or both process and energy-related CO_2 emissions if the project involves capacity construction or upgrades.

Data needs

Which boundary is chosen for the emissions baseline will affect the data needed to construct the emissions baseline (and will also have an impact on what data need to be monitored to assess project performance and calculate emissions credits).

Given the equations outlined above, an emissions baseline for energy efficiency, process change or input fuel change project types would therefore need to focus on the following items (assuming it was being drawn up per ton of clinker produced):

i)   quantity of fuel(s) used (in terms of energy);

ii)   emission factor(s) of fuel(s) used;

iii)   quantity of electricity consumed; and

iv)   emission factor of electricity consumed.

This information should be broken down for each major process step.

Blending-type projects would need data on:

v)   clinker to cement ratio before the project;

vi)   clinker to cement ratio during the project;

vii)   information on which additives are used and how they are prepared; and

viii)   amount of clinker produced by the project site.

If blending was the only aspect of an existing plant that was being considered as a potential project, data items i-iv would not be needed and an emissions baseline could consider just items v to viii. If, however, increased blending was part of a larger project, data on i-viii would be needed.

The quantity of fuel and electricity used in cement manufacture depends mainly on the technologies used in the different stages of manufacturing (see Table 2-5), but also on potentially site-specific data such as the moisture and silica content of raw materials[33]. (Moreover, the choice of technology may be determined by these site-specific data).

---

[33] The energy intensity of the pyroprocessing step can vary between two sites that use the same technology. In particular, kilns using raw materials with a high silica content will need to operate at a higher temperature (*e.g.* nearer 1500°C than 1400°C) than those kilns using raw materials with a lower silica content. The silica content of raw materials can vary slightly depending on the source of those raw materials (*i.e.* the chemical composition of limestone and other raw materials used may vary slightly depending on the source of these raw materials). If the variation in energy-intensity that is caused from such variations in silica content is high, it may be decided that the silica content (or kiln temperature) is a critical factor that needs to be specified when determining an emissions baseline for a CDM/JI project in the cement sector.

70

Table 2-5

Variations in fuel and electricity intensity of different components of the cement manufacturing process

Manufacturing step	Unit	Range	Lower intensity technology (typical value of "best practice")	Higher intensity technology (typical value)
Blasting/transport of raw materials	GJ/t clinker	0.023 (est. avg.)	-	-
Crusher	kWh$_e$/t input#	0.3 -1.6	Roller crusher (0.4-0.5) or Gyratory crusher (0.3-0.7)	Hammer crusher (1.5-1.6)
Grinder (raw materials)	kWh$_e$/t input#	12 - 22	Roller press (integral), (12)	Ball mill (22)
Kiln (electricity use only)	kWh$_e$/t clinker	26 - 30	5-stage pre-heater, pre-calciner (26)	Semi-dry (30)
Kiln (direct fuel use)	GJ/t clinker	2.9 - 5.9*	Short kiln, 5-stage pre-heater, pre-calciner (2.9-3.2)	Wet kiln (5.9)
Grinder (clinker)	kWh/t cement**	24.5 - 55	Roller press (24.5)	Ball mill (55)
Sub-total (elec.)	kWh$_e$/t clinker	70.8 - 124		
Sub-total (fuel)	GJ/t clinker	2.9 - 5.9		
Total***	GJ/t clinker	3.69 - 7.25		

Source: drawn from data included in IEA GHG R&D, 1999

An estimated 1.5-1.75 t input are needed for 1t output.

* Shaft kilns, found in China, have a range of 3.7 - 6.6 GJ/t clinker.

** Data for Portland cement, 95% clinker, 3500 Blaine. More finely ground cement, or cement with additives that need grinding (*e.g.* blast furnace slag) would require more electricity for this grinding step. For example, grinding portland cement to 4000 Blaine with a roller press requires 28 kWh/t (IEA GHG R&D 1999), whereas grinding portland cement to 3500 Blaine with the same technology requires only 24.5 kWh/t (Cembureau 1997).

*** Assuming generation efficiency of 33% and 1.65t raw material input needed for 1t output.

Thus, in order to set up a baseline for a cement plant, default figures for energy use could be estimated from the technology used in different process steps. However, since energy consumption in the three major process steps and therefore GHG emissions, may vary by ±15% within one technology type (Cembureau 1997), defaults may need to be adjusted with information on actual energy use, if this is available.

Obtaining the emission factor for the fuel(s) used should be a straightforward step. If site- or country-specific values are known they could be used. Otherwise, IPCC defaults (IPCC 1996) could be used and result in only small errors. (Given the uncertainty surrounding the number of credits generated by an emission baseline, the small variation in carbon content within a fuel type is of little importance).

The quantity of electricity consumed in cement manufacture should also either be known or easily measurable. The missing and most difficult component is therefore the emission factor of electricity generation avoided by the project. Calculating the emission factor for the electricity used can require detailed information to do accurately. Simple pro rata estimations could be made per country, for example by using annual fuel input data and type. More detailed estimations (*e.g.* distinguishing between demand for baseload and peak electricity and between different electricity systems within a country) may also be appropriate in some cases. (This topic is the subject of the Electricity Case Study.) Alternatively, emission reductions from electricity avoidance could be omitted from the calculation of emission credits, as in the French/Czech AIJ project.

Energy consumption at the lowest end of the range corresponds to clinker production at different GHG intensities, depending on which fuels are used and how efficiently electricity is generated. For example, using residual fuel oil and gas-fired electricity would result in energy-related emissions of 248 kg CO_2/t clinker, whereas using coal and coal-fired electricity would result in energy-related emissions of 341 kg CO_2/t clinker.

Data quality and availability

The data needed to construct an emissions baseline is different for different project types. The data quality and availability will also differ.

For projects relating to energy use, emission factor(s) would be needed to "translate" baselines[34] from energy use to emissions. As previously indicated, default emission factors for direct fuel use are available (IPCC 1996) and estimations of, or methodologies to, determine the GHG-intensity of electricity may also be available for some countries (see Electricity Case Study). CO_2 emission factors for other fuels (*e.g.* tyres) that may be

---

[34] Or project data.

used in cement manufacture are less widely available, but may not be needed if their energy content is known[35].

Energy efficiency and process change projects

Different types of data could be used as the basis on which to calculate emission baselines for energy efficiency and process change type projects. These can be grouped as two major types:

- technology-based data (*e.g.* fuel use per process step for a given technology or "best practice");

- sector-specific data (either technologies and processes in place or energy use) for a country. This data could include the types of technology and historical or projected trends in technology use, which processes are used and whether there is any trend in process use (*i.e.* whether process changes happen in BAU investment), the energy used in cement manufacture, the types of cement produced and the amount of clinker produced.

Technology-based data (*i.e.* energy use for different technology types) is widely available for the technologies used in raw materials preparation and pyro-processing. Thus, standardising the energy use component of an emissions baseline would be relatively simple if this baseline were set per ton of clinker produced. Basing this energy component on the performance of recently installed technology (which is similar worldwide) would obviate the need to gather country-specific data on the manufacturing technologies used, their performance and their ages. Thus, a default (international) value for energy use could be allocated to different components of the clinker manufacturing process. The energy use of the process step(s) involved in a JI/CDM project would also be monitored and the difference would define the maximum number of CERs/ERUs that could be transferred. However, determining a baseline purely on technology-based data does not take into account the potentially significant site-specific variations ($\pm 15\%$) that may occur in operating similar technologies at different sites (Cembureau 1997).

Technology-based data on cement grinders is also available. However, the energy required to grind cement depends not only on the technology used, but also on the fineness required for the cement produced (and on whether or not any additives are ground before or with the clinker). Thus, any standardised energy value set for the cement grinding step would need to distinguish *e.g.* between cements of different fineness.

Some country and *sector-specific data* may also be relatively easily available (such as total energy used in the cement sector, by fuel type, for a given country in a given year). However, a breakdown of how much electricity is used in the different process steps is

---

[35] IEA GHG R&D 1999 gives the energy content for the following alternative fuels as follows (MJ/kg): scrap tyres, 21; plastics, 33; waste oil, 38; paper residues, 6; and waste solvents 18-33.

less readily available[36]. This means that it may not be possible to estimate the national average electricity intensity of the different process steps within a country. Thus, estimating the electricity intensity of individual process steps by technology type in countries with many types of cement producing plants (*e.g.* India and China) would be impossible with only sector-specific electricity consumption figures.

Fuel input change projects

The GHG mitigation of a fuel input change project is proportional to the amount of "alternative" fuel used. This amount will therefore need to be monitored in order to calculate the CERs/ERUs accruing from a project. Thus, historical data on which alternative fuel is used and in what quantities, will be available at the project level for a JI/CDM project (although such data may not be available at a national level).

The use of "alternative" fuels can vary significantly from year to year[37], depending on, for example, relative fuel availability and prices. Thus, levels of historical alternative fuel use may not provide an accurate indication of future alternative fuel use for plants already in use and are obviously not available at all for greenfield projects.

Blending type projects

Data on cement production by product type is also patchy. It exists for some larger developing countries, but not for smaller ones (Price *et. al.* 1999) or for some countries with economies in transition (Phylipsen *et. al.* 1998). Moreover, the type of cement produced may vary substantially from plant to plant as well as from country to country[38]. The clinker content of any one cement type can also vary by up to 25 percentage points for composite cements (although variation is much smaller for Portland cement). Thus, the cement produced by a particular plant may diverge significantly from the "average" or most common cement produced in that country in the same year, so rendering inappropriate comparison to an "average". However, the operator of a particular cement plant should know how much clinker and cement that plant produces in a year (although this may change from year to year). Thus, project-specific values should be used to determine the baseline clinker use for plants already producing clinker as these data are both more available and more accurate. Equivalent figures are of course not available for greenfield plants.

---

[36] Since almost all direct fuel use is in the pyro-processing step, the lack of a breakdown is less problematic for direct fuel use: it can all be assumed to be used for pyro-processing.

[37] Jan-Willem Bode, Ecofys, personal communication, 18.4.2000.

[38] Christopher Boyd, Lafarge, personal communication, 20.3.2000.

Recommendations

➔ For energy-efficiency type projects and potentially also for process change type projects, a standardised value for the baseline energy use of the raw material preparation and pyro-processing steps in cement manufacture should be based on the technology performance of new technology additions/upgrades rather than country-specific sectoral data. Thus, standardised values would be based on *e.g.* kilns with a 5-stage pre-heater precalciner. However, country-specific data may need to be used for China, which has an atypical technology structure.

➔ Projects that change the production process technology would probably also need to include some country-specific information (*e.g.* on whether or not process changes are happening under BAU conditions) in order to help indicate the "additionality" or not of the project. This information could be both qualitative (*e.g.* whether this has happened already) and quantitative (how often/regularly).

➔ For fuel change type projects, at sites already in operation, historical site-specific data on which alternative fuel is used and in what quantities, will be available (although previous use of such fuels is not necessarily a good indication of future use). Thus, no standardisation of such information is needed. However, given the potential day-to-day variability in the quantities of alternative fuels used, it may be best to use annual or multi-year averages when determining emission baselines. For greenfield projects, rules of thumb should be developed that link potential alternative fuel use with distance from alternative fuel sources.

➔ Similarly, for blending type projects, data on clinker and cement production before and during a project are likely to be both easily available at the project level and more accurate (and available) at this level than at the country level. Thus, project-specific information should be used to determine the baselines for this project type for plants already in operation. For greenfield plants, assessing levels of additive use that are additional is difficult, although rough rules of thumb may be able to be developed that link cement type produced, proximity of sources of additives and levels of additive use.

➔ The energy required to grind additives (*e.g.* blast furnace slag) should be reported explicitly and separately from the cement grinding step in order to ensure that it is included in both the baseline and monitoring of blending-type projects.

2.4 Potential baseline assumptions

This section examines both the level at which the baseline could be set and the time for which emission credits could accrue to different energy-related and "blending" projects.

2.4.1 Energy efficiency and process change projects

Both energy efficiency and process change projects could reduce the energy intensity of clinker manufacture. Energy efficiency measures can be taken in any of the three major steps of cement manufacture (raw materials preparation, pyro-processing, cement grinding) and could be part of a plant's refurbishment or as an "additional" investment to a planned new plant. Process changes can occur in raw materials preparation or pyro-processing and are only likely to occur for plants currently in operation. Both process and energy efficiency projects could affect the fuel and/or electricity intensity of cement.

A question of debate is whether or not greenfield projects and refurbishment projects should be judged against the same baseline. Arguments for treating greenfield and refurbishment cement projects in a similar fashion include:

- It can be difficult to draw the line between a large-scale refurbishment project and a greenfield project.

- Setting less stringent baselines for refurbishment projects may create incentives for relatively inefficient plants to continue operating.

Arguments for different treatment for greenfield and refurbishment projects are that:

- Refurbishment of older plants could substantially reduce their GHG emissions, although it may not bring them to as high an energy efficiency as new plants. Creating only one baseline for greenfield and refurbishment projects would either make the majority (and possibly all) refurbishment projects ineligible for JI/CDM status - if it was set at the level of new plants, which would drastically the reduce the number of potential JI/CDM projects in the cement sector. Alternatively, it would allow new BAU operations to generate (non-additional) credits.

- Not all technologies are suitable for both refurbishment and greenfield projects (for example, Cembureau's BAT document suggests that different types of grinders should be installed for new plants than for plant upgrades).

- Not all old plant layouts are amenable to allow changes from a wet process to a dry process, so improvements on the existing process would be ineligible for JI/CDM status.

This argument has both political and technical components and may sensibly be resolved in different ways for different JI/CDM project types. Ideally, if there were separate standardised baselines for greenfield and refurbishment projects, they would on average require the same level of effort by a manufacturer in order to perform better than the baseline.

Table 2-6

Suggested baseline energy components and other
assumptions for energy-related projects in the cement sector

Process step	Energy use (units)
Raw materials preparation	16* kWhe/t raw material input (or 27 kWhe/t clinker[1])
Pyro-processing[2]	3.0 GJ/t cli + 26* kWhe
Cement grinding (new plants)	28.2 kWh/t cement (assuming a roller press, 1-4% moisture content and ground to 3500 Blaine[3])
Cement grinding (capacity upgrades)[4]	36.8 kWh/t cement (assuming a two-stage grinder with roller press, 1-4% moisture content and ground to 3500 Blaine)
Additive grinding	32.8 kWh/t

Source: Adapted from data in Cembureau 1997 and * IEA GHG R&D 1999

[1] Assuming 1.65 t raw materials needed for 1t clinker. This value does not include energy use for drying the raw materials.

[2] This does not include energy use for grinding the fuel

[3] Producing cement with different characteristics (*e.g.* fineness) is likely to require another standardised energy value.

[4] Cembureau (1997) indicates that different technologies would be used for new plants and for capacity upgrades.

The figures in this table represent the lower end (*i.e.* higher energy consumption) of the range of energy requirements for cement manufacture using the most energy-efficient of "standard" technologies.

Given that the norm for new installations worldwide is a dry process kiln with a 5-stage pre-heater and a pre-calciner, this technology should generally be assumed as the baseline for new plants. Non-AIJ refurbishment projects also install this technology (Ruth *et. al.* 2000, Cement Hranice 2000). This technology corresponds to an energy use in the different process steps as outlined in Table 2-6.

2.4.2   Fuel input change projects

Projects that change the fuel inputs could be of two types - either they focus on the direct fuel use (in the pyro-processing step), or they could aim to reduce the GHG-intensity of electricity used in any of the three process steps[39].

In the first type of fuel input project, alternative fuels such as different types of waste (tyres, hazardous waste, or even "animal flour" - parts of animals not used in the food or other industries) could substitute for the use of fossil fuels. Use of alternative fuels is possible in all cement kilns because of the high temperature reached and is routinely used in some plants (for example, in countries where landfilling waste is difficult/prohibited, or where sources of hazardous waste are not too distant from the cement works). The proportion of fuel energy demand from waste fuels has recently been increasing in some countries (IEA GHG R&D 1999).

The amount and type of fuel that would otherwise have been used would represent the baseline. Once assumptions have been made for these factors, IPCC defaults for emission factors and methodology can be used to assess the GHG equivalent of a baseline. However, determining the baseline level of alternative fuel use is difficult, given the variability in actual and potential use of alternative fuels. For plants already in operation, the level of - and/or trend in - alternative fuel use for that particular plant over one or more years may be an appropriate baseline assumption[40]. For greenfield plants, the level of alternative fuels that would have otherwise been used is difficult to assess, given variations between different plants. It may be possible to draw up a rule of thumb linking alternative fuel use with other factors, such as proximity to sources of these fuels, but this would need further research.

> **Recommendations**
>
> → Assessing the quantity of baseline alternative fuel use is tricky, particularly for greenfield plants. However, once these assumptions have been made, IPCC default methodologies and emission factors can be used to calculate the baseline.
>
> → No international standardisation is possible on the *values* of the GHG mitigation potential of different "alternative" fuels because the impact of the fuel used depends on the GHG intensity of the alternative fuel and the GHG intensity of the fuel being displaced.

---

[39] The second type of project should be treated as an electricity-sector project and a baseline developed accordingly.

[40] However, testing additionality of alternative fuel use is difficult even for plants already in operation because of variations in alternative fuel use at a site over time. It is further complicated by the fact that alternative fuel use potential is not equal for different sites within a country (as the potential depends on the proximity to sources of alternative fuels).

2.4.3   Blending projects

Process emissions from calcination are significant and estimated by the IPCC at 507 kg CO_2/t clinker produced (IPCC 1996). Reducing the proportion of clinker in cement would lower its GHG-intensity as clinker is by far the most GHG-intensive component of cement. A US cement producer (Holnam 1999) indicates that increased cement blending can "significantly and painlessly" reduce CO_2 emissions in cement manufacture. The GHG-intensity of cement could also in theory be lowered if the process CO_2 emissions could be "captured". However, no such process is in use as capturing and storing the large quantities of CO_2 emitted from cement manufacture (half a million tons of CO_2 per year just from process emissions from a plant producing 3000t clinker/day) would be costly.

Materials that could be added to clinker could include either by-products of other processes, such as fly ash (from coal-fired power stations) and blast furnace slag (from iron and steel production), or natural materials, *e.g.* pozzolana and limestone. The GHG impacts of potential additives are significantly lower than those of clinker: fly ash only needs to be transported, whereas pozzolana, limestone and blast-furnace slag need to be transported and ground.

Analysis here and elsewhere (*e.g.* Ruth *et. al.* 2000) indicates that the potential GHG reductions from cement blending may outstrip those from energy efficiency by a significant margin. Use of extenders is increasingly being undertaken by some cement works such as those in Nigeria, Malaysia (Blue Circle 2000), Panama and Columbia (Cemex, 1998) as a means to reduce the environmental impact of cement use. However, increasing the use of extenders is not always feasible, such as in cases where there is no nearby source of such materials. (Transporting such low-value materials over long distances would be too expensive).

Thus, the use of extenders may vary significantly between different cement works within a country because of the differences in the relative locations of cement works and sources of additives and because of variations in demand for different cement types (for a given plant). So while a clinker/cement ratio may be known at the national level, it may mask significant variations between plants and therefore be misrepresentative at the level of an individual plant. Moreover, the clinker production to cement production ratio may vary significantly within a country (and plant) from year to year - see Table 2-7 (Price *et. al.* 1999). These fluctuations of "what would have happened otherwise" could potentially give rise to significant amounts of gaming when setting an emissions baseline for one particular facility or for a group of facilities.

Table 2-7

Clinker to cement ratio in key developing countries (1980, 1990, 1995)

	1980	1990	1995
Brazil	0.81	0.74	0.80
China	0.73	0.74	0.70
India	0.85	0.84	0.90

Source: Price *et. al.* 1999

The volume of cement production means that small changes in the clinker proportion assumed in an emissions baseline would have large effects on the number of credits generated by a project. For example, if a factory producing 1 Mt clinker per year reduced the clinker content of its portland flyash cement by 10 percentage points, *e.g.* from 94% to 84%, it could reduce its clinker production by 100,000t. Using equation 3 (section 2.3), this could equate to 50,000t process CO_2 emissions and at least 22,000 t energy-related CO_2 avoided[41] (or almost US$200,000 equivalent if the carbon value is US$10/ton). Alternatively, clinker production could be maintained and cement production raised by approximately 126,700 t/y, which should create additional revenue.

Moreover, wider variations than this example are possible, as a single type of cement can have a clinker content that varies by up to 24 percentage points. Setting a standardised clinker content for any particular type of cement would be arbitrary and could be used to create significant numbers of non-additional credits unless the value chosen was at the bottom of the range (in which case, some additional projects would not qualify for credits).

Establishing a credible standardised value for a baseline clinker/cement ratio may therefore not be possible at a national level (and it may even vary from year to year for individual plants). However, some other standardisation formula could possibly be used. (For example, cement type T at plant no more than D distance from a source of potential additives should have a clinker content no greater than X %[42]). However, even estimating the clinker content of cement of a particular type is subject to significant error because of the potential variation in clinker content within a cement type.

---

[41] Using the GHG-conservative assumptions that the fuel used directly is oil and the electricity used has a GHG intensity of zero.

[42] If such a formula were to be used, the indication of which type of cement is produced would have to be fairly specific so that the clinker content varies by no more than 15 percentage points within one cement category. For example, a producer of Portland fly-ash cement (clinker content 65-94%) should specify whether the cement produced is equivalent to the Cembureau classifications CEM II/A (80-94%) or CEM II/B (65-79%).

2.4.4   Baseline lifetime

The technical lifetime of a cement works can be many tens of years: up to 50 years is common. The actual lifetime of a cement works is often determined by the lifetime of the quarry that is used to supply raw materials (limestone) to the works. Different pieces of equipment may be replaced during the life of a cement works and at different times. Thus, a cement plant may have up to two major "revampings" (refurbishments) during its lifetime. However, major pieces of equipment (*e.g.* pre-heater and grinders) would normally only be considered for potential modernisation after 20-25 y or even longer for the kiln[43] although they may continue operating for much longer[44].

Refurbishing parts of a cement plant after a certain number of years, irrespective of the country in which the plant is located, is BAU practice both in Europe and elsewhere for some larger, private cement manufacturers. Refurbishment of existing plants also occurs in plants in developing countries such as India, China and Brazil (Price *et. al.* 1999, Schumacher and Sathaye 1999). However, the exact timing of any refurbishment is likely to depend on the detailed operating performance of a plant, as well as the financial capacity of the plant's owner. Whether or not a refurbishment of a plant occurs will also depend on the remaining lifetime of the quarry that supplies the plant.

Routine refurbishment has implications for the lifetime over which a project could accrue emissions benefits. If the potential availability of ERUs/CERs hastens a modernisation project that would otherwise have occurred later, emission credits should not accrue to the project for its entire life, but only for the number of years that the project was hastened. For example, if factory A was planned to be refurbished in 2005, but was refurbished in 2001 because the availability of ERUs/CERs made the project more feasible, it should receive credits for 4 years. Of course, determining this number with precision is almost impossible in practice, as it would involve scrutiny of company-specific decisions and priorities, which are likely to be confidential.

It may be possible to develop "rules of thumb" for timelines for energy-efficiency and process change type projects in the cement sector, *e.g.* by using the current age of a plant as an indication of whether and when it would have otherwise been refurbished. Alternatively, projects with more stringent baselines (such as those based on best available technology performance) may be allocated lifetimes that are longer than projects with less stringent baselines (such as those based on the lower end of the range of best practice).

However, great care would need to be taken when setting any rules of thumb in order to avoid creating perverse incentives that would, for example, reward installing inefficient

---

[43] Personal communication, Michel Picard, Lafarge, 10.1.00 and Malte Becker, Cembureau, 3.4.00.

[44] Personal communication, M. Bigum, FLS Industries, 6.4.2000

technology or creating overly lax baselines, *e.g.* by allowing a project whose additionality is questionable to generate credits over a long time. Moreover, any rules of thumb may need to be different for different pieces of equipment within any one industry. It is likely that any rules of thumb developed for one equipment type in one industry may not be appropriate for the same equipment type in another industry. The Iron and Steel Case Study indicates that this arbitrary approach is unlikely to be useful for determining timelines in the iron and steel sector.

In addition, the timeline for a project may depend on what technology the project is replacing. For example, a fixed 5y crediting lifetime may be suitable for a project that refurbishes an existing 20y old plant so that it includes a 5-stage pre-heater pre-calciner, as it could be judged that this project hastens BAU investment. However, a project that refurbishes an existing 20y old plant so that it includes a 6-stage pre-heater pre-calciner, or that installs similar equipment in a greenfield project, goes beyond current BAU investment and so it may be appropriate to allocate a longer crediting lifetime to this project. Alternatively, this latter project could have a baseline that is fixed for a longer time period with the possibility of continuing after a baseline revision. Making the fixed lifetime longer for a project that installs advanced technology would help encourage the take-up of this technology.

The Czech/France AIJ project has an initial baseline lifetime of 5y, although this may be extended (the different documents containing information on this project were not clear). The lifetime for the China/Japan project is 20y and based on the technical lifetime of the equipment installed rather than on the projected lifetime or refurbishment plans for equipment that it replaced.

The economic benefits of potential JI/CDM emission credit revenues from energy efficiency or process change project types are likely to be tiny in comparison to the total costs and revenues involved in those projects. The economic benefits of GHG mitigation from a particular project are thus likely to have only a marginal impact on company decisions on if and when to refurbish a particular plant and on the equipment used for a new plant[45].

The feasibility of other potential project types in cement manufacture (such as blending and fuel input changes) can change significantly over a short period of time because of policy changes in the project-site country. For example, changes in legislation regarding waste disposal may mean that waste can no longer be landfilled. This may make waste incineration more common and/or profitable than it was before. This will affect the additionality of cement plants that incinerate waste. The feasibility of blending cements can also change for policy or for other reasons. For example, construction of a coal-fired plant near to a cement plant would provide a potential supply of additives and such a construction could make blending a possibility somewhere where it had not been a possibility before. Thus, the crediting lifetime of blending or fuel-input changes could in

---

[45] The extent of this impact could usefully be explored further in additional analysis.

theory extend throughout the lifetime of the cement manufacturing plant. However, baselines for these project types would need to be revised at regular intervals to take into account policy changes and other potential changes that impacts actual or potential supply of alternative fuels or additives in order to ensure that they remained credible.

Economic benefits of potential JI/CDM revenues

This example illustrates the magnitude and importance of potential JI/CDM revenues that could be generated from a project that increases energy efficiency or changes the production process in a cement works.

For example, the range in electricity use for clinker production is 70.8 - 109 kWh/t clinker produced (Table 2-5). Major refurbishment of an inefficient plant may lead to energy efficiency improvements that reduce electricity consumption by 30 kWh/t clinker produced. This would avoid 10-30 kg CO_2 emissions, depending on the assumptions used to calculate the CO_2 intensity of avoided electricity. Taking the highest assumption (corresponding to emissions of 1 kg CO_2/kWh, *i.e.* inefficient coal-fired production) and assuming a price for avoided C emissions of US$10-25/t C (US$2.7-6.8/t CO_2) would give a benefit of 8-20 cents/t clinker produced. This corresponds to an extra income of US$240-600/day for a standard new plant with capacity of 3000 t clinker/day, assuming that the baseline is continued operation of the old plant, which may or may not be a valid assumption. However, these JI/CDM revenues are tiny compared to the revenues of that plant, which would be of the order of US$110,000-US$210,000/day depending on the assumptions of clinker cement content (70-95%) and price of cement (US$35-50/t) used.

Recommendations

➜ The age of any technology to be replaced in a JI/CDM project may influence the crediting lifetime of a project and should be reported by the project developer.

➜ Which technology is installed and, potentially, which technology is being replaced, should influence the crediting lifetime for an energy-efficiency or process change type project. For cement projects where BAU technology is used to refurbish a relatively young plant, the crediting lifetime should be limited, *e.g.* fixed at 5-10y. In projects where advanced (beyond BAU) technology is installed, the crediting lifetime could be longer (*e.g.* 8y) and/or the baseline revisable.

➜ Credits should be calculated on a yearly basis.

➜ The crediting lifetime for fuel input change and blending type projects could be longer than that for energy efficiency and process change type projects, but would need to be regularly revised in order to ensure that it remained credible.

2.5   Potential stringency of baselines

Decisions on which technology and/or energy use to use as the basis for calculating baselines has significant impact on the number of credits generated from a particular project. Thus, an emissions baseline set at the level of an "average plant" (including both wet and dry plants) would be higher and therefore generate many more ERUs/CERs for an investor, than a baseline set at the emissions level of an "average dry process plant". The gap between "average plant" performance and "average dry process plant" performance will obviously be greater for countries with a greater proportion of wet/semi-wet plants, such as India and China. However, given that recent industry trends towards investment is in highly energy-efficient plants, the most realistic and credible baseline is likely to be equivalent to a "5-stage preheater, precalciner dry process plant", *i.e.* even lower (more stringent) than that of "average dry process" plants.

The difference in energy requirements of different cement plants and potential baseline energy levels for fuel use in pyro-processing varies considerably (Figure 2-4). The figure also illustrates the significant improvements in energy efficiency that have occurred over the 1990s (such as in the Czech Republic) and the differences between the average value for all plants, all dry plants and recent additions (*e.g.* in India). The "recommended baseline" for this process step is 3.1 GJ/t clinker (towards the lower end of the 2.9 - 3.2 GJ/t clinker "best practice" range and a lower energy efficiency than some new plants installed under BAU conditions, see *e.g.* Ruth *et. al.* 2000).

The figure also presents possible baseline values for the fuel input into the pyro-processing step[46]. The fuel use in this step varies from 2.93 (Rajashree) to 5.14 (Tianjin, pre-project) GJ/t clinker produced. This compares to an estimated best practice (dry process) kiln fuel use in a standard kiln, *i.e.* dry process 5 stage preheater pre-calciner, of 2.9 - 3.2 GJ/t clinker. A solid line and a dotted line in the figure shows this range of "best practice".

The figure also shows that the energy consumption of the AIJ project in Cízkovice and of the potential AIJ project in Tianjin, do not have the highest energy efficiency of the different plants examined. For example, plants recently constructed in India, Mexico and Thailand (none of which were constructed as part of an AIJ or potential CDM project) all have higher energy efficiencies (lower energy consumption) in the pyro-processing step.

---

[46] Not enough consistent data were available to carry out a similar analysis for electricity use.

Figure 2-4

Different plant performances and potential baseline values for pyro-processing

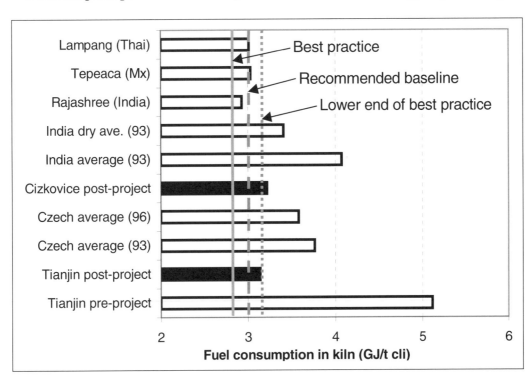

Sources: Data on China from NEDO 2000, data on Czech plants from UNFCCC 1997, data on Indian average performance from Schumacher and Sathaye 1999, other data from Ruth *et. al.* 2000. Data on "best practice" and lower end best practice from Cembureau 1997.

This creates a problem as to where to set the standardised values to be used in an emissions baseline. Should it be at the higher (most energy-efficient) end of "best practice"? If so, none of the plants considered would be eligible to generate emission credits, even though they are amongst the newest and most efficient plants in operation and in the case of the Rajashree plant install technology superior to that of standard best practice[47]. Alternatively, could the baseline be set at the lower (less energy efficient) end of "best practice", *e.g.* 3.2 GJ/t clinker production? If so, four of the five plants considered would be eligible to generate credits (although the AIJ project would not), even though three of these four eligible plants were constructed as part of BAU plans.

However, the plant at Tianjin has greatly improved its energy intensity as the result of a process change (the existing shaft kiln was replaced). As indicated in section 2.3, this

---

[47] The Rajashree plant has a 6-stage preheater.

process change project may sensibly be judged against a different baseline than Cízkovice and other energy-efficiency type projects. This is because although the Tianjin project ultimately improves the energy efficiency of production, it does this by changing the manufacturing process, rather than just modernising existing equipment with a more efficient version. In this and similar cases, basing a baseline on the upper range of "best practice" might be too stringent to stimulate a large volume of investment in more efficient plant and in turn worthy emission reduction investments. The project developers in Tianjin chose to assess the number of potential credits from the plant according to a baseline based on the plant's previous performance, *i.e.* 5.14 GJ fuel input/t clinker[48]. This effectively assumes that this plant would not have been refurbished or scrapped. However, given the restructuring of the cement industry in China (outlined in section 2.2.3), this may not be the case. To take this uncertainty into account, a more stringent baseline could be applied, such as the average between an "energy efficiency" project and previous plant performance. This would equal 4.02 GJ fuel input/t clinker for the Tianjin plant.

Figure 2-5

The effect of different baselines for different project types on potential credits

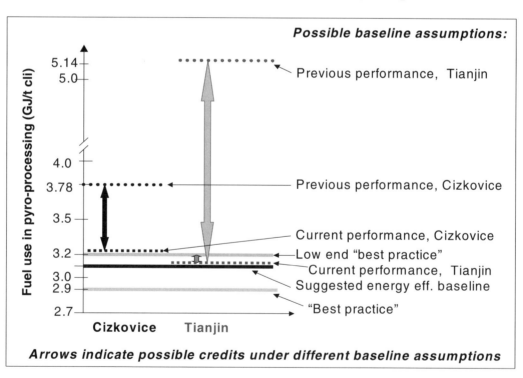

---

[48] The project developers accounted for the fact that increased electricity use of the new kiln offset some of the reductions from decreased direct fuel use. This section assesses only the affect of direct fuel use.

Small differences in baseline energy use per ton of clinker produced can make a large difference to the number of credits obtained by a project (Figure 2-5) because of the large volumes of cement manufactured by a plant and is quantified in Table 2-8 for four plants. Figure 2-5 shows that, for example, the Cízkovice plant could only generate credits under an energy efficiency baseline if it were compared to the performance of the plant operating before the project and not if compared to "best practice". The figure also illustrates the relatively high energy use of some manufacturing processes and the potential energy efficiency gains that could be made by encouraging process change.

For the energy efficiency projects, no credits would be obtained if the high end of best practice is used as an energy baseline. The number of credits obtained could more than double for the plants in India and Mexico depending whether or not a value of 3.1 or 3.2 GJ/t clinker was used for the baseline. However, for an individual project, credits could range from 0 to 30,660 t CO_2/y depending on which baseline is used (see table for assumptions on baseline and production levels). If the value of 1 t CO_2 was US$10, the total volume of credits that could be generated by the Tepeaca plant[49] could be worth between US$0 and US$293,000 per year for each year of the crediting lifetime of the project. (This would be a net present value of almost US$1.1m assuming a crediting lifetime of 5y and a discount rate of 17%).

Table 2-8

The effect of different standardised energy baseline values on the number of credits

Plant	Capacity (t/d)	Kiln energy use (GJ/t clinker)	Credits (t CO_2/y) at full capacity compared to:		
			Best practice	Lower end best practice	Other
Tepeaca (Mexico)	6500	3.03 (fuel oil)	0	29300	12070*
Rajashree (India)	3500	2.93 (coal)	0	30660	19306*
Cizkovice (Cz)	2700	3.22 (waste oils and used tyres)	0	0	0
Tianjin (China)	620	3.14 (anthracite)	0	1264	18400**

* 3.1 GJ/t clinker for potential "energy efficiency" projects (*i.e.* Tepeaca, Rajashree, Cizkovice)

** Average of "best practice" and pre-project performance for the process change project at Tianjin (*i.e.* 4.02 GJ/t cli).

The process change project at Tianjin, would barely generate any credits (1264 t CO_2/y) if judged against an energy efficiency baseline, but would generate substantially more if judged against a process change baseline (15 times as many credits, in the example below). The variation in credits would have a consequent effect on the value of credits

---

[49] If this plant were proposed and approved as a CDM project.

obtained from a project and potentially on the likelihood of other similar projects being undertaken.

Despite an energy intensity that is higher than other plants, the plant at Cízkovice has relatively low CO_2 emissions per ton of clinker produced (Figure 2-6). This is because Cízkovice uses waste fuels (assumed as CO_2-neutral) as well as fossil fuels in the pyro-processing step, whereas the other plants use fossil fuels only. Thus, the plant at Cízkovice may be eligible to generate emissions credits as a "fuel input change" type project. (Not enough information was available to assess how many credits should be generated by fuel switching).

Figure 2-6

CO_2 intensity of pyro-processing in selected plants

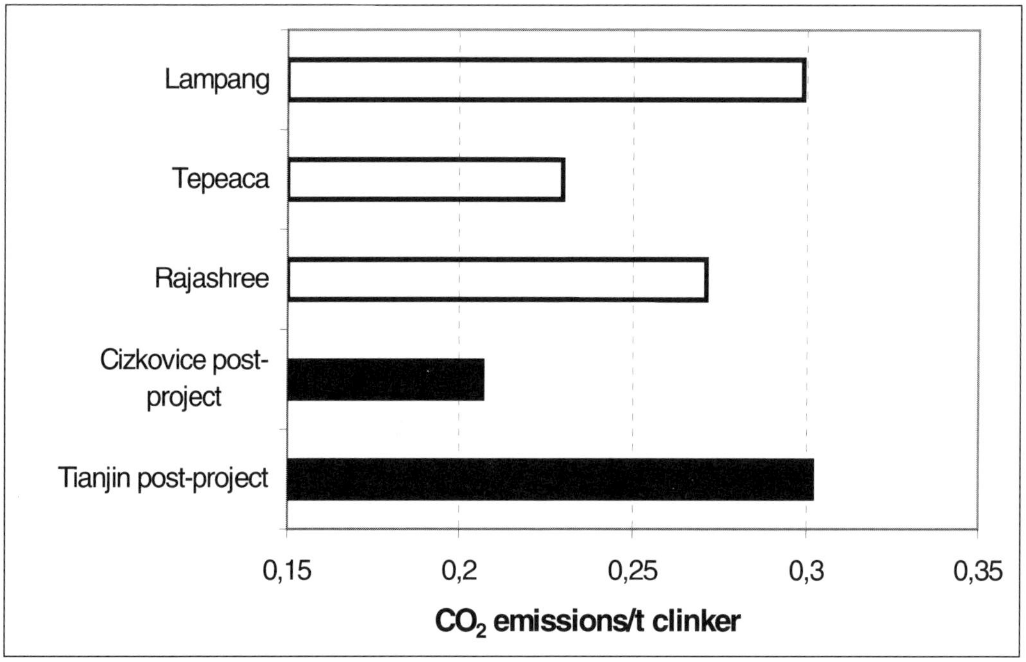

Sources: Data on China from NEDO 2000, data on Czech plants from UNFCCC 1997, other data from Ruth *et. al.* 2000.

Whichever format for a standardised value is chosen for an individual process step, the level of credits generated under the "cement production" level and the "major process step" level could be significantly different. This is what would be expected intuitively for projects that have opposite effects on fuel and electricity use. For example, initial data indicates that the Tianjin plant would qualify for credits for relatively low electricity use under a baseline set at either the best practice or low end of best practice level. This would occur despite the project almost doubling the electricity intensity of cement production compared to the pre-project level. However, the same plant would only qualify for credits in the pyro-processing step if compared to the top end of best practice (even though the project significantly reduces fuel consumption).

This section illustrates how important the baseline unit and aggregation is in assessing the relative environmental performance of different projects. It also illustrates that changes in the way an individual plant operates may make it potentially eligible for up to four different types of JI/CDM projects.

Note on additionality of projects

The most difficult aspect of assessing potential JI/CDM projects in the cement sector could be in determining whether or not the proposed project is "additional" to what would otherwise occur at the time of investment. This is because the cement industry is a sector which is operated by private, highly competitive companies and where energy costs form a large part of total costs. Thus, it could reasonably be expected that business as usual investment is energy-efficient.

For example, the additionality of the French/Czech AIJ project was questioned by the French government, particularly since the energy efficiency improvements to existing plants occurred before the project was put forward as a potential AIJ project. Nevertheless, the project was finally accepted as an AIJ project by both host and investor country governments (although with a lower baseline than that originally suggested and with a limited lifetime: 5 years).

The difficulty in determining the additionality or not of projects, the fact that cement production is high volume and highly energy-intensive and the differences between the energy (and GHG) intensity of old and new plants could lead to many non-additional credits being obtained if baselines are lax. Thus, baselines for all energy efficiency type projects should be based on marginal (new) additions rather than averages across all vintages of facilities.

Recommendations

➜ A standardised baseline value for the energy required to manufacture cement should be set towards the lower end (*i.e.* higher energy consumption) of the best practice range for energy-efficiency type projects, *e.g.* 3.1 GJ/t clinker direct fuel use. If a project developer can demonstrate that their project only affects one process step, the baseline could be calculated for that step. If, however, the project affects both the fuel and electricity intensity of cement manufacture and more than one process step, the project developer should calculate the aggregate effect of the project for energy-related emissions from the whole manufacturing process.

➜ For process change type projects (which are by definition only applicable for refurbishment projects) the baseline may need to be somewhat less stringent than for energy efficiency type projects in order to encourage a greater number of projects. This level may vary from country to country, although a standardised methodology for calculating the baseline level could be developed. However, basing a baseline on the continued operation of an inefficient plant would lead to a lax baseline and many potentially non-additional credits.

➜ In order to better attest to the additionality of projects, some qualitative or quantitative "additionality checks" may be needed (such as asking for indications of regulatory or behavioural additionality), in addition to the baseline "test". This might usefully be explored further in additional work.

➜ Given the continued improvement in energy intensity (and therefore GHG-intensity) of different parts of the cement manufacturing process under BAU investment, any multi-project baselines for this sector may need to be updated frequently (*e.g.* every few years). Alternatively, baselines established in year n for projects approved in that year could be modified and used for projects that start in subsequent years (*e.g.* n+1, n+2) by applying an autonomous energy improvement factor to the original baseline. (Or both types of adjustments could be used, for example by using assumed energy efficiency improvements - a downwards sloping baseline - in between more "major" baseline updates).

2.6   Conclusions

Cement manufacture is an energy-intensive process and results in significant quantities of both energy-related and process CO_2 emissions. There are four main types of potential JI/CDM projects in the cement sector: energy efficiency, process change and fuel input changes (all energy-related) and blending (not energy-related).

There are three main process steps in production of the cement intermediate, "clinker": preparation of raw materials, pyro-processing and grinding the clinker. Each of these main steps can be divided into two or more discrete sub-processes that could be the subject of a JI/CDM project. However, it is recommended that emission baselines be established at the main process step level or at the clinker manufacturing level (which would encompass emissions from all three main steps).

Elements of emission baselines for potential JI/CDM projects in cement manufacture could be standardised to a certain extent, depending on the project type. This is outlined below. Changes in the way an individual plant operates may make it potentially eligible for more than one different type of JI/CDM project in the cement sector.

For *energy-efficiency projects* in cement manufacture (*e.g.* replacing an existing pre-heater with a more efficient one), standard energy values for different manufacturing steps could be established. The energy used for each of these steps is essentially governed by the technology used. Therefore, a standard emissions baseline could be based on the energy use for a "standard" technology, *e.g.* that installed under BAU investment conditions (which is a good indication of what would have happened otherwise). These standardised energy values could apply internationally to both existing and new plants. Basing a standardised energy value on technology-specific data has the advantage that such data are readily available (and could be easily updated, if necessary). However, this level of aggregation also has disadvantages. For example, such baselines would reward large plants that benefit from economies of scale more than small plants. Standardised values would be simpler to set up for direct fuel use in the pyro-processing step, *e.g.* 3.1 GJ fuel input/t clinker produced, than for electricity use in the different steps, as this can vary significantly within technologies.

However, emission baselines for each of these steps would, by definition, need to be expressed in terms of emissions. A standardised value for CO_2 emissions/ton clinker, unlike a standardised energy value, cannot be drawn up across countries because it would need to incorporate assumptions about, for example, which fuel is used in the cement kiln and which fuels are used to generate electricity at what efficiencies. "Translation" from a standardised energy value to GHG emissions would therefore need to be carried out using some project-specific and/or country-specific data for these variables. This could be done by using *e.g.* IPCC emission inventory methodologies to calculate fuel-related emissions and suggested methodologies (see Electricity Case Study) to calculate emissions from avoided electricity use.

For projects that change the production process (*"process change" projects*), *e.g.* conversion of an existing plant from the wet process to the dry process, standardised energy values could also be drawn up. However, these may need to be drawn up at a higher level of disaggregation (such as by country, rather than internationally) than energy-efficiency type projects. This disaggregation would allow for regional variations in plant conversion rates (*e.g.* because of lack of capital availability) to be taken into account, *i.e.* would essentially allow process change projects to have a less stringent baseline level than energy efficiency projects.

For *fuel input change projects* (*e.g.* using waste fuels to displace fossil fuel use in the pyro-processing step), assessing the quantity of waste fuels that would have otherwise been used is difficult, as this can vary significantly over time as well as from plant to plant. This difficulty is exacerbated for new plants, where historical "alternative fuel" use data is not available. However, it would not be possible to set international default values for the GHG mitigation potential of different "alternative" fuels because the fuels they are displacing varies. For greenfield projects, rules of thumb should be developed that link potential alternative fuel use with distance from alternative fuel sources. Nevertheless, once the amount of alternative fuel use, its emission factor and what it is displacing has been established, a standard methodology to "translate" this into GHG equivalent is available in the IPCC inventory guidelines. It may be possible to estimate at a national or multi-country level which fuels are likely to be displaced by alternative fuels, but this would require further analysis.

For all energy-related projects, baselines should be expressed in terms of energy use per ton clinker produced for each of the three main process steps. Since the characteristics of "cement" can vary widely, expressing standardised baselines in terms of tons of cement would not lead to comparable values across projects. An internationally standardised baseline value for the energy required to manufacture cement should be set towards the upper end of the best practice range for energy-efficiency type projects, *e.g.* 3.1 GJ direct fuel use /t clinker. This value compares to estimated best practice of 2.9 - 3.2 GJ/t clinker and performance of 2.93 - 3.10 GJ/t clinker in new cement plants using standard technology. It may be more appropriate for process change type projects to have a less stringent baseline (*i.e.* at a higher energy level), in order to encourage conversion from highly inefficient plant types.

Because of the high volume of cement production, the number of credits generated by a particular project is highly sensitive to small changes in baseline value. For example, the hypothetical level of credits that could be obtained from two recently constructed cement plants in India and Mexico was examined. These plants have not requested AIJ or CDM approval, but if they did, they could qualify for credits under certain baseline assumptions. Moreover, the number of credits obtained could more than double depending whether or not the baseline was based on a value of 3.1 or 3.2 GJ fuel use/t clinker. The value of these credits could be more than US$300,000 per year for an individual plant, if the value of 1t CO_2 was US$10.

Energy-related emissions of CH_4 and N_2O combined represent less than 0.5% of total CO_2-equivalent energy-related emissions. The importance of the variability in energy use and therefore energy-related CO_2 emissions, is an order of magnitude higher ($\pm$15%). Thus, omitting estimations of CH_4 and N_2O will simplify the baseline-setting procedure without having a significant impact on either the stringency of the emissions baseline or on the uncertainty of credits. It is therefore recommended that baselines for energy-related projects in cement manufacture should include energy-related CO_2 emissions only. Since process-related CO_2 emissions are not impacted by energy-related projects, they would not need to be included in the emissions baseline for energy-related projects either.

For *blending projects,* it would be difficult to set either international or national standards for the clinker content of cement produced because the clinker content of cement varies significantly within and between countries, cement plants and cement types and can change significantly from year to year. Moreover, data on clinker and cement production before and during a project are likely to be both easily available at the project level (for plants already in operation) and more accurate (and available) at this level than at the country level. However, needing a project-specific number on which to base credits from blending projects increases the opportunity for gaming by the project proponents. Blending projects would need little if any technology input and are also relatively cheap (given the proximity of a potential source of additives). Emission baselines for any blending-type projects may need to include components related to both energy-related and process CO_2 emissions. These components should be separated for transparency and verification purposes. Baselines for blending projects should be reported in terms of energy-related and process CO_2 emissions per ton cement produced.

This study recommends quantifying the major emission sources that are influenced by a project for both energy and non energy-related projects in the cement sector. For energy projects, the major emission sources are the three major process steps: raw materials preparation, pyro-processing and cement grinding. Process CO_2 emissions are unchanged by energy-related projects and so could be omitted from the project baseline for simplicity. For blending projects, process emissions, emissions from additive preparation, as well as energy-related emissions in the three major process steps should be included in the project boundary. Emissions from other activities related to cement manufacture (such as transport of raw materials, bagging and transport of finished cement) could be addressed by applying a constant multiplier to the quantified emission sources. Attempting to quantify small sources by using a multiplier addresses both simplicity and leakage concerns, although it is approximate and may therefore raise some accuracy issues.

Determining the lifetime of potential JI/CDM projects in the cement sector is extremely tricky, because there are no general standards (across different countries and companies) about the technical lifetime of equipment or how long it is used for before being refurbished. For example, some companies may replace kilns after 25y, whereas others will continue operation until the supply of raw materials is exhausted. Refurbishment (or not) of existing plants will also depend on the competitiveness of the cement supply market.

The long technical life (>50y) of cement plants mean many existing cement plants manufacture cement using old and inefficient technology. Although refurbishments, often combined with capacity increases, are undertaken under commercial business-as-usual conditions, refurbishment of such plants also could be a potentially promising area for JI/CDM projects.

It may be possible to set up rough "rules of thumb" to help determine the crediting lifetime of energy efficiency and process change projects. However, great care would need to be taken in order to avoid creating either non-additional credits or perverse incentives that rewarded installing inefficient technology. The best way of doing this may be to opt for either relatively short crediting lifetimes for energy efficiency and process change projects (*e.g.* 5-10y) or baselines that are revised relatively frequently (*e.g.* 5y) for all project types. However, any multi-project baseline used for the cement sector may need to be updated frequently (*e.g.* every few years) in order to reflect trends in BAU energy intensity, fuel use and blending practices within the cement industry.

Determining whether or not a project is truly "additional" may be as difficult as determining for how long an "additional" project should receive credits for. Thus, it may be useful to ask for some qualitative additionality checks when assessing whether or not a proposed project is eligible for JI/CDM status. These could include, *e.g.* indications of policy, regulatory or behavioural additionality of the proposed project. The use of qualitative additionality checks in conjunction with a quantitative baseline "test" could help to reduce the risk of non-additional projects generating emissions credits.

2.7   References

Blue Circle, 2000, List of environmental commitments, (www.bluecircle.co.uk)

Cembureau, 1991, *Cement Standards of the World*, Cembureau, Brussels, Belgium

Cembureau, 1997, *BAT reference document,* Cembureau, Brussels, Belgium

Cembureau, 1999, *Climate Change: a message from Europe's cement industry,*
    (www.cembureau.be)

Cement Hranice, 2000, Cement Hranice prichází novým výrobkem, (www.cement.cz)

Cemex, 1998, Environmental Health and Safety report, (www.cemex.com)

Holderbank, 1999, Hong Chong cement plant, (www.engineering.hmc.ch)

Holnam, 1999, *Cement, Concrete and Greenhouse Gas,*
    (www.holnam.com/environment/greenhouse.htm)

IEA Greenhouse Gas R&D Programme (IEA GHG R&D), 1999, *The reduction of
    greenhouse gas emissions from the cement industry,* Report Number PH3/7,
    Cheltenham, UK

IEA, 1997, Energy Statistics and Balances of Non-OECD Countries, Paris, France

IFC, 1999, Project descriptions in the cement sector,
    (www.worldbank.org/pics/ifcers/cne04955.txt)

IPCC, 1996, *Revised 1996 IPCC Guidelines for National Greenhouse Gas Inventories*,
    IPCC/OECD/IEA

Lawrence Berkeley National Laboratory (LBNL) 1999, INEDIS data base on cement
    production

Marland, G, T Boden and A Brenkert, 1998, *Revised Global CO_2 Emissions from Fossil
    Fuel Burning, Cement Manufacture and Gas Flaring, 1751-1995,* Carbon Dioxide
    Information and Analysis Center, Oak Ridge National Laboratory, TN, US.

NEDO, 2000, *Basic Survey Project for Joint Implementation etc.: Feasibility study for
    the diffusion of fluidised bed cement kiln system in China* (unofficial translation
    from Japanese)

NEDO, 1998a, *Basic Survey Project for Joint Implementation etc.: Feasibility Study for the Promotion of a Fluidized Bed Cement Kiln System in China*

NEDO, 1998b, *Basic Survey Project for Joint Implementation etc. :Waste Heat Recovery Power Generation Plant for a Cement plant in China*

Phylipsen, GJM, K Blok and E Worrel, 1998, *Handbook on International Comparisons of Energy Efficiency in the Manufacturing Industry,* Utrecht

Price, Lynn, Ernst Worrel, Dian Phylipsen, 1999, *Energy Use and Carbon Dioxide Emissions in Energy-Intensive Industries in Key Developing Countries,* paper presented at the Earth Technologies Forum, Washington D.C., 1999

Ruth, Michael, Lynn Price, Ernst Worrell, 2000, *Evaluating Clean Development Mechanism Projects in the Cement Industry Using a Process-Step Benchmarking Approach*, Report number LBNL-45346, Lawrence Berkeley National Laboratory, United States

Sathaye, Jayant and Ashok Gadgil, 1999, *Role of Development Banks in Promoting Industrial Energy Efficiency: India Case Studies,* Report number LBNL-43191, Lawrence Berkeley National Laboratory, US, (www.lbl.gov).

Schumacher, Katja and Jayant Sathaye, 1999, *India's Cement Industry: Productivity, Energy Efficiency and Carbon Emissions*, Report number LBNL-41842, Lawrence Berkeley National Laboratory, US, (www.lbl.gov).

UNFCCC, 1998, Activities Implemented Jointly under the Pilot Phase (Czech/France project report), (www.unfccc.de)

WEC, 1995, *Efficient Use of Energy Utilizing High Technology: An Assessment of Energy Use in Industry and Buildings,* World Energy Council, London, UK

Worrell, Ernst, Rob Smit, Dian Phylipsen, Kornelius Blok, Frank van der Vleuten, Jaap Jansen, 1995, International Comparison of Energy Efficiency Improvement in the Cement Industry, *Proceedings ACEEE 1995 Summer Study on Energy Efficiency in Industry,* Washington D.C.

3. ELECTRICITY GENERATION CASE STUDY

3. ELECTRICITY GENERATION CASE STUDY[50]

3.1   Executive summary

The objective of this case study is to examine baseline methodologies in the context of the possibilities and implications of developing multi-project[51] or standardised baselines in the electricity generation sector. To do so, it considers, through a quantitative analysis using detailed electricity data, recent capacity additions in the electricity generation sectors of three countries with different national circumstances: Brazil, India and Morocco[52]. Compared to highly aggregated multi-project baselines (e.g. including all plants operating in a country), less aggregated multi-project baselines are likely to provide a better reflection of business-as-usual investments and thus be a more credible evaluation of what would happen without Clean Development Mechanism/Joint Implementation projects in the electricity sector.

The examination of multi-project baselines in the context of electricity generation projects is important and timely, as:

- Electrification is often linked to sustainable development priorities;

---

[50] This paper was prepared by Martina Bosi of the IEA Secretariat. The author is grateful for comments and oversight from Jonathan Pershing and advice from Olivier Appert, Maria Argiri, Pierre Audinet, Richard Baron, Laura Cozzi, Lawrence Metzroth, Hans Nilsson, John Paffenbarger, Bénédicte Riey, Karen Tréanton, Jocelyn Troussard, Kristi Varangu and David Wallace (IEA), as well as comments and suggestions from Jan Corfee Morlot, Jane Ellis and Thomas Martinsen (OECD). Shigemoto Kajihara (Japan), the US delegation to the Annex I Expert Group and Robert Kleiburg of Shell International also provided very useful suggestions.

[51] "Multi-project" baselines could be developed, for example, to assess, in a standardised manner, the emission reductions associated with similar electricity projects operating in similar circumstances. The advantages of developing these standardised baselines (as opposed to project-specific baselines) could include increased transparency and consistency, as well as the potential to reap economies of scale from the resources spent on the baseline-setting process.

[52] The three countries examined in the context of this case study are potential hosts of Clean Development Mechanism (CDM) projects. It is expected, however, that the issues and insights from this case study would also be applicable in the context of Joint Implementation (JI), although the application of its conclusions to Annex I Parties might warrant further examination.

- The electricity sector is projected to grow significantly, particularly in non-OECD countries, during the next two decades;

- World CO_2 emissions from the electricity sector represent over one third of world annual energy-related CO_2 emissions and are projected to increase at an annual rate of 2.7% between 1995 and 2020 (IEA, 1998);

- Projections also indicate significant capital expenditures on new power plants in the non-Annex I region, which could potentially include CDM projects;

- The electricity sector seems particularly well-suited to the development of multi-project baselines; and,

- Electricity multi-project baselines would facilitate the calculation of the greenhouse gas (GHG) mitigation potential of other projects (*e.g.* energy efficiency projects).

The development of electricity multi-project baselines requires making decisions on certain key underlying assumptions. One of the first steps is to define the boundary of an electricity generation JI or CDM project. Although a fully comprehensive approach would argue for boundaries to include all life-cycle emissions related to electricity generation, this broad boundary definition is generally considered impractical for the development of CDM/JI emission baselines. It seems preferable, as demonstrated in this case study, to define the boundaries around the direct GHG emissions from the combustion of fossil fuels to generate electricity (which represent the bulk of life-cycle emissions associated with electricity generation).

The development of a multi-project baseline is necessarily based on either historical or projection data. There are inherent uncertainties associated with forecasts and projections, as well as discrepancies between projections and forecasts of different origins. Consequently, this case study constructs the multi-project baselines from historical data on recent investments in electricity plants/units, as well as on plants/unit under construction at the time of data collection. This choice of data set, which only considers recent plants, offers a good proxy for "what would occur without CDM/JI projects" in the electricity sector. However, baseline updates at regular intervals will be crucial to ensure that future projects are compared to multi-project baselines that credibly reflect the electricity generation situation at that time.

It is recommended to calculate multi-project baselines on a rate basis, *i.e.* tonnes of CO_2 emissions per GWh of electricity produced (instead of on total emissions, *e.g.* tCO_2). The total number of years for which a multi-project baseline will be considered adequate to reflect "what would occur otherwise" (*i.e.* the crediting lifetime) will be critical to determining the total amount of emission units that could be expected from a CDM or JI project in the electricity generation sector. Determining up-front the crediting lifetime associated with a multi-project baseline would also enhance transparency and consistency among similar types of projects, in addition to providing some certainty for the project sponsors (investors and host country).

There is no truly objective crediting lifetime for electricity multi-project baselines. Subjective assessments of what would be considered appropriate will need to be made. Various economic and technical factors/criteria (*e.g.* technical lifetime, economic lifetime of power plants, time required to pay off the debt, *etc.*) can be considered when making this assessment. However, these factors need to be balanced out with environmental considerations. This case study suggests a crediting lifetime for electricity multi-project baselines of around 10-15 years.

For example, this would mean that project developers could count on the same multi-project baseline for the agreed 10-15 year period. However, this does not necessarily mean that all future projects implemented in the subsequent 10-15 years would use that same baseline. In this context, it may be appropriate to consider periodically updating electricity multi-project baselines approximately every 5 years, for example, in order to reflect ongoing developments in the electricity sector.

The case study focuses on new electricity investments. Reliable data on timing of refurbishment or fuel switching of power plants is very scarce. However, estimates of economic lifetime frequently include normal refurbishments and updating of equipment. Nonetheless, some experts suggest that the multi-project baseline crediting lifetime be different for new projects and for refurbishment projects. This differentiation could be justified because the expected remaining lifetime of a plant being refurbished would normally be presumed to be shorter than the lifetime of a new power plant. Also, a distinction may be considered useful to take into account the difference in capital investments (which are typically lower for refurbishment projects) and thus the different size of incentive needed to stimulate more climate-friendly investments. However, some major refurbishments in the electricity sector can be quite capital intensive and come close to (or even match) investments for new power projects. Also, some refurbishment and greenfield electricity projects can have very similar greenhouse gas reduction benefits (*e.g.* fuel switching from coal to gas and a new gas plant). Thus, making a distinction between "refurbishment" and "greenfield" electricity projects may be difficult. Furthermore, it is important that both types of electricity projects be treated in a consistent manner in order to create a level playing field and avoid unwanted incentives in the electricity generation sector. This issue could usefully be explored further.

A crucial element to take into account in the development of multi-project baselines is the quality and availability of data. Ideally, the following plant-specific data:

- Commissioning date (in order to determine whether the plant/unit should be used in the sample of recent capacity additions);

- Type of technology (*e.g.* internal combustion engine, combined cycle gas turbine, *etc.*);

- Source of electricity generation (*e.g.* natural gas, water, bituminous coal, *etc.*);

- Generating capacity (measured in MW - it is a necessary input to calculate the electricity production in MWh);

- Load factor (for what portion of total possible hours in a year is the plant/unit in operation - this is necessary to determine the electricity production in MWh);

- Conversion efficiency (for fossil fuels);

- Emission factors (to convert into GHG emissions).

A lot of this data is available for each plant/unit (at least in the case of this case study)[53]. In circumstances where requisite information is not available, assumptions, based on expert advice from IEA secretariat and national experts, are used in lieu of actual data on these variables.

CO_2 emissions (calculated based on the type of fuel used by each plant) represent more than 99% of energy-related GHG emissions for electricity generation. Methane (CH_4) emissions are small and can be calculated based on the type of technology of each plant using IPCC default emission factors. Emissions of N_2O, also very small, were not estimated, as default emission factors are only available for few types of technologies. Robust multi-project baselines are likely to be possible without the inclusion of N_2O data.

Current data constraints need to be taken into account in decisions on baselines for electricity projects, but should not necessarily be considered a barrier. Independent assumptions, based on expert advice, can be made where data is not available. Moreover, the emergence of the CDM and JI mechanisms may stimulate the monitoring, reporting and publication of more detailed and reliable data.

This case study examines, quantitatively, various aggregation options to set multi-project baselines for electricity generation projects. Country-based multi-project baselines may be suitable in many countries. Multi-country baselines for groups of small neighbouring countries with similar circumstances may also be possible and useful. Similarly, large countries where regions are quite different may demand the development of sub-national multi-project baselines in order to be more credible.

---

[53] The plant samples used for this case study exclude CHP-type plants. Making conversion efficiency assumptions for CHP plants is complicated, as there is no standardised way of accounting for the production of both heat and power by these plants (for example, accounting for only the power produced by those plants would make them appear less efficient than they really are). Once appropriate conversion efficiency levels of CHP plants are developed, CHP plants could be included in the electricity generation baselines. The exclusion of CHP plants should not significantly affect the assessment and development of multi-project electricity baselines based on recent capacity additions, as CHP-type plants represented very small portions of recent capacity additions in the countries examined.

After having put in place a workable database, for any region or country being examined, assumptions or choices have to be made as to which electricity multi-project baseline would be most appropriate. This case study examines multi-project baselines based on recent capacity additions, according to: (i) all sources; (ii) only fossil fuels; (iii) source-specific; (iv) region-specific; and (v) load-specific. The implications of these baseline assumptions, in terms of stringency, vary from country to country. However, some general insights can be drawn from the case study:

- For Brazil and India, source-specific multi-project baselines (*e.g.* comparing different coal fired plants to a coal-specific baseline) yield the largest volume of emission credits from clean coal plants, *i.e.* coal-specific multi-project baselines lead to least stringent levels of any multi-project electricity baseline. Using such a baseline may not be considered, by some, as consistent with the environmental objective of the CDM. In fact, source-specific multi-project baselines, particularly in the case of coal, may cause concerns in terms of the overall environmental effectiveness of the project-based mechanisms. However, these baselines may be very useful in promoting a cleaner use of coal than would otherwise occur, which for countries like India and China, with huge coal reserves, could be an important variable in promoting a more environmentally benign electricity infrastructure.

Brazil may serve as an example of large countries with varied circumstances within their borders (a characteristic that also applies to India). In these cases, it may be appropriate to consider the further development of separate multi-project baselines for different regions within a country. At a minimum, the development of separate multi-project baselines for off-grid, isolated electricity systems would be useful.

- Developing separate multi-project baselines for peak and baseload electricity was done in the case of India, based on expert advice to make relevant assumptions. Given that the majority of recent plants are assumed to generate baseload electricity, the multi-project baseline for baseload electricity is very similar to the country's multi-project baseline using all sources. However, the multi-project baseline for peaking electricity is quite a bit higher, due to the typically lower efficiency of the gas and oil-fuelled power plants generating peak electricity. Developing a separate multi-project baseline for peaking electricity may be desirable, as those plants are typically different from baseload plants. However, caution is needed in making assumptions on which plant type would constitute the "peaking electricity generation" for a given country and preferably would only be done with advice from in-country experts.

This case study provides a series of quantitative examples (Figures 3-6, 3-7 and 3-8 in particular) of the implications on stringency of different electricity multi-project baselines in the context of Brazil, India and Morocco.

- The evaluation of "stringency" based on "average" performance depends on what exactly the "average" represents. For example, there is a significant difference between multi-project baselines based on the average emission rate of recent capacity

103

additions including all sources and multi-project baselines based on the average emission rate of recent fossil fuel capacity additions. In this case study, using Brazil as the example, the latter would lead to a baseline of 808 tCO_2/GWh, while the former would lead to a baseline of 108 tCO_2/GWh. The "average emission rate" of recent capacity additions including all sources may be viewed as sufficiently stringent in some cases or perhaps too stringent in others (*e.g.* Brazil where recent capacity additions consist largely of non-GHG emitting hydropower plants). Nonetheless, it may be worth considering further the potential options and implications for better than average electricity multi-project baselines. For example, a better than average multi-project baseline could be defined as x% below the average multi-project baseline using recent capacity additions (including all sources). Other potential options may be to define it as better than the 75th percentile, for instance, or setting the baseline at one or two standard deviations below the average emission rate.

- However stringent a multi-project baseline for electricity generation projects is, non-emitting sources would always be below the baseline level and therefore theoretically eligible to generate emissions credits. This is irrespective of whether they are part of the business-as-usual trend in that country's electricity generation sector. It might thus be useful to consider a "hybrid" approach to assessing the GHG additionality of those zero-emitting projects. For example, it may be worth considering an activity additionality test, which would screen out projects or types of power plants that have a significant probability of generating non-additional emission credits. In order to focus on larger plants that have the potential to lead to larger volumes of non-additional emission credits, another option would be to require large zero-emitting projects to go through a more elaborate evaluation process. Small renewable projects would only need to pass the multi-project baseline test.

The details of the overall CDM decision-making process have yet to be agreed-upon by the international community. However, the final decision on which multi-project baseline(s) is/are most appropriate and at what level of stringency, can be expected to be a decision tailored to national circumstances, based on environmental, economic, administrative and data availability criteria. Further consideration might be warranted to determine whether and, if so, what type of guidance could be developed internationally to ensure consistency among similar projects in similar circumstances.

This case study considers the potential volume and value of emission credits that could be earned by a hypothetical new best available technology (BAT) gas plant in India and how they could affect the economic feasibility of the project. In the example examined, the revenues from the emission credits (calculated at both 5 US\$/tCO_2 and 10 US\$/tCO_2) would help increase the potential revenues from the hypothetical new BAT gas plant, but would not be sufficient to make it economically feasible. At a 5% discount rate, the CDM credits contribute to reducing the net deficit of the hypothetical new Indian gas plant by 16% if emission credits are worth 10 US\$/tCO_2.

The evaluation of the contribution of the emission credits from a potential CDM project critically depends on the assumptions made (*e.g.* cost and revenues of the project, type of financing, discount rate, *etc.*). Another key factor, which cannot be generalised, is each investor's financial criteria (*e.g.* rate of return). It is thus not possible to draw general conclusions on the potential volume of projects under different multi-project baseline options. However, if the example of this case study can be representative of projects more broadly, the CDM impact on investment decisions could be relatively small: proposed CDM projects may need to be already very close to meeting the basic feasibility criteria from an investor's point of view in order for the emission credits to have an impact on the investment decision. In this case, the CDM could be viewed as a means of improving the ranking of the proposed project against other competing investment options.

3.2   Context

Options for Project Emission Baselines (Ellis and Bosi 1999) included case study simulations with multi-project baselines in the electricity generation sector. These multi-project baselines for Brazil and India were derived from 1996 national electricity generation (including all existing capacity) and CO_2 emissions data. That case study demonstrated, *inter alia,* that the environmental stringency of a multi-project baseline is dependent on assumptions used and independent of baseline approach, *i.e.* multi-project, hybrid or project-specific. The case study also illustrated the significance of different national circumstances in a determination of the absolute level of the baseline and the resulting amount of emission credits that might accrue from its use.

Ellis and Bosi (1999) also acknowledged that alternative multi-project sectoral baselines could be appropriate in different regions or countries. For example, the construction of multi-project baselines in the electricity generation sector might be based on the emissions performance of recently constructed plants. Compared to highly aggregated multi-project baselines (*e.g.* including all plants operating in a country), less aggregated multi-project baselines are likely to provide a better reflection of business-as-usual investments in that sector and thus be a more credible evaluation of what would happen without CDM/JI projects.

The case study presented here builds on this earlier work and further examines baseline methodologies in the context of the possibilities and implications of developing multi-project or standardised baselines in the electricity generation sector. To do so, it considers recent capacity additions in the electricity generation sectors of three countries with different national circumstances: Brazil, India and Morocco[54]. This case study also draws

---

[54] The three countries examined in this case study are potential hosts of CDM projects. It is expected, however, that the issues and insights from this case study would also be applicable in a JI context, although it may warrant further examination.

on a number of studies, including the findings of Tellus Institute *et. al.* (1999), which includes a very useful analysis of baselines in the electricity generation sector.

3.3   Broad overview of sector

The electricity generation sector provides key services (*e.g.* lighting, heating, power) that maintain and enhance countries' economic activity, as well as maintain and increase populations' standards of living.

Reliable supply of electric power is a key input for the industrialisation process of developing countries' economies. In many developing countries, the growth rate of this sector is higher than that of the overall economy, as electrification is often closely linked to development priorities (*e.g.* in Brazil and India).

The 1998 World Energy Outlook (IEA 1998a) projected an annual growth rate of 3.0% from 1995 to 2020 for world electricity generation. The non-OECD share of world electricity generation is projected to increase from 40% in 1995 to 53% in 2020. Non-Annex I generating plant capacity is expected to roughly double in 2010, compared to 1995 and nearly triple by 2020, representing an addition of about 1500 GW of new capacity in this time-frame[55]. According to IEA (1998a) projections, by 2020, this translates into US$1699 billion (1990 prices) in capital expenditure on new generating plants in the non-Annex I region. World CO_2 emissions from the power generation sector represent over one third of world annual energy-related CO_2 emissions and are projected to increase at an annual rate of 2.7% between 1995 and 2020. Although coal is projected to maintain its position as the most widely used source for electricity generation, natural gas-generated electricity grows at the highest rate during the projection period (*i.e.* up to 2020). The use of renewables in electricity generation is projected to increase but it is expected to remain a relatively small portion of total generation throughout the period.

Notwithstanding the different fuel or energy sources (*e.g.* coal, oil, hydro, *etc.*), electricity output is considered homogeneous. One kWh of electricity provides the same service[56] (*e.g.* lighting, heating, *etc.*) everywhere in the world. In a given country or region, the fuel or energy source used for electricity generation depends on factors such as the availability and proximity to the fuel or energy supply, reliability, prices of fuel and technology, as well as government policies. Electricity imports may also play a significant role in a country's electricity supply. National circumstances (including resource endowments and distance between the resource and the consumption centres) help explain differences between countries' electricity generation - and large countries with diverse geographic territories and more than one electricity grid may also have different electricity generation mixes between regions. Many utilities within different countries rely on a mix of

---

[55] *i.e.* an increase from 832 GW in 1995, to 1592 GW in 2010 and to 2387 GW in 2020.

[56] Assuming equipment/appliances have same efficiency levels.

generating plant types in order to hedge against fluctuations in the prices of fuels and uncertain growth rates in electricity demand, as well as to match changing load requirements (*i.e.* peak versus baseload).

Figure 3-1(a)

World electricity generation by region

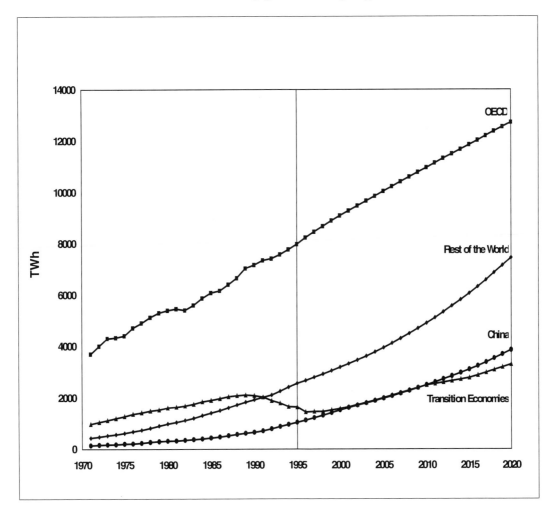

Source: IEA, 1998a

Different power production technologies, combined with different inputs, result in different greenhouse gas (GHG) emissions by unit of electricity output. The different energy sources used to generate electric power, as well as the type of technology along with their conversion efficiency levels, are key factors in determining the GHG emissions associated with power generation. Hydroelectric, wind and nuclear plants, for example

107

will not emit any GHG emissions while generating electricity with technologies using fossil fuels (*i.e.* coal, oil and natural gas) can result in significant GHG emissions[57].

Figure 3-1(b)

World electricity generation by fuel

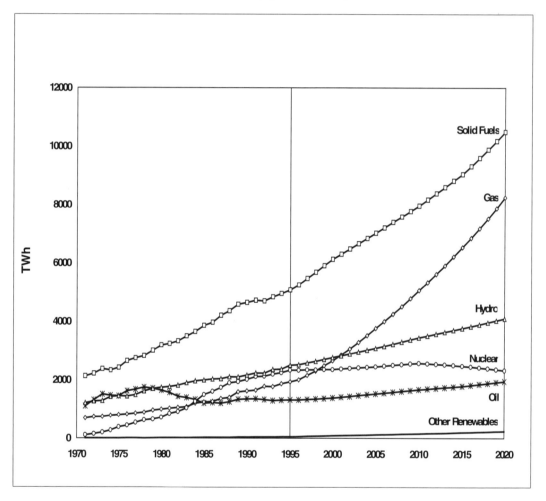

Source: IEA, 1998a.

Several AIJ projects were based in the electricity generation sector, although most did not seek to use standardised methodologies to set emissions baselines. In terms of JI/CDM potential, the power sector is viewed by many as a good candidate to host projects. Tellus

---

[57] While the electricity generation from these sources are essentially non-emitting, life cycle analyses indicate none have "zero" emissions. For example, land inundation in hydro-power reservoirs releases methane, while processing uranium is often undertaken with fossil fuels.

(1999) concludes: "the power sector is likely to be fertile territory for CDM projects as well as being relatively well-suited to benchmarks".[58] A Pew Center report (Pew Center, 1999) also concludes that there is a significant potential for emission reduction in the power sector: "if developing countries adopt different policies and planning methods for their power generation sectors, technologies other than those included in "business-as-usual (BAU)" projections could provide lower local and global environmental impacts and produce similar or even higher economic benefits".

A number of different types of electricity projects, in the context of CDM and JI, could be undertaken. For example (IEA, 2000 forthcoming):

(i)   Installing a new plant (*i.e.* greenfield);

(ii)   retiring an existing plant and replacing it with a new one;

(iii) fuel switching (*e.g.* from coal to gas) that may require minor or major replacement of equipment;

(iv)   refurbishment of equipment at existing facilities (*e.g.* replacing existing basic generation technologies, such as boiler or turbine, with a more recent technology); or

(v)   housekeeping type projects (*e.g.* improvements to processes, *etc.* that do not involve installing generation equipment).

This case study is based on data from new plants and is most likely applicable to the types of electricity projects (i) to (iv).

3.3.1   Brazilian electricity context

Electricity generation totalled 307.3 TWh in 1997 (IEA, 1999a) in Brazil. The growth rate of Brazilian electricity consumption (4.7% p.a. between 1990 and 1997) is greater than the country's GDP growth rate (3.1% p.a. during the same period). The predominant source of electricity generation is hydro, generating 90.8% of total electricity in 1997. The other sources include oil (3.2%), non-hydro renewables (2.9%), coal (1.8%), nuclear (1%) and natural gas (0.4%). However, Brazil's predominant reliance on hydro is expected to slowly decrease (although remaining the main source of power), as the competitivity of new hydro is reduced due to relatively high transmission and construction costs for remaining sites. In addition, around half of Brazil's remaining hydro potential is located in the Amazon area, which may not be considered appropriate for reservoir development. Brazilian authorities are thus planning a thermoelectric transition program to help meet increasing electricity demand. The Brazilian Ten-Year

---

[58] The term "benchmark" used in some studies on baselines is equivalent to "multi-project baselines", which is the term used in this case study to describe emissions baselines that can apply to more than one project.

Expansion Plan: 1999-2008 is counting on increased involvement of the private sector in the electricity sector to develop the hydropower potential in parallel with the construction of new thermal plants. This thermoelectric expansion should be fundamentally based on the use of natural gas, mineral coal and, in the case of isolated electricity systems, petroleum derivatives (Electrobrás *et. al.*, 1999). The expansion of the nuclear program remains within the public sector, which plans to have two additional nuclear units (Angra II[59] and Angra III) come on stream by 2005.

Figure 3-2

Total electricity generation in Brazil (all existing capacity in 1997): 307.3 TWh

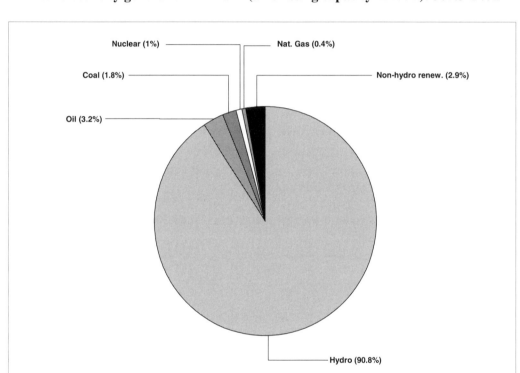

Source: IEA (1999a)

Significant natural gas reserves in South America (*e.g.* in nearby Bolivia) and plans to construct pipeline infrastructure in South America that would go into Brazil make it likely that natural gas will be readily available and competitive for some of the new power facilities. Thus, the current very low percentage of Brazilian electricity generated by natural gas can be expected to increase. The extent and rate of this increase is difficult to

---

[59] Angra II was under construction at the time of producing the Ten-Year Expansion Plan 1999-2008.

predict, however, as it will largely depend on private sector investment (as opposed to government plans).

3.3.2 Indian electricity context

Electricity consumption in India is also growing (7% p.a. between 1990 and 1997) faster than economic activity (5.5% p.a. during the same period); it has more than doubled in the last 10 years. According to IEA statistics (IEA, 1999b), Indian electricity generation in 1997 totalled 463 TWh.

The lack of an inter-connected electricity grid across the country means that states with surplus power do not transfer that surplus to states facing power shortages. Furthermore, the Indian distribution and transmission system is under significant strain due to fluctuations in frequency and voltage. This combined with the poor quality of the transmission lines, result to power losses amounting to approximately one fifth of generated electricity.

The electricity sector attracted more than a sixth of all Indian investments over the past decade (Shukla *et. al.*, 1999). Despite these investments in power addition, the power generating supply is still insufficient to meet electricity demand in India. Increasing the proportion of the population connected to the electricity grid is one of the development goals of the Indian government. In its Ninth Five-Year Plan (1997-2002) (Government of India, 1997), the Indian government evaluates that the capacity addition requirement during the 1997-2002 period to be about 46,814 MW, but assesses that a capacity addition of the order of 40,245 MW would be feasible during the Plan period.

India is a very large and populated country with significant regional differences within its borders (*e.g.* in resource endowments, electricity demand, *etc.*). It has large reserves of coal and was the world's third largest coal producer in 1998. On the other hand, India has few oil or gas reserves, although the share of gas in India's total primary energy supply is growing quickly (from 2.8% in 1990 to almost 4% in 1997) and gas use in power generation is projected to grow significantly (IEA, 2000). Using domestic coal for electricity generation is generally cheaper than using imported fuels due to high tariffs and volume import restrictions. It is, therefore, not surprising that coal-fired electricity generates the great majority (73% in 1997) of Indian electricity. However, recent developments, such as reduced restrictions on fuel imports, inadequate expansion of coal mining capacity, as well as greater foreign investments, have resulted in an increase in the use of natural gas for power generation. Lower capital costs, shorter construction periods and reduced environmental impacts also benefited natural gas plant construction. Over the last 25-30 years, the capacity share of large hydro has declined, while nuclear power capacity is growing slowly (with the aim of using India's significant thorium resources). The contribution of non-hydro renewables is relatively small, but increasing in specific markets and in certain regions of the country (mainly Tamil Nadu and near Mumbai

(Bombay) along the Southern coasts). India's Ninth Five-Year Plan (1997-2002) includes a target of 3000 MW for non-hydro renewable capacity.

3.3.3   Moroccan electricity context

According to IEA statistics (1999b), Morocco's electricity output totalled 13.1 TWh in 1997, with 45% coming from coal, 39% from oil and 16% from hydro. Approximately half of Morocco's population lives in rural areas where basic services, including electricity, are scarce. The Government is putting in place an ambitious plan to raise the electrification rate in rural areas from 21% in 1994 to 60% in 2003 (Resource Publications (PTY) Ltd., 1999).

The country has some coal reserves in the north-east which are mostly used for electricity generation (Royaume du Maroc, 1998), but still has to import significant amounts of coal and oil for its electricity generation. Coal and hydroelectricity[60] production is encouraged. The Moroccan government is also examining the feasibility of building, with private sector involvement, a large combined cycle power station using imported natural gas from neighbouring Algeria. In addition, the Government is encouraging the development of renewable energy in the form of wind and solar electricity. While solar is being considered mainly for remote villages not connected to the nation-wide network (in the context of Morocco's rural electrification program), Moroccan authorities are planning to connect wind power generation to the national electricity grid (Resource Publications (PTY) Ltd., 1999). Morocco is also conducting a feasibility study on the use of biomass fuelled electricity generation based on energy crops or agricultural residues.

3.4   Baseline construction: Environmental performance

This section examines key issues for the construction of electricity multi-project baselines.

3.4.1   Key underlying assumptions

The development of electricity multi-project baselines requires making a number of assumptions/choices on the parameters to be used. Assumptions on boundaries, data sets, baseline lifetime and the technology and fuel are examined below.

---

[60] The hydro potential is estimated at 5 billion kWh, but only 40% was being exploited in 1998 (Ibid).

Boundaries

In order to take into account the complete GHG impacts associated with a particular electricity generation project, it would be necessary to set boundaries around a project in a way that would include all life-cycle emissions related to the project. For example, emissions associated with the extraction of gas, coal or oil from the ground, or with the production of biomass fuels, emissions released during the transportation and emissions generated during the transmission of electricity should all be within the full life-cycle boundaries of an electricity generation project[61].

However, this type of broad project boundary definition is generally viewed as impractical for the development of CDM/JI emissions baselines. For example, in the case of electricity generated with imported fuels, the current international emission inventory guidelines allocates the emissions from the extraction of these fuels to the producing country and not to the importing country. In fact, the Tellus (1999) report points out that "full fuel-cycle analysis is neither straightforward nor simple and could result in double-counting if CDM projects occur at more than one point in the fuel chain". Information is not available, however, to be able to determine whether the greater risk is that of double-counting or that of leakage from full-life cycle emissions that would not be accounted for in the baseline calculation. This issue may require further analysis.

A more practical option appears to be to define the project boundary around the direct emissions associated with electricity generation. In essence, this would mean establishing the project boundaries to include only the GHG emissions from the combustion of fossil fuels, which is where the bulk of GHG emissions come from, as indicated in Table 3-1 below. This would be the case even in a full life-cycle analysis of GHG emissions associated with the generation of electricity using different fossil fuels (European Commission, 1995).

This approach is also favoured in the Oeko-Institut (2000) report, which concludes, "… it seems preferable that life-cycle emission should not be included in the baseline estimate". JIRC (2000) states that one of the lessons learned from the Dutch AIJ experience is that system boundaries should be determined clearly and that the common policy was "not to credit the project with extra emission reductions realised outside and beyond the control of the project", also suggesting that the boundaries should be set around the direct emissions of an electricity generation project.

---

[61] More information on life-cycle emissions of various energy technologies can be found in the IEA Greenhouse Gas Implementing Agreements. Furthermore, the European Commission (Directorate-General XII, Science , Research and Development) produced a series of studies under the title Externe: Externalities of Energy (1995), providing useful information on the assessment of externalities and life-cycle analysis associated with energy.

Table 3-1

Relative importance of Greenhouse Gases

Type of GHG	CO_2	CH_4	N_2O	Others	Σ
Shares in Total anthropogenic GHG	82%	12%	4%	2%	100%
Contribution of Energy Sector	96%	35%	26%	n/a.	85%
Main Source within Energy Sector	Fuel Combustion	Fugitive emissions	Fuel Combustion	n/a.	

Source: UNFCCC, Second compilation and synthesis of second national communications, FCCC/CP/1998/11/Add.1, September 1998

Direct greenhouse gas emission from the combustion of fossil fuels to generate electricity are carbon dioxide (CO_2), which represent the bulk of the direct GHG emissions (more than 99%) and relatively small amounts of methane (CH_4) and nitrous oxide (N_2O). As IPCC default emission factors for N_2O are not available for most types of electricity generation plants, the quantitative examples of multi-project emission baselines presented in this case study are based on a narrow boundary around direct CO_2 and CH_4 emissions associated with electricity generation of the different plants/units[62].

Historical or projection data

There are different views on the utility of data based on projections as a basis for developing multi-project baselines. For example, Hagler Bailly (1998) recognises the relevance of using newer units to develop "marginal benchmarks", but notes that in the case of countries that need new capacity (such as developing countries), it may be appropriate to develop a forward-looking multi-project baseline, or to incorporate an efficiency trend from the historical data. However, developing an efficiency trend can be relatively subjective, as it is difficult to predict how and at what rate technologies that are at different stages of development will increase their efficiencies. Furthermore, government policy, which can also influence developments in the electricity sector, cannot be considered static and may stimulate changes over time, which throw forecasts off. For example, policy decisions working to increase market liberalisation of countries'

---

[62] Further examination of the boundary issue in the case of emissions from electricity generation could be useful; for example, exploring the possibilities and implications of accounting for indirect GHG emissions occurring outside the defined boundary.

electricity sectors can significantly change developments compared to a previous situation dominated by state-owned monopoly utilities.

Tellus (1999) concludes that projections of power sector behaviour are very sensitive to underlying assumptions; they therefore prefer to use historical performance data (on recent capacity additions) for developing multi-project baselines. Similarly, Ellis and Bosi (1999) note that while projections may be viewed as a better reflection of what would happen under a future business-as-usual (BAU) scenario than baselines based on historical data, projections' inherent speculative nature may make them more open to gaming than baselines constructed using historical data.

Because of the inherent uncertainty associated with forecasts and projections and the discrepancies between projections or forecasts by different groups, this case study proposes to construct baselines from historical data on recent investments in electricity units, as well as on units currently under construction. Tellus (1999) notes that an averaging period of 3 to 5 years appears adequate for the construction of baselines based on recent capacity additions in the electricity sector. CCAP (2000) suggests that a multi-project baseline for new projects may represent the average emission rate of new plants during the last 5 to 10 years. This case study defines "recent investments" (or capacity additions) as those plants or units that began operating in 1995 or later, as well as those plants that were under construction at the time of collecting the data (*i.e.* 1998-1999). The use of disaggregated and recent data should enable the construction of credible emission baselines reflecting what would likely occur without the CDM/JI in individual countries.

However, as discussed in the following section, the updating of multi-project baselines at regular intervals will be important to ensure that developments in the electricity sector are being captured for the assessment of future projects. For example, although Brazil's electricity generation via natural gas[63] can be expected to increase (although it is difficult to project the importance of this), it's potential future trend is not captured by the data used for this case study. Baseline updates will thus be crucial to reflect this trend as it occurs and to ensure that future electricity projects continue to be compared to a credible baseline.

---

[63] Eletronorte, an electric energy utility which belongs to the Brazil's Eletrobras System, notes on its website (www.eln.gov/br/home35.htm) recent studies' findings that natural gas may be "the most convenient fuel source for the thermal units both technically and economically to substitute the diesel consumption due to the large gas reserves available in the Amazonas State". Consequently, although they are continuing to plan that their capacity additions will be using diesel oil, they expect that these new plants will fuel switch to gas sometime in the future.

115

Lifetime

Crediting lifetime

The calculation of potential emission baselines for projects in the electricity generation sector in this case study is based on tCO_2/GWh per year. The total number of years for which a multi-project baseline will be considered adequate to reflect "what would occur otherwise" (*i.e.* crediting lifetime) will be key to determining the total amount of emission units that could be expected from a CDM or JI project in the electricity generation sector. Determining up-front the crediting lifetime associated with a multi-project baseline would also enhance transparency and consistency among similar types of projects, in addition to providing some certainty for the project sponsors (investors and host country). A recent Dutch study on baselines (JIRC, 2000) suggests considering the development of a generic list of time horizons based on the type of projects; the electricity generation projects could be one "type" of project and the lifetime for this type could differ from that of forestry projects, for example.

The AIJ Pilot Phase includes several electricity generation projects. The proposed lifetime over which these projects are expected to generate GHG reduction benefits is generally long[64], but there is no consistency between the AIJ projects[65]. For example:

- the Dutch hydro power project in Bhutan has a 10 year lifetime (based on the economic lifetime of the project);

- the Doña Julia hydroelectric project in Costa Rica uses a project lifetime of 15 years (with possible 5 year extensions);

- the US solar-based rural electrification project in Honduras is based on an "estimated service life" of 20 years;

- the US Bio-Gen biomass power project in Honduras is based on its expected operational lifetime of 20 years;

- the fuel-switching Decin project[66] in the Czech republic uses a project lifetime of 26 years;

- the Australian Fiji Grid Connected Photovoltaic project estimates CO_2 reductions over 20 years (*i.e.* the technical lifetime of the equipment);

- the German Latvia windpark project uses a 10 year lifetime (consistent with length of the depreciation period);

---

[64] Justifications for the timelines used for AIJ projects are not always provided in the reports (www.unfccc/program/aij).

[65] See Ellis (1999) for greater discussion on the different timelines used in the AIJ pilot phase.

[66] This is a CHP-type plant.

116

- the Costa Rican Aeronergia Wind Project calculates emission reduction benefits over 4 years (to take into account Costa Rica's policy goal to phase out fossil fuels by 2001).

Seeking to set objective crediting timelines for electricity baselines is challenging. There are various criteria/factors that can be considered, for example:

- technical lifetime of electricity project equipment;
- economic lifetime of power plants;
- the time needed to pay off the debt;
- the depreciation period.

There is no one set of generic technical lifetime data for power plants. The design lifetime of major components of power plants tend to be around 30 years, but in many cases the economic lifetime of power plants may be longer depending on the maintenance and prevailing economic conditions. For example, the NEA/IEA (1998) study used a common economic lifetime of 40 years for new state of the art baseload power plants (*i.e.* coal, gas and nuclear plants) in its reference cases. However, the Oeko-Institut (2000) Report notes the uncertainty on whether a manufacturer's recommended technical lifetime would be valid for all countries, given that the technical lifetime typically depends on various factors such as maintenance and climatic influences. Nonetheless, the report concludes, based on the technical literature on lifetime estimates for biomass power plants, that 15 years seemed like a "realistic choice" for the technical lifetime of wood waste power plants in Zimbabwe.

Indian experts[67] have suggested using 20-40 years for the technical lifetime of different types of power plants in India, with 20 years viewed as appropriate for internal combustion (reciprocating engine or diesel engine) plants; 25 years for wind turbine generators and gas/combustion turbines; 30 years for steam turbines (boilers), nuclear plants and gas turbines in combined cycle; and 40 years for hydro plants.

Brazilian experts[68] have suggested using 15 to 50 years for the technical lifetime of different types of power plants in Brazil, with 15 years for gas turbines, 15 years for internal combustion engine plants, 25 years for steam turbines, combustion turbines, gas turbines in combined cycle and nuclear plants, 30 years for wind turbine generators and 50 years for hydro plants.

---

[67] Recommendations received (March, 2000) from experts of the Indian Institute of Management, Ahmedabad, India.

[68] Recommendations received (April, 2000) from experts of the Agência Nacional de Energia Eléctrica (Aneel), Brasília, Brazil.

Recent IEA work has examined the issue of capital stock turnover (IEA, 2000 forthcoming). Although the focus of this work is on capital turnover in OECD countries and thus may not provide an accurate picture of the situation in countries with economies in transition and developing countries, it may nonetheless offer interesting insights for the crediting lifetime of emission baselines for JI/CDM electricity projects. The IEA forthcoming report indicates that one estimate for the lifetime of power plants can be the economic useful life for accounting purposes[69]. According to UNIPEDE information (1993), the economic useful lives for new thermal power plants (*i.e.* that burn fuel directly to produce steam) range from 15 to 40 years and from 16 to 30 years for nuclear plants. The median economic useful life for these two types of new power plants is 25 years. (This is within the technical lifetime ranges estimated by the Brazilian and Indian experts above.)

Statistics exist in some OECD countries on the age of their power plants. For instance, the average retirement age for all types of power plants in the US is about 38 years[70] and the median retirement age of coal-fired plants in the European Union was around 34 years. However, these figures do not tell the whole story and are likely to be underestimated. In the case of the US, plants that were retired tended to be relatively small; while the older but larger plants continue to operate with ongoing maintenance. In the case of the EU, the figure obtained for the retirement age was largely influenced by the early retirement of coal fired plants in the UK, due to a combination of environmental requirements and changed market conditions. In fact, the report notes that large coal-fired power plants could continue to operate almost indefinitely on relatively modest maintenance schedules. Furthermore, the lifetime of components[71] (*e.g.* turbines, boiler piping and superstructure and steam pipes) may also surpass the average retirement age of smaller older plants. There is not sufficient experience with combined-cycle gas turbines (CCGTs) to assess the typical lifetime of this technology. It is expected, however, that the main CCGT component that would require refurbishment would be the turbine blades, but some manufacturers believe that this should not be prior to 11 years of operation (IEA, 2000 forthcoming).

In addition to purely technical factors, increased competition in the electricity sector (through privatisation and deregulation of electricity markets, as is currently being experienced in many OECD countries) can be, in some cases, an incentive to extend the lifetime of power plants. In fact, the extension of plant lifetime may involve lower capital risks than investing in a new power plant. The ongoing electricity market reform of

---

[69] In some countries, this reflects the depreciation period that national tax authorities allow utilities to apply to their capital stock.

[70] This figure, based on the US Energy Information Administration database, includes average retirement ages of 58 years for hydro plants, 38-45 years for steam turbines (depending on fuel used), 31-33 years for internal combustion engine generators and 21 years for nuclear power plants.

[71] Many power plant components deteriorate very slowly under baseload operation.

OECD countries may not be entirely relevant for developing countries: while the former have significant over-capacity, the latter are rather suffering from under-capacity (as mentioned in section 3.3).

Turning to economic and financial considerations, the depreciation period is not the same for all electricity projects and varies by country. The time needed to pay off the debt depends on the financing of the project (*e.g.* bonds, bank loans, or equity) and profitability. In general, 10 to 15 years is the maximum time for private bank loans, whereas corporate bonds can have a length of 15 to 30 years and government loans can be for 20 to 30 years. However, Oeko-Institut (2000) points out that, in some cases, particularly in some developing countries, commercial loans are not always available for particular projects[72]. Consequently, the "typical" payback time of loans used for a project may not be appropriate to determine the crediting lifetime associated with a baseline.

The crediting lifetime for multi-project electricity baselines has to take into account the need to provide project investors with sufficient certainty on the number of years for which they can take into account revenue flow from emission credits and to create an incentive to invest in more climate-friendly power projects. However, some (*e.g.* CCAP, 2000) argue that this is shorter than the typical lifetime of power project investments. Given that the electricity generation sector in each country is not static, it is also important, from an environmental perspective, to be somewhat conservative, in the creation of emission credits in order to ensure lasting climate change benefits.

This discussion and analysis is mostly focussed on new electricity investments. Reliable data on timing of refurbishment or fuel switching of power plants is very scarce. However, estimates of economic lifetime frequently include normal refurbishments and updating of equipment.

Some experts have suggested that the crediting lifetime be different for new projects and for refurbishment projects. For example, the Dutch program recommends 5 years for good-housekeeping projects, 10 years for refurbishment/retrofit projects and 15 years for greenfield projects and no distinction is made between projects in different sectors. However, others (*e.g.* CCAP submission to UNFCCC, January 2000) indicate that the crediting lifetime could vary by project type and/or by sector.

One of the rationales for having different crediting lifetimes associated with baselines for refurbishment and greenfield projects is that the expected remaining lifetime of a power plant being refurbished would normally be presumed to be shorter than the lifetime of a new greenfield plant. Making a distinction may also be considered useful to take into account the difference in capital investments (which is typically lower for refurbishment projects) and thus the different size of incentive needed to stimulate more climate-friendly investments. However, some major refurbishments in the electricity sector can be

---

[72] This is also true for countries with economies in transition.

quite capital incentive and come close (or even match) investments for new power projects. Also, some refurbishment and new electricity projects can have very similar greenhouse gas reduction benefits (*e.g.* fuel switching from coal to gas and a new gas plant). Thus, while some electricity projects may be easily labelled "greenfield" or "refurbishment", it may be difficult for others (*e.g.* the replacement of turbines and fuel switching at an existing plant can be considered very similar to installing a new plant). This means that if a distinction were to be made between "refurbishment" and "greenfield" electricity projects, it would need to be specifically defined.

It may be necessary to further explore the options and implications of distinguishing between refurbishment and new projects in terms of the baseline crediting lifetime[73]. However, given that this case study is based on data of new recent capacity additions as a proxy for "what would occur otherwise" in the electricity sector of different countries, this distinction is not made here.

Based on the various studies examined and different criteria and objectives, the international community may wish to consider the possibility of setting a crediting lifetime for electricity generation baselines around 10 to 15 years. This is less than the typical lifetime of electricity plants, but it would nonetheless ensure that revenues from emission credits could accrue during the first years of the project, when it is most important to pay off debts. From an environmental perspective, this timeframe is likely to provide sufficient certainty in the decision-making process of project developers and investors, for consideration of greater climate-friendly projects, while still being environmentally cautious by not extending the current assessment of "what would occur otherwise" too far into the future[74]. It may also be considered important to stay relatively close to the planning horizon of the UNFCCC negotiations: commitments are currently only specified until 2012, but the Kyoto Protocol specifies that negotiations on commitments for subsequent commitment periods shall start no later than 2005.

Using a baseline fixed for 10-15 years would mean that at the start of the electricity project, project developers would know that they could count on using the same multi-project baseline for the agreed crediting timeline. However, this does not necessarily mean that all future electricity projects implemented in the subsequent 10-15 years would also use that same multi-project baseline.

---

[73] The treatment of "good house-keeping" projects in the electricity sector would also need to be examined further.

[74] From an environmental perspective, it may be useful to further examine the potential trade-off between (i) more or less stringent baseline levels; and (ii) longer or shorter baseline crediting lifetimes.

Timing of baseline updates

Setting a baseline crediting timeline up-front is expected to provide greater certainty to project developers and also potentially stimulate earlier climate change investments, particularly if it is expected that the multi-project baseline will be updated (perhaps more stringently) in the future for subsequent projects.

Regardless of the crediting timeline chosen, multi-project baselines are likely to need regular updates for future electricity projects, particularly if key factors become sufficiently important to improve GHG intensity of electricity generation. For example, Tellus (1999) mentions factors such as advances in combustion technology and increased competition in power markets that would require updating multi-project baselines if they are to continue to provide an adequate representation of "what would occur otherwise". Other potential factors could include effects of reforms of energy sector policy and changes in investment conditions in potential CDM/JI host countries.

It may be desirable, as a starting point, to consider periodically updating electricity multi-project baselines, *e.g.* every five years. This would mean, for example, that electricity projects implemented more than 5 years after the development of the first set of electricity multi-project baselines would be assessed against updated multi-project baselines, as the first set of electricity baselines would be considered as having expired. Five-year intervals appear reasonable in seeking to strike a balance between, on the one hand, seeking to reflect business-as-usual developments in countries' electricity sectors over time (particularly if baselines are developed with historical data, as in this case study) and, on the other, managing the overall baseline development costs (through updates at a reasonable frequency).

Technology and fuel

The technology (and its conversion efficiency) of a plant/unit and its source of electricity (*e.g.* coal, wind, oil, *etc.*) are the two key variables determining the GHG-intensity of electricity production. These variables depend on various factors, such as resource endowments, price of fuels, access to technologies, infrastructure, maintenance, *etc.* in a given country or region.

The database used in this case study to develop multi-project baselines based on recent capacity additions includes information on the fuel used by each individual unit, as well as the type of plant. However, assumptions, based on different sources and expert advice, had to be made for the conversion efficiency of each type of technology. Ideally, it would have been better to produce conversion efficiency assumptions for each individual plant/unit in the sample used for the case study. However, this type of detailed information was not possible to develop here. Instead, country-specific assumptions were made for the different types of technologies. For the purpose of this study, it is thus

121

assumed that all plants using the same technology in a given country have the same conversion efficiency[75] (see Annex C).

3.4.2   Data needs, quality and availability

Establishing multi-project baselines for power generation based on national average performance figures using all existing electricity generation capacity can be quite straightforward[76], as data are available for more than 100 countries[77]. For example, for all three countries examined in this case study, it is possible to draw national sectoral baselines for power generation with 1997 data (Annex D includes examples of such baselines, using all existing capacity, based on weighted average for all sources or weighted average for fossil fuel only).

Although simple to draw (and a useful basis for comparison), this national multi-project baseline design may not be considered, in many cases, the best way of reflecting "what would occur otherwise" in the power sector, as:

- Capital investments in the power sector have a relatively long lifetime (see section on *Lifetime* for more details), but the type of new investments and fuel mix tends to change over time. Consequently, a national baseline based on a country's entire power generation capacity in a given year (*e.g.* 1997) can include 30-year old plants that would not be at all representative of typical investments made in more recent years.

- Some larger countries have very different electricity generation mixes, reflecting sub-national differences in availability and cost of sources for power generation within their borders. As a result, a single national electricity generation multi-project baseline may not be considered appropriate to reflect some (potentially significant) regional differences in both total existing generating capacity as well as more recent power investments.

There is, therefore, a strong rationale to try and develop a more disaggregated multi-project baseline for the power sector. As pointed out in Tellus (1999), a multi-project baseline based on recent capacity additions provides a more accurate estimate of what would occur without a JI or CDM electricity project than does a multi-project baseline based on all existing capacity. Of course, the trade-off is that the analytical work to

---

[75] Seeking plant level data or making disaggregated assumptions for conversion efficiencies of different plants within a country would improve the accuracy of the multi-project baselines.

[76] This does not imply that the collection of information needed to develop this data is a simple exercise.

[77] See, for example, annual IEA statistics on Energy Balances of Non-OECD Countries and CO_2 Emissions from Fuel Combustion.

support multi-project baseline estimation based on recent additions requires more data gathering and time to prepare.

In this case study, the sample of plants used to develop multi-project baselines based on recent capacity additions consisted of power plants/units in Brazil, India and Morocco that started operating in 1995 or later, or that are currently under construction.

The development of electricity multi-project baselines based on recent capacity additions, as developed in this case study, requires plant specific data on those recent plants/units included in the sample used to calculate the multi-project baseline:

1. Commissioning year (in order to determine whether the plant/unit should be used in the sample of recent capacity additions).

2. Type of technology (*e.g.* internal combustion engine, combined cycle gas turbine, *etc.*);

3. Energy source used for electricity generation (*e.g.* natural gas, water, bituminous coal, *etc.*);

4. Generating capacity (measured in MW - it is a necessary input to calculate the electricity production in MWh);

5. Load factor (what portion of total possible hours in a year is the plant/unit in operation - this is necessary to determine the electricity production in MWh);

6. Conversion efficiency (for fossil fuels);

7. Emission factor(s) of energy source(s) used (to convert into GHG emissions).

Some of this data, at least for the countries examined in this case study, is readily available for each plant/unit, while some is not, which means that some estimates or assumptions need to be made.

The data for this case study is drawn from the Utility Data Institute (UDI)/McGraw-Hill (1999) *World Electric Power Plants Data Base*. This data base includes information on individual electric power plants world-wide, except for two types of power plants: (i) most reciprocating engines or gas turbines identified in primary sources as "emergency", "standby", or "back-up"; and (ii) all gas turbines or internal combustion engines on offshore platforms. Due to the difficulty in data collection, the UDI database may not necessarily include, for all countries, fully comprehensive coverage for all wind turbines, internal combustion engines and mini-and micro-hydro units. Although the coverage may not be comprehensive for some countries, it is nonetheless considered representative[78].

---

[78] Information based on personal communication with Chris Bergesen of McGraw Hill (March, 2000).

The UDI/McGraw-Hill (1999) database includes, albeit with a small lag (1 to 2 years), information on the electricity source, capacity, technology and on-line date for each unit[79]. The database, however, does not include information on the conversion efficiency and load factors for the different types of plants. Assumptions, based on IEA expert advice (and subsequently checked with experts from Brazil and India), were made for these two key variables.

It was not possible to develop reasonable load and efficiency assumptions for CHP-type (combined heat and power) plants, as literature on this type of information, particularly for Brazil and India, is quite scarce[80]). So, the plant samples used for this case study exclude CHP-type plants. Nonetheless, this omission, due to unavailable data and the difficulty in making reasonable assumptions[81], should not significantly affect the development of multi-project electricity baselines based on recent capacity additions. In fact, CHP-type plants which started operating after 1994 or are currently under construction (UDI/McGraw-Hill database) represented, in the case of Brazil, only 3.8% (*i.e.* 9 plants) of the total number of plants in the Brazilian sample and 0.9% (*i.e.* 169.5 MW) of the total capacity originally considered for this case study. In the case of India, twenty-three CHP-type plants were taken out of the case study sample, but they represented only 598 MW (*i.e.* 1.7% of total electricity capacity originally considered for the multi-project baseline based on recent capacity additions).

In the end, this case study's multi-project baseline analysis on recent electricity capacity additions is based on[82]:

- 229 power plants/units representing a generating capacity of 19,040 MW in Brazil (out of a total of 1070 existing plants/unit representing 82,287 MW of generating capacity in Brazil);

- 13 power plants/units representing a generating capacity of 1,452 MW in Morocco (out of a total of 94 existing plants/unit representing 4,709 MW of generating capacity in Morocco); and

---

[79] There were a few "unknown" or "unspecified" values for certain key variables for some plants in the database. This required additional research by the author in order to determine the correct data or to make realistic assumptions.

[80] There are no CHP-type plants in the Moroccan database used for this case study.

[81] Making conversion efficiency assumptions for CHP plants is complicated, as there is no standardised way of accounting for the production of both heat and power by these plants (for example, accounting for only the power produced by those plants would make them appear less efficient than they really are). Once appropriate conversion efficiency levels of CHP plants are developed, CHP plants could be included in the electricity generation baselines.

[82] See Annex II for more details on the data sample used for this case study.

- 617 power plants/units representing a generating capacity of 35,770 MW in India (out of a total of 2,441 existing plants/unit representing 125,951 MW of generating capacity in India).

The CO_2 (calculated based on the type of fuel used by each plant) and the CH_4 emissions (calculated based on the type of technology of each plant) associated with the production of electricity can be easily estimated using IPCC default emission factors. Emissions of CH_4 associated with fuel combustion for the generation of electricity are very small, representing less than 1% of CO_2 emissions. Emissions of N_2O (small) were not estimated, as default emission factors are only available for few types of technologies.

The multi-project baselines are based on rates (*i.e.* tCO_2/GWh), as suggested in various studies[83], instead of on total emissions (*e.g.* tCO_2).

3.4.3   *Aggregation*

The literature surveyed in this work generally examines emissions baselines for electricity generation in individual countries and not worldwide. For example, the electricity case study simulations in Ellis and Bosi (1999) highlighted the potential significance of differing national circumstances (*e.g.* resource endowments) on GHG emissions associated with electricity generation. Tellus (1999) points out to the absence of a clear/consistent worldwide trend in the electricity sector and also concludes that multi-project baselines based on individual countries' circumstances might therefore be most appropriate. This suggests that there is some acceptance that developing emission baselines on a country basis is appropriate. Of course, this would not preclude the possibility of developing baselines on a multi-country basis for a group of small neighbouring countries with similar circumstances. Similarly, large countries where regions are quite different may demand the development of sub-country multi-project baselines in order to accurately reflect "what would occur otherwise".

This case study examines various options, with quantitative comparisons, to set country-based multi-project baselines for electricity generation projects.

3.4.4   *Baseline calculation*

Developing a national-type of baseline using nationally aggregated data derived from all existing electricity capacity (Ellis and Bosi, 1999), for example, is a relatively straightforward exercise. For a given country and for the latest year for which data are available (*e.g.* 1997), it consists of summing the weighted average CO_2 emission contribution (per unit of electricity production) of each source of electricity:

---

[83] Ellis and Bosi (1999), Hagler Bailly (1998) and Tellus *et. al.* (1999).

Equation 1:

$$CO_2 \; per \; unit \; of \; production \; = \sum_{i=1}^{n} \left[\frac{CO_2 \; emissions_i}{\sum_{i-1}^{n} electricity \; production_i} \right]$$

Where: i represents each electricity source (*e.g.* coal hydro, nuclear, natural gas) used in the country;

- CO_2 Emissions for electricity source "i" are measured in tonnes of CO_2 (*e.g.* this data is available in CO_2 Emissions from Fuel Combustion reports published yearly by the IEA);

- Electricity production by electricity source "i" is all the electricity produced, measured in GWh, in a given country in a given year by the energy source (*e.g.* this data is available in The Energy Balances of Non-OECD Countries reports[84] published yearly by the IEA).

Developing a more disaggregated multi-project emission baseline for electricity generation based on recent capacity additions, as is the focus of this case study, requires more detailed data and more elaborate calculations. The multi-project baseline (measured in tGHG (*i.e.* tCO$_2$-equivalent)/GWh) using recent capacity additions is calculated by summing up the weighted average GHG contribution by unit of electricity generation of each recent plant:

Equation 2:

$$GHG \; emissions \; per \; unit \; of \; production \; = \sum_{z=1}^{n} \left[\frac{GHG \; emissions_z}{\sum_{z=1}^{n} electricity \; production_z} \right]$$

Where: z represents each individual electricity plant/unit in the database;

- GHG emissions for each plant/unit "z" are measured in tCO$_2$-equivalent (with disaggregated information, it is possible to calculate CH_4 emissions, as well as CO_2 emissions, using IPCC methodologies and default factors);

- Electricity production for each recent plant/unit "z" is measured in GWh.

Unlike equation (1) based on nationally-aggregated data for a given year where CO_2 emissions and electricity production (GWh) figures are readily available, equation (2)'s electricity output (GWh) and GHG emissions have to be calculated. Data (GWh and GHG emissions) are not generally readily available at such a disaggregated level; they

---

[84] Similar data also exists for OECD countries in separate IEA reports.

had to be estimated in this case study. Annex I contains information on the individual steps that were taken, in this case study, to calculate disaggregated multi-project electricity baselines based on recent capacity additions.

3.5   Potential baseline assumptions

3.5.1   National average GHG performance (per unit of output) of all existing electricity capacity

Emission baselines based on national average 1997 GHG performance per GWh of all existing plants, either including all sources or only fossil fuels, are presented in Annex D. In the case of all three countries examined in this case study, there is a significant difference between national multi-project baselines based on all existing capacity using all sources and only fossil fuel sources for the same country. Moreover, each country's different national circumstances lead to significant variances between countries' baseline emission levels.

While baselines based on all existing capacity are easy to develop and provide an interesting basis of comparison, the case was made earlier that they do not provide a satisfactory representation of the business-as-usual electricity situation. The focus of the rest of the analysis will thus be on baselines based on recent capacity additions.

3.5.2   National average GHG Performance (per unit of output) of recent capacity additions (after 1994)

As was the case for multi-project baselines based on all existing national capacity (above), there are significant variances between the three countries when examining baselines based on recent capacity additions. It is interesting to note that calculating multi-project baselines using recent electricity capacity additions provides a different picture, compared to the baseline calculation based on total existing capacity, for all three countries examined in this case study[85]. The trends, however, do not all move in the same direction: in some cases, recent capacity additions are towards more GHG-intensive electricity generation; while in others, the recent trend is towards less GHG-intensive

---

[85] Care has to taken when comparing the baselines calculated using the two types of data: all existing electricity capacity and recent electricity capacity additions, as the data sources (IEA and UDI/McGraw-Hill) are different. One other difference, albeit small, may stem from the fact that, in this case study, recent baselines from UDI/McGraw-Hill data include CH_4 as well as CO_2 emissions, while the IEA data is based only on CO_2. However, given that CH_4 emissions are so small in comparison to CO_2 emissions from fuel combustion, the fact that one baseline includes CH_4 while the other does not, is not expected to be the cause of any significant variance between the two baselines.

electricity generation, confirming that there is no global consistency in the development of electricity generation capacity. Thus, a country-focussed approach to establishing multi-project baselines in the electricity sector appears warranted.

Different designs of multi-project baselines based on recent capacity additions are examined for each of the three countries. The final decision on which multi-project baseline(s) is/are most appropriate and at what stringency level can be expected to be a political decision based on environmental, economic, administrative and data availability criteria. The analysis below examines various designs of multi-project baselines that could be considered in such a decision-making process. Electricity projects that lead to emissions below the baseline level are assumed, in this case study, to be "additional to what would occur otherwise" and could thus generate emission credits.

The analysis starts by looking at multi-project baselines based on recent capacity additions[86] using (i) all sources, as well as (ii) recent fossil fuel-based capacity additions (See Annex E for details). Other types of baseline disaggregation are also examined subsequently: (iii) source-specific baselines; (iv) sub-country (regional) baselines; (v) peaking and baseload baselines.

Multi-project baselines using recent capacity additions: all sources and only fossil fuels

Figure 3-3 presents weighted average baselines based on the emissions (tonnes of CO_2 equivalent) per electricity production (GWh) of each plant.

The variances between the countries' multi-project baselines are much greater for the recent capacities including all sources than for the recent capacities including only fossil fuels. Given that plant-level data for conversion efficiency and load factors were not available and that only country-specific assumptions could be made, it is possible that, in reality, variances between countries' multi-project baseline levels would be larger than those calculated, but this cannot be verified.

---

[86] CHP-type plants were excluded from the sample due to difficulty in finding consistent assumptions for load and efficiency factors.

Figure 3-3

**Multi-project baselines using recent
capacity additions: All sources and fossil fuel only**

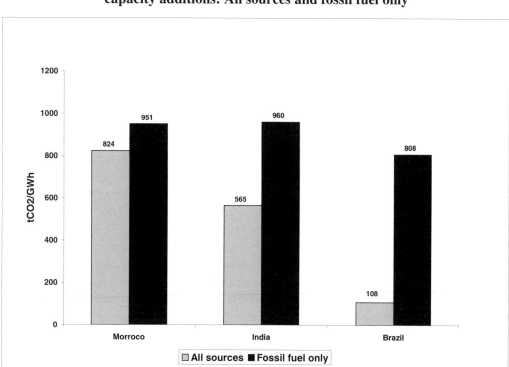

Brazil

A Brazilian national baseline based on recent capacity additions (including all sources) is equal to a weighted average of 108 tCO_2/GWh (the emissions of the different plants included in the sample range from 0 tCO_2/GWh for the hydro, nuclear and non-hydro renewable plants to 953 tCO_2/GWh for steam turbine plants using bituminous coal). A comparison of this baseline with a national baseline using all existing electricity capacity in 1997, which is equal to 49 tCO_2/GWh[87], highlights the recent Brazilian trend of electricity investments being made, in larger proportions than historical investments, in fossil fuel power plants. Although the baseline based on recent capacity additions is 47% greater than the one based on all existing capacity, only non-emitting electricity projects could generate emission credits under the recent capacity additions including all sources baseline. All other electricity projects would generate emission levels greater than the 108 tCO_2/GWh baseline. This means that electricity generated by natural gas, which is

---

[87] From IEA (1999a); includes only emissions of carbon dioxide.

129

foreseen to increase in Brazil in the near future, would not "pass" this baseline test even if it were best-available-technology (BAT) that might not otherwise be installed.

For Brazil, a multi-project baseline based on recent fossil fuel capacity additions, which represent 11% of the sample's total recent capacity, would be equal to 808 tCO_2/GWh (this is about 11% lower than a similar baseline based on all fossil fuel existing capacity in 1997, but almost eight times greater than a multi-project baseline based on recent capacity including all sources). Brazil's fossil-fuelled electricity generation is thus experiencing a trend towards a lower GHG-emitting mix. Obviously, a greater volume of projects that generate credits can be expected under a "recent fossil fuel capacity additions" multi-project baseline, than under a "recent all sources capacity additions" multi-project baseline. However, since the majority of recent capacity additions are expected to continue to be hydro-based, using a multi-project baseline based on recent fossil fuel capacity additions may not be considered a credible baseline, at least in the short-term.

India

A national Indian multi-project baseline based on recent capacity additions including all sources would be equal to 565 tCO_2/GWh (which is 38% lower than the same baseline using all 1997 existing capacity in India). Such a baseline is thus a clear reflection of the improvements in GHG intensity of recent investments in power plants in India. Under this multi-project baseline based on recent capacity additions including all sources, natural gas plants would be the only fossil fuel plants being able to generate emissions below the emission baseline and thus be able to generate emission credits.

An Indian multi-project baseline based on fossil fuel recent capacity additions amounts to 960 tCO_2/GWh (*i.e.* 14% lower than the same baseline using all 1997 existing power generating capacity in India). The power plants included in this baseline represent 48% of the total recent capacity included in the Indian sample.

Morocco

Morocco's baseline based on the weighted average of recent electricity capacity additions, including all sources, amounts to 824 tCO_2/GWh, which is almost 11% greater than the same baseline using all 1997 existing capacity. A Moroccan baseline based on recent fossil fuel capacity additions, which represent 73% of Morocco's total recent capacity, equals to 951 tCO_2/GWh (28% higher than the same baseline calculated using all 1997 existing capacity). This suggests that the business-as-usual investments, inasmuch as they can be approximated by the recent capacity additions used in this case study, are actually increasing the GHG-intensity of Morocco's electricity generation compared to historical power investments.

Multi-project baselines using recent capacity additions: source-specific

Another potential way to establish multi-project baselines may be to set them according to the source of electricity generation of recent capacity additions. Tellus (1999) concludes that disaggregated multi-project baselines, according to fuel or technology, could help reduce the potential likelihood of free rider projects. On the other hand, source-specific multi-project baselines would not encourage fuel switching for electricity generation, which may be, in many cases, the most desirable electricity generation option from a greenhouse gas mitigation point of view.

The calculated values (in tCO_2/GWh) for source-specific multi-project baselines based on recent capacity additions for Brazil, India and Morocco are presented in Table 3-2 below. These can be compared to values for estimated Best Available Technology, based on performance averages from OECD countries:

Table 3-2

Multi-project baselines based on recent capacity additions: Source-specific

	Brazil (tCO_2/GWh)	India (tCO_2/GWh)	Morocco (tCO_2/GWh)	Best available technology* (tCO_2/GWh)
Coal	954	1,085	954	781-786**
Oil	761	661	791	Not available
Natural Gas	426	418	None	382
Other electricity sources	0.0	0.0	0.0	0.0

*Best Available Technology (BAT) values are taken from the Case Study Simulations with Multi-Project Baselines in Ellis and Bosi (1999), based on NEA/IEA (1998).
**The higher value is for India and the lower value is for Brazil. (Ellis and Bosi (1999) did not include multi-project baseline simulations for Morocco).

131

Source-specific multi-project electricity baselines, as defined in Table 3-2, would mean that projects in the form of best-available technology coal power plants could generate 299 emission credits per GWh (assuming one credit equals 1 tCO_2 reduced below the baseline level) in India and 173 credits/GWh in Brazil and Morocco[88]. However, projects in the form of best available technology (BAT) gas plants would generate a slightly larger volume of emissions credits (*i.e.* 44 emission credits) in Brazil than in India (36 emission credits). As hydro, nuclear and non-hydro renewables do not generate GHG emissions, electricity projects based on these sources would need another basis of comparison (one suggestion on how to potentially deal with this situation is a "hybrid" approach discussed in section 3.6).

Table 3-3 compares these results with the emission credits that could be generated by the same BAT projects. This could be done by using baselines drawn up using the performance of source-specific capacity additions and the performance of a weighted average for recently installed fossil plants.

Table 3-3

**Potential emission credits (per GWh)
generated by projects in BAT coal and BAT gas under different
multi-project electricity baselines based on recent capacity additions**

	Brazil Baseline :			India Baseline:		
	all sources	*fossil fuels only*	*source-specific*	*all sources*	*fossil fuels only*	*source-specific*
BAT Coal Plant	0	27	173 (coal)	0	174	299 (coal)
BAT Gas Plant	0	426	44 (gas)	183	578	36 (gas)

According to the calculations presented in Table 3-3, projects in BAT coal generation would not generate emission credits in either Brazil, or India if the multi-project baseline was based on recent capacity additions including all sources. Compared to that same multi-project baseline (*i.e.* all sources), BAT gas projects would not generate emission credits in Brazil, but would generate 183 emission credits per GWh in India. It is also worth noting that if multi-project baselines were source-specific, clean coal (BAT) plants in both India and Brazil could generate a significantly larger volume of emission credits than BAT gas plants, even though the latter plants emit substantially lower levels of GHG emissions than the former. In fact, in both Brazil and India, it is under source-specific multi-project baselines that clean coal plants could generate the largest volume of emission credits. This outcome may not be considered by some as consistent with the

---

[88] Assuming the performance of BAT would be the same in Morocco as estimated for Brazil.

environmental objective of the CDM. In fact, source-specific multi-project baselines, particularly in the case of coal, may cause concerns in terms of the overall effectiveness of the CDM, although they may promote a cleaner use of coal - which for countries like India and China, with huge coal reserves, could be an important variable in promoting a more environmentally-benign electricity infrastructure and lead to GHG emission levels lower than would otherwise occur.

Multi-project baselines using recent capacity additions: sub-national

For large countries with different circumstances within their borders and different power grids based in these different regions, multi-project baselines in the electricity sector may need to be disaggregated below the country-level in order to provide a credible representation of "what would have happened otherwise". This is likely to be the case for countries such as India and Brazil. For countries such as Morocco, *i.e.* a relatively small country with a small number of recent electricity capacity additions, it is probably not necessary to develop sub-national electricity baselines.

However, developing disaggregated baselines on a sub-national basis can increase the data needs and time required to develop the baselines, as databases do not always specify which electricity system is associated to each individual plant. In this case study, implications of such disaggregation is presented for Brazil, where the Brazilian Electricity System is divided into three separate subsystems[89]:

(i)   The South/Southeast/Midwest Interconnected System;

(ii)   The North/Northeast Interconnected System; and

(iii)   The Isolated Systems (which represent 300 locations that are electrically isolated from the interconnected systems)[90].

In order to examine the potential implications of setting sub-national multi-project baselines, this case study includes emission baselines developed for these three main Brazilian electricity systems. The Isolated Systems in this case study are represented by those systems in the Northern Region (*i.e.* Amazonas, Roraima, Randônia, Amapá and Acre States) which represent approximately 85% of the Isolated Systems[91] (this region is thus referred to as "North Isolated" system in this case study).

---

[89] Source: Petrobras and the Brazilian Ministry of Mines and Energy (1999).

[90] In these isolated systems, about 50% of the locations have a daily supply period of less than 24 hours and rationing still persists (Ibid).

[91] As the database used for this case study did not specify the electricity system which was associated to each individual plant, it was not possible to determine exactly which system plants in other states belonged.

Table F3-1 of Annex F indicates quite clearly the detailed differences that exist, in terms of electricity generation, between the three Brazilian systems. Figure 3-4 below presents the variances between Brazil's three sub-national baselines (including all sources). Unlike the other two systems that use mainly hydro, the smaller North Isolated system is based almost exclusively on oil-fired (diesel) electricity, translating into a higher multi-project baseline level. This means that a single Brazilian baseline based on total recent capacity additions (of all regions) does not provide a very accurate reflection of the situation in the Isolated Systems.

Figure 3-4

Multi-project baselines using recent
capacity additions: Brazil's regions (all sources)

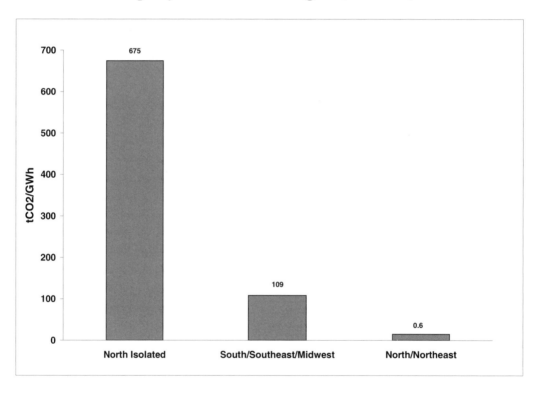

In fact, according to the data used for this case study and the breakdown made between the three regions[92], multi-project baselines using all sources would be equal to 675 tCO_2/GWh for the North Isolated system (representing 3% of Brazil's electricity generation by recent capacity additions), 0.6 tCO_2/GWh for the North/Northeast system (17% of Brazil's electricity generation by recent capacity additions) and to 109 for the

---

[92] The allocation of each individual plant to one of the three main electricity systems in Brazil may not be completely accurate.

large South/Southeast/Midwest system (accounting for 80% of Brazil's electricity generation by recent capacity additions). It is not surprising, therefore, that as the latter system is where the bulk of Brazil's electricity capacity and demand is concentrated, it is practically identical to the national Brazilian baseline using recent capacity additions including all sources.

As Brazil can be shown as an example for other large countries with different circumstances within their borders (*e.g.* India[93]), it may be appropriate to consider further the development of separate multi-project baselines for different regions within a country. At a minimum, the development of separate multi-project baselines for off-grid, isolated electricity systems would be useful.

Multi-project baselines using recent capacity additions: load-specific

Tellus (1999) concludes that while aggregated electricity multi-project baselines could provide desirable incentives for switching to lower or non-emitting sources, disaggregated approaches to multi-project baselines could be more effective. Also, in considering disaggregation possibilities examined above, the authors believe that another interesting option may be to distinguish between baseload and peakload plants. This disaggregation might be particularly useful to create incentives to improve the efficiency of peaking units which are typically less efficient than baseload units. It may also be useful for the assessment of GHG reductions from certain energy efficiency projects.

This option for disaggregated multi-project baselines certainly merits careful consideration, but it must be noted that the data needed to make this breakdown between the different plants operating in a country is difficult to obtain. However, reasonable general assumptions could be made about the types of power plants normally used to generate peak and baseload electricity.

Based on expert advice, a distinction between peaking plants (defined as all internal combustion engines and combustion turbines) and baseload plants (all other types) was made for India in order to test the options of developing peak load and baseload multi-project electricity baselines within a country. As shown in Figure 3-5 a multi-project baseline for India's *peaking* plants would be equal to 789 tCO_2/GWh; while a multi-project baseline for *baseload* plants would be almost 30% lower, at 556 tCO_2/GWh. The multi-project baseline for recent *baseload* capacity additions is essentially the same as the Indian multi-project baseline based on all recent capacity additions (including all sources) which was evaluated at 565 tCO_2/GWh. This is to be expected given the very large proportion (71%) of recent capacity additions in India assumed to be used to generate baseload electricity (they account for 96% of the total recent electricity generation).

---

[93] More time and information would be needed to develop region-specific electricity multi-project baselines for India, but there are no *a priori* reasons why it could not be possible.

Natural gas and oil are the typical sources used to generate peaking electricity. As a direct consequence of the lower conversion efficiency assumed for these plants and used for peaking electricity generation, the multi-project baseline level for peaking plants is naturally higher than the Indian gas-specific (418 tCO$_2$/GWh) and oil-specific (661 tCO$_2$/GWh) multi-project baselines, which are based on all plants (*i.e.* both peaking and baseload). However, a *peaking* multi-project baseline for India is lower than an Indian multi-project baseline based on *fossil fuel* recent capacity additions (960 tCO$_2$/GWh).

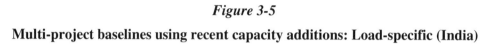

Figure 3-5

Multi-project baselines using recent capacity additions: Load-specific (India)

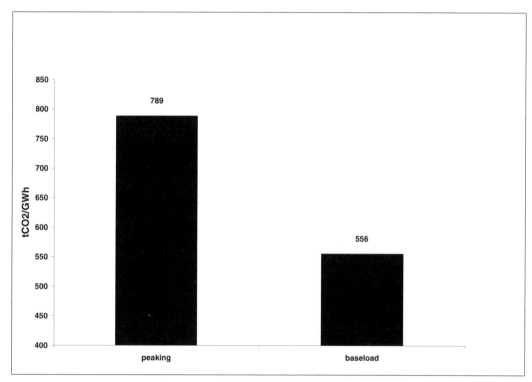

Caution has to be used when making assumptions for developing the peaking multi-project baseline. Setting an appropriate performance standard for peaking plants in developing countries poses particular challenges (compared to Annex I countries). In many cases where there is a supply shortage, power plants designed to generate peaking electricity are actually operated as mid-range or baseload plants. The Brazilian electricity situation provides a good example of typical peaking plants used to supply baseload electricity, as Brazil's North Isolated system relies almost exclusively on the types of plants normally used to generate peaking electricity. In fact, all the internal combustion engine units and 10 out of the 12 gas/combustion turbine units included in the database of recent Brazilian capacity additions for this case study are located in the North Isolated system. It is not realistic, at least in this case, to define a multi-project baseline for Brazilian peaking units as being composed of these two types of plants.

The development of peaking multi-project baselines therefore requires a careful consideration of each country's electricity situation, particularly in the case of developing countries experiencing power supply shortages.

3.6 Potential stringency of baselines

Ellis and Bosi (1999) concluded, "the maximum effectiveness of the project mechanisms (as opposed to individual projects) is unlikely to be achieved with […] overly stringent baselines". Furthermore, maximising environmental stringency ought to be traded off against the desire to maximise the overall global environmental benefits from JI and CDM, where a greater number of good projects will be more beneficial for the environment than a smaller number of individually better projects.

Multi-project electricity baselines based on *recent* capacity additions provide a more accurate picture of what is happening under a business-as-usual scenario than multi-project baselines based on all existing capacity. However, they do not necessarily provide a more stringent multi-project baseline level. Not surprisingly, using multi-project baselines using *recent* capacity additions based on all sources results in a lower baseline level (because of the inclusion of zero-emitting nuclear, hydro and other renewables in the that baseline) than if the baseline calculations are based only on fossil fuel sources.

Figures 3-6, 3-7 and 3-8 below show, for Brazil, India and Morocco, the different stringency levels associated with various multi-project baseline options and their implications, in terms of the potential to generate emissions credits with different electricity sources.

Tellus (1999) remarks that better-than-average multi-project baselines are more promising and could help reduce the potential magnitude of free-ridership[94], although better-than-average multi-project baselines may increase the probabilities of missed emission reduction opportunities in the electricity sector.

Nonetheless, by definition, an average baseline based on all sources would mean that about half the power plants included in the sample used to develop the baseline would emit emissions below the average emission level. Consequently, the level of the average multi-project baseline (all sources) may be considered not sufficiently stringent to ensure long-term, additional greenhouse gas reductions. Of course, there could be exceptions to

---

[94] For more discussion on the issue of free-ridership in the context of different emissions baselines for the project-based mechanisms, see Ellis and Bosi (1999).

the general rule. For instance, the Brazilian example is particularly interesting in this context, as the level of the weighted average multi-project baseline using recent capacity additions, including all sources, is significantly more stringent than all the other baselines options presented in the three figures below.

The evaluation of "stringency" based on "average" performance depends on what exactly the "average" represents. For example, there is a significant difference between multi-project baselines based on the average emission rate of all recent capacity additions (all sources) and multi-project baselines based on the average emission rate of fossil fuel recent capacity additions. The former formulation of the "average emission rate" may already be viewed sufficiently stringent in some cases and perhaps too stringent in others (*e.g.* Brazil).

Still, it may be worth further considering in some cases the potential options for better than average multi-project baselines. For example, a better than average multi-project baseline could be defined as x% below the average multi-project baseline using recent capacity additions (including all sources). Other potential options may be to define it as better than the 75th percentile, or setting the baseline at one or two standard deviations below the average emission rate[95].

Figure 3-6

Brazil: Implications of multi-project baselines using recent capacity additions

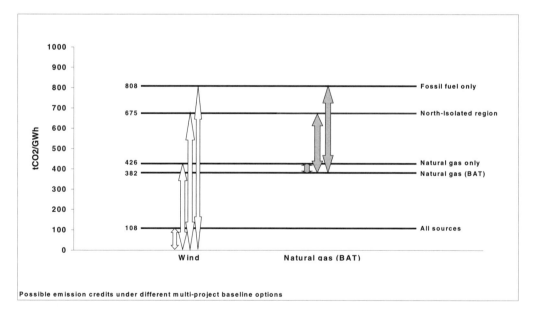

Possible emission credits under different multi-project baseline options

---

[95] This was suggested by CCAP (2000) for retrofit projects for which credits would be calculated based on the average emission rate of all existing projects.

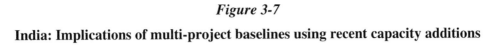

Figure 3-7

India: Implications of multi-project baselines using recent capacity additions

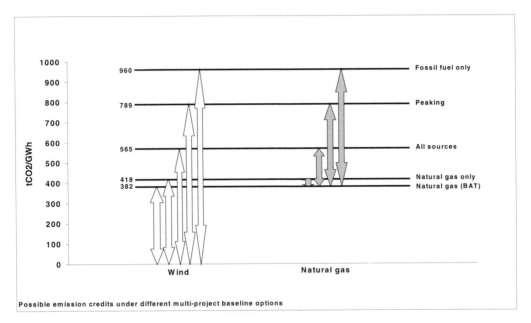

Figure 3-8

Morocco: Implications of multi-project baselines using recent capacity additions

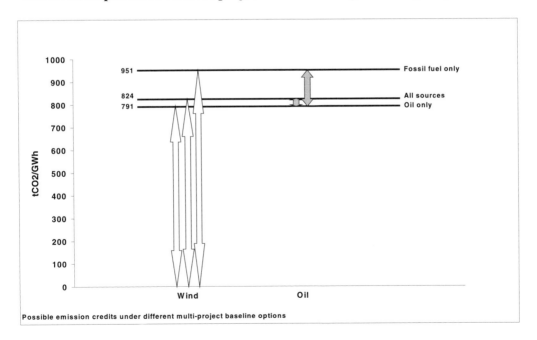

Under all the different options examined to develop multi-project baselines for electricity generation projects, non-emitting sources would, theoretically, be eligible to generate emissions credits, although they may simply be part of the business-as-usual trend in the country's electricity generation sector. Tellus (1999) suggests that it might be useful to consider a "hybrid [multi-project] approach for the power sector". This could be done, for example, by having an activity additionality test which would screen out projects or types of power plants that have a significant probability of generating non-additional emission credits. Another expert, Erik Haites[96], also suggests a kind of hybrid approach taking the form of a more elaborate evaluation process - not a different baseline - but would limit it to "large" projects to avoid creating an insurmountable burden for small projects. UNIDO (2000) also recommends adding "additionality" checks, of a qualitative nature, to the baseline test in order to make a better assessment of the JI/CDM nature of proposed projects. Such approaches may merit further consideration.

This case study and the multi-project baselines constructed based on recent capacity additions are focussed on new power plants (and not improvements to existing power plants). While further consideration should be given to whether (and if so, how) greenfield projects should/could be treated differently than refurbishment projects in the electricity sector (in terms of different crediting different timeline, or different stringency level of the same baseline assumption, for example), it is important that both types of electricity projects be treated in a consistent manner in order to create a level playing field and avoid unwanted incentives in the electricity generation sector. For example, given that many developing countries are projected to increase significantly their electricity production to meet currently unmet or future demand, it would be important not to create a negative bias against greenfield project (versus refurbishment projects), as this could be a disadvantage for countries experiencing rapid electricity growth in their efforts to attract CDM investments.

3.7   Potential volume of projects

One of the main criteria for evaluating the success of JI and CDM is likely to be the number of additional climate-friendly projects that these Kyoto mechanisms were able to stimulate. Baseline stringency is a key determinant of electricity project volumes. The potential volume of projects in the electricity sector will depend on the number of emission credits and their value, that can be expected from electricity projects. Total project volumes (through a more or less significant global supply of credits) will also influence the international price of each emission credit. Furthermore, baseline stringency determines the magnitude of credit revenue streams from any one project and thus whether these revenues affect project feasibility.

---

[96] Based on his presentation at the IPIECA Workshop on Issues, Barriers and Opportunities for Practical Application of the Kyoto Mechanisms, Milan, Italy, April 6 and 7, 2000.

Clearly the more stringent the baseline level, the fewer (if any) the calculated emission reductions and, hence, the credits earned by an electricity project. Compared to a scenario where the same electricity project would earned more emission credits, the value of each emission credit will have to be higher, as the total volume is smaller under a more stringent emission baseline, to change business-as-usual behaviour.

The box below illustrates, through simple calculations and a series of assumptions, the potential volume and value of the emission credits earned by a hypothetical CDM electricity project. The example is based on a new BAT natural gas plant in India compared to the Indian multi-project baseline based on recent capacity including all sources. Compared to a multi-project baseline based on fossil fuel only recent capacity, this is a relatively stringent baseline level. The crediting lifetime associated with the multi-project baseline is assumed to be 10 years[97], meaning that the project developers can expect, from the start, a certain volume of credits (assuming the electricity project performs as planned, *i.e.* emitting 382 tCO_2/GWh) for this period. After that, the project may potentially still earn emission credits if its GHG emissions are below the level set by the updated baseline, but this was not taken into account.

The total annual costs (including investment, operation and maintenance, as well as fuel costs) and electricity revenues of the new Indian plant are presented based on both a 5% and 10% discount rate[98] to show the impact of the financing terms on the economic feasibility of a potential electricity project. Neither of these discount rates allows the project to go ahead, on economic grounds, as the costs are greater than the revenues.

Compared to the Indian multi-project baseline based on recent capacity including all sources (*i.e.* 565 tCO_2/GWh), the new BAT gas plant would reduce emissions by 183 tCO_2/GWh, so 183 emissions credits could be earned per year. The annual value of these emission credits, discounted at 5%, would be worth 604,847US$ if emission credits were worth 5US$/$tCO_2$ or 1,225,138US$ US$/year if emission credits were worth 10US$/ tCO_2[99]. While certainly significant in absolute terms, the revenue from the sale of the potential emission credits from such a CDM project need to be examined in relative terms.

According the example provided in the box below, the annual value of the emission credits relative to estimated annual electricity revenues (discounted at 5%), represent 9.6% if emission credits are worth 5US$/$tCO_2$ and 19% if emission credits are worth

---

[97] Further analysis could include comparing implications of different crediting timelines, *e.g.* 10 and 15 years.

[98] The discount rates seek to reflect private and public financing practice.

[99] The emission credits price assumption of 5 or 10 US$ per tonne of CO_2 is consistent with various model results. For example, the survey of modelling results by Baron (in IEA, October 1999) indicates 7.6 US$/$tCO_2$ is the average estimated price of emission credits under "global trading" (which includes CDM).

10 US$/tCO$_2$. The revenues from the CDM credits would thus help increase the potential revenues from the hypothetical new BAT gas plant, but would not be sufficient to make it economically feasible. At a 5% discount rate, the CDM credits contribute to reducing the annual net deficit by 16.2% if emission credits are worth 10 US$/tCO$_2$.

Of course the evaluation of the contribution of the emission credits from a potential CDM project critically depends on the assumptions made. In addition, this example does not take into account each investor's criteria (*e.g.* internal rate of return, net present value, capital efficiency, payback period, risk evaluation, *etc.*), which can be expected to raise the feasibility threshold. The magnitude of the impact of the CDM emission credits would certainly be different if the price of emission credits were much higher and the volume of emission reductions and thus emission credits were also greater (*e.g.* comparing a zero-emitting project to the same baseline as in the example in the box below).

It is, in fact, impossible to draw a general conclusion on the potential volume of projects under different multi-project baseline options, as results will vary according to the type of project, its total net cost, the volume of emission credits, the price of emission credits as well as the financing terms and feasibility criteria. Nonetheless, this example provides insights on the potential small contribution of the CDM credits (at the credit prices generally estimated by models) on electricity investments and confirms what others have concluded (*e.g.* Lanza 1999 in IEA 1999): in order for the emission credits to have an impact on the investment decision, proposed CDM projects may need to be already very close to meeting, or have already met, the basic feasibility criteria from an investor's point of view.

3.8   Insights and conclusions

Standardisation of emission baselines

Standardisation of emission baselines (or multi-project baselines) for electricity projects in the context of the Kyoto Protocol's JI and CDM is possible and desirable to increase transparency and consistency between similar projects in similar circumstances and to reduce overall transaction costs of the mechanisms. Multi-project electricity baselines will also facilitate the calculation of the GHG mitigation potential of other projects, such as energy efficiency projects.

What could the CDM potentially be worth for a BAT CCGT gas plant in India?

Assumptions

The CDM project is assumed to be a 50 MW CCGT plant, generating 325 GWh per year with a conversion efficiency of 52.9%; a load factor of 0.75 and emissions of $382tCO_2/GWh$ at a cost of 4.77cents/kWh (Ellis and Bosi, 1999). The baseline is drawn up using the average GHG intensity of recent capacity additions (all sources), *i.e.* 565 tCO_2/GWh. A ten-year lifetime is assumed.

The Economic life of the plant is taken to be 40 years and the Indian electricity tariff at 4.5 cents/kWh**. The effect of two discount rates (5% and 10%) and two prices of emission credits (CERs) (5 and 10 US$/$tCO_2$) are calculated.

Calculations

Cost of new Indian plant:
- Cost per GWh* = 47,700 US$/GWh (@ 10% discount rate) or 42,520 US$/GWh (@5% discount rate)
- Cost per year = 15,507,270 US$ (*i.e.* 47,700US$/GWh * 325.1 GWh per year) or 13,823,252 US$ (*i.e.* 42,520 US$/GWh*325.1GWh per year)

Revenue from new Indian plant's electricity generation (without emission credits):
- Revenue per GWh = 45,000 US$/GWh
- Revenue per year = 6,274,005 US$ (@5% discount rate); ; 3,558,622 US$ (@10% discount rate)

Net deficit of new Indian plant (without emission credits):
- (7,549,247 US$) @ 5% discount rate; or (11,948,648 US$) (@ 10% discount rate)

Volume of emission credits:
- Number of emission credits/GWh = 183 (*i.e.* 565 tCO_2/GWh - 382 tCO_2/GWh)
- Number of emission credits per year = 59,493 (*i.e.* 325.1 GWh/year * 183 emission credits/GWh)

These 59,493 credits are worth 297,465 US$ at 5 US$/$tCO_2$; or 594,930 US$ at 10 US$/$tCO_2$. The value of annual discounted emission credits are indicated in the following table.

(continued)

What could the CDM potentially be worth for a BAT CCGT gas plant in India?

(US$)

Discount rate	Annual Discounted Generation Costs (000 $)	Annual Discounted Revenues (without credits) (000 $)	Annual Discounted Revenues minus costs (000 $)	Discounted Revenues (incl. emission credits) minus costs (annual) (000 $)		Value of annual discounted CERs (000 $)	
				5 $/tCO$_2$	10 $/tCO$_2$	5 $/tCO$_2$	10 $/tCO$_2$
5%	13,823	6,274	(7,549)	(6,944)	(6,324)	605	1,225
10%	15,507	3,559	(11,949)	(11,467)	(10,974)	481	975

* Cost figures based on NEA/IEA (1998): as no India-specific data was available, costs estimated to be similar to those of Korea (as in Ellis and Bosi 1999);

** Tariff for 1997; source: From Pew Center (1999), based on TERI Energy Data Directory and Yearbook 1998/1999.

Data set

Developing multi-project baselines using recent capacity additions provides a closer reflection of what would happen in the electricity sector under a business-as-usual scenario than more aggregated approaches. For example, a multi-project-baseline based on all existing capacity would include emissions from all plants, including those from old inefficient plants that started operating 15-25 years ago, although such plants and technologies are no longer routinely installed in BAU investments today. This would not happen when using multi-project baselines based on recent electricity capacity additions.

Boundaries

For practical reasons and in order to avoid double counting of emission reductions, it appears appropriate to set project boundaries around direct emission impacts (ideally all GHGs, but CO_2 emissions would be sufficient) of electricity generation for the development of multi-project baselines.

Historical or projection data

Given the inherent uncertainties associated with energy and electricity projections, particularly in the case of rapid growth and increased liberalisation, it appears reasonable and possibly less controversial (in terms of avoiding a debate on what is the "accurate" projection) to develop multi-project baselines for the electricity sector using recent historical data. This data, in the context of developing electricity multi-project baselines, could be defined as recent capacity additions based on additions over the last 3 to 5 years, as well as those currently under construction, in any one country (or, depending on the size of the country, region within a country or group of small countries). Taking into account only capacity additions in the most recent years would increase the likelihood that the multi-project baselines reflect business-as-usual investments in the electricity sector.

Crediting lifetime

The decision on the timeline during which a particular electricity multi-project baseline will be valid for potential projects needs to be specified up-front to provide greater certainty to project developers and increase transparency and consistency between similar projects. The timeline would need to take into account the relative inertia of electricity capital stock as well as the need to ensure additional and long-term GHG reductions. The consideration of various factors (*e.g.* technical lifetime, economic lifetime or debt payback period) combined with various objectives (*e.g.* environmental, economic and practicality) should guide the determination of the crediting lifetime associated with an electricity multi-project baseline. Nonetheless, a baseline crediting lifetime of around 10-15 years may be considered appropriate.

It is unclear whether a distinction, in terms of crediting lifetime, should be made between "greenfield" and "refurbishment" projects and if it were made, how it could be defined adequately. Such a distinction was not made in the case study (as it was based on new capacity additions), but this issue may merit further investigation.

Timing of baseline updates

Given the non-static nature of developments in the electricity sector, it is important to update the multi-project baselines at regular intervals in order to ensure that future electricity projects use an adequate multi-project baseline, reflecting the electricity situation at that time. However, in order to gain economies of scale from the development of multi-project baselines and minimise overall baseline development costs for JI and CDM, updates need to be made at reasonable intervals. It appears reasonable to periodically update the electricity multi-project baselines, such as every 5 years.

Aggregation

With respect to the level of aggregation, multi-project electricity baselines appear to be more reliable if they are country-based electricity profiles in order to take into account the different national circumstances. Sub-country multi-project electricity baselines may be appropriate for large countries and multi-countries may be adequate for a group of small countries.

Data quality and availability

In general, the more disaggregated the standardisation, the greater the data requirements, with implications on overall costs of developing baselines. However, disaggregated standardisation, based on plant-level data of recent capacity additions, as was done in this case study, is generally a better reflection of "what would occur otherwise" than baselines based on highly aggregated data and is thus recommended.

The development of disaggregated electricity multi-project baselines based on recent capacity additions requires the following information for each plant/unit included in the sample to develop the multi-project baseline:

1. Commissioning year;
2. Type of technology;
3. Source of electricity (*i.e.* fuel used);

4. Generating capacity;

5. Load factors;

6. Conversion efficiency; and

7. Emission factor(s) for fuel used.

The database used for this case study includes data, for each plant, on the commissioning year, the type of technology, the generating capacity and the source of electricity. Reasonable assumptions, based on expert advice, were made for the load factor and the conversion efficiency, albeit at a country-level (and not specific to each individual plant within a country).

The IPCC Guidelines for National Greenhouse Gas Inventories should be used when developing multi-project electricity baselines. These will provide basic assumptions about carbon content of fuels and energy content factors to provide comparability in the baseline construction.

It is normal for databases to have some "unknown" or "unspecified" values that require some research to find the correct value or to estimate it. Current data constraints need to be taken into account in decisions on baselines for electricity projects, but should not be considered a barrier. Assumptions, based on expert advice, can be made where data is not available. Moreover, the emergence of the CDM and JI mechanisms may stimulate the monitoring, reporting and publication of more detailed and reliable data. The process to develop electricity multi-project baselines should thus be viewed as an evolving one, improving over time.

Potential baseline assumptions:

Different assumptions can be used to develop multi-project baselines based on recent capacity additions. This case study examined multi-project baselines based on recent capacity additions, according to: (i) all sources; (ii) only fossil fuels; (iii) source-specific; (iv) region-specific; and (v) load-specific. The implications of these baseline assumptions, in terms of stringency, are different for different countries (Figures 3-6, 3-7 and 3-8 provide good illustrations of the different implications).

In the case of Brazil and India, clean coal plants could generate the largest volume of emission credits under source-specific multi-project baselines. This outcome may not be considered, by some, as consistent with the environmental objective of the CDM. In fact, source-specific multi-project baselines, particularly in the case of coal, may result in perverse incentives (*e.g.* for example, reducing the relative incentive to develop alternative cleaner technologies such as natural gas). Of course, such baselines might promote a cleaner use of coal than would otherwise be the case - which for countries like

147

India and China, with huge coal reserves, could be an important variable in promoting a more environmentally-benign infrastructure.

With Brazil serving as an example for other large countries with different circumstances within their borders (*e.g.* India), it may be appropriate to further consider the development of separate multi-project baselines for different regions within a country. At a minimum, the development of separate multi-project baselines for off-grid, isolated electricity systems would be useful.

Developing separate multi-project baselines for peak and baseload electricity was done in the case of India, based on expert advice and assumptions. Given that the majority of recent plants are assumed to generate baseload electricity, the multi-project baseline for baseload electricity is very similar to the country's multi-project baseline using all sources. However, the multi-project baseline for peaking electricity is quite a bit higher, due to the typically lower efficiency of the gas and oil-fuelled power plants generating peak electricity. Developing a separate multi-project baseline for peaking electricity may be desirable, as those plants are typically different from baseload plants. However, caution has to be taken when making assumptions on which plant type would constitute the "peaking electricity generation" sample and seeking country experts' advice is strongly recommended.

Potential stringency of baselines

Multi-project baselines based on recent capacity additions provide a good reflection of "what would happen otherwise" but are not necessarily more stringent than multi-project baselines based on all existing capacity. This is because recent capacity additions are not always lower GHG-emitting power plants. A good example of such as situation is Brazil where the main source of power generation is hydro, but the share of hydro is slowly diminishing (and this is projected to continue) due to increases in thermal power facilities.

Thus, the same multi-project baseline approach implies different levels of stringency in different countries.

The evaluation of "stringency" based on "average" performance depends on what exactly the "average" represents. For example, there is a significant difference, in terms of the level, between multi-project baselines based on the average emission rate of recent capacity additions including all sources and multi-project baselines based the average emission rate of recent fossil fuel capacity additions, with the former being more stringent than the latter. In fact, the "average emission rate" of all recent capacity additions may be viewed sufficiently stringent or perhaps too stringent in some cases (*e.g.* Brazil).

Still, it may be worth further considering the potential options and implications for "better-than-average" electricity multi-project baselines. For example, a better than average multi-project baseline could be defined as emitting x% below the average multi-project baseline using recent capacity additions (including all sources). Other potential options may be to define it as better than the 75th percentile, or setting the baseline at one or two standard deviations below the average emission rate.

Regardless of the stringency of the multi-project baseline for electricity generation projects, non-emitting sources would be eligible to generate emissions credits, although they may simply be part of the business-as-usual trend in countries' electricity generation sector. It might thus be useful to consider a "hybrid" approach to assessing the GHG additionality of those zero-emitting projects. For example, it may be worth considering an activity additionality test, which would screen out projects or types of power plants that have a significant probability of generating non-additional emission credits. In order to focus on larger plants that have the potential to lead to larger volumes of non-additional emission credits, another option would be to require large zero-emitting projects to go through a more elaborate evaluation process. Small renewable projects would only need to pass the multi-project baseline test.

This case study did not make a distinction between baselines for greenfield and refurbishment projects. A preliminary view is that it does not seem necessary or practical to distinguish between baselines for refurbishment and greenfield power projects. Nonetheless, further consideration should be given to whether (and if so, how) greenfield projects should/could be treated differently than refurbishment projects in the electricity sector (in terms of different crediting, different timeline and/or different stringency level of the same baseline assumption, for example). A practical definition to make this distinction would be needed. Furthermore, it is important that both types of electricity projects be treated in a consistent manner in order to create a level playing field and avoid unwanted incentives in the electricity generation sector. The details of the overall CDM decision-making process have yet to be agreed-upon by the international community. However, the final decision on which multi-project baseline(s) is/are most appropriate and at what level of stringency, can be expected to be a decision tailored to national circumstances, based on environmental, economic, administrative and data availability criteria. Further consideration might be warranted to determine whether and, if so, what type of guidance could be developed internationally to ensure consistency among similar projects in similar circumstances.

Potential volume of projects

It is not possible to assess quantitatively the volume of electricity projects that could be stimulated under various electricity multi-project baselines.

Clearly, the more stringent the emission baseline, the fewer (if any) the GHG reductions and, hence, the emission credits earned by an electricity project.

This case study provides a quantitative example of the potential volume and value of emission credits that could be earned by a hypothetical new BAT gas plant in India and how they could affect the economic feasibility of the project.

The evaluation of the contribution of the emission credits from a potential CDM project critically depends on the assumptions made (*e.g.* cost and revenues of the project, type of financing, discount rate, *etc.*). A key factor, which cannot be generalised, is each investor's financial criteria (*e.g.* internal rate of return, payback period, risk assessment). It is thus not possible to draw general conclusions on the potential volume of projects under different multi-project baseline options, but if this case study is representative of other projects, the CDM impact (based on the emission credit prices generally estimated by models) on investment decisions could be relatively small.

ANNEX A

Calculation of multi-project electricity baselines based on recent capacity additions (*i.e.* those that started operating after 1994 and those currently under construction)

The calculation is based on the IPCC suggested methodology. The first step is to calculate the electricity production of each individual plant/unit in the database:

Equation A3-1

$$Electricity\ production(MWh)_z = Capacity(MW)_z * Load(hours\ of\ operation\ per\ year)_z$$

It is then necessary to calculate the fuel consumption used to generate the electricity:

Equation A3-2

$$Fuel\ consumption\ (GJ)_z = \frac{electricity\ production(MWh)_z}{efficiency_z} * 3.6$$

The CO_2 emissions are then calculated using the IPCC default emission factor for each energy source and the IPCC suggested fraction of carbon oxidised:

Equation A3-3

$$CO_2\ emissions\ _z(GgCO_2) = \left[\frac{fuel\ cons._z(TJ) * emission\ factor\ _z(tC/TJ)}{1000} * fraction\ carbon\ oxidised\ _z \right] * \frac{44}{12}$$

The gigagrams of CO_2 emissions $(GgCO_2)$ for each plant are then converted into tonnes of CO_2 emissions (tCO_2). $(1Gg = 1t)$

The methane emissions (CH_4) for each plant are calculated using the IPCC default emission factors for each type of electricity generation technology:

Equation A3-4

$$CH_4\ emissions_z\ (kgCH_4) = fuel\ cons_z\ (TJ) * emission\ factor_z\ (kg/TJ)$$

The kilograms of CH_4 emissions $(kg\ CH_4)$ for each plant need to be converted into CO_2 emissions equivalent $(kt\ CO_2)$ by multiplying by the 100-year global warming potential of 21[100]. These CO_2 equivalent emissions then need to be translated into tonnes of CO_2 equivalent (tCO_2).

---

[100] IPCC, Second Assessment Report (1997)

Total GHG emissions for each individual plant are calculating by adding the CO_2 emissions and the CH_4 emissions (translated into emissions CO_2 equivalent).

The GHG emissions per unit of electricity output (in tCO_2/GWh) for each plant are obtained in the following way:

Equation A3-5

$$GHG\ per\ unit\ of\ output\ (tCO_2/GWh)_z = \left[\frac{GHG\ emissions\ (tCO2)_z}{electricity\ output\ (GWh)_z} \right]$$

The multi-project electricity baseline based is the sum of all the weighted average GHG emissions per unit of electricity production associated with each individual plant:

Equation A3-6

$$Baseline\ (tCO_2/GWh) = \sum_{z=1}^{n} \left[\frac{GHG\ emissions\ _z}{\sum_{z=1}^{n} electricity\ production\ _z} \right]$$

Where:

z represents each power plant in the database used to develop the multi-project electricity baseline.

152

ANNEX B

Recent electricity capacity additions in Morocco, Brazil and India

Figure B3-1

Brazil: Recent electricity generation capacity
(1995, 1996, 1997, 1998 & plants under construction)

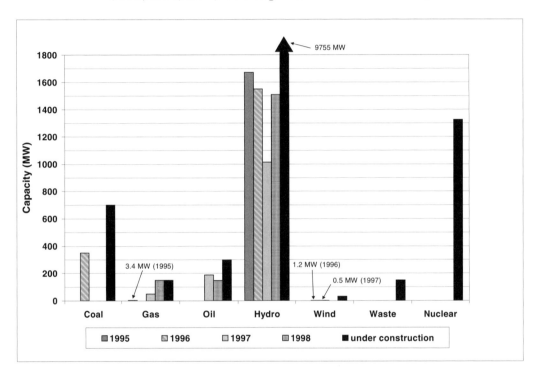

Source: UDI/McGraw- Hill (1999)

Table B3-1

Brazil: Number of recently added generating units (excludes CHP plants)

Source	1995	1996	1997	1998	Under const.	Total
Coal	0	1	0	0	2	3
Gas	1	0	1	1	1	4
Oil	0	0	19	4	93	116
Nuclear	0	0	0	0	1	1
Hydro	7	9	11	8	64	99
Wind	0	1	1	0	3	5
Waste	0	0	0	0	1	1
Total	8	11	32	13	165	229

153

Figure B3-2

India: Recent electricity generation capacity
(1995,1996,1997,1998 & plants under construction)

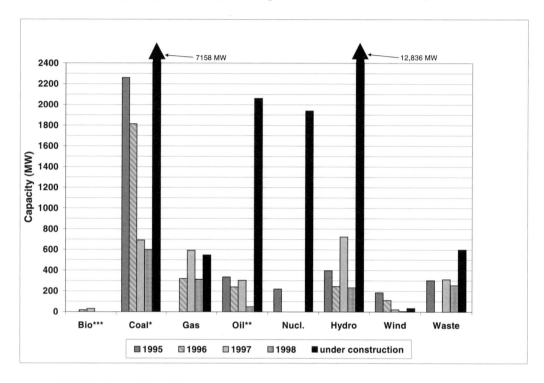

Source: UDI/McGraw-Hill, 1999

*incl. coke oven gas, blast furnace gas & coal gas
**incl. naphtha & petroleum coke
*** Biomass includes bagasse

Table B3-2

India: Number of recently added generating units (excludes recent CHP plants)

Source	1995	1996	1997	1998	Under const.	Total
Coal	8	10	10	5	35	68
Gas	0	14	15	2	4	35
Hydro	11	27	20	7	125	190
Oil	46	46	39	4	35	170
Nuclear	1	0	0	0	6	7
Wind	105	17	5	2	2	131
Biomass	0	1	1	0	0	2
Waste	2	0	5	2	5	14
Total	173	115	95	22	212	617

Figure B3-3

Morocco - Recent Electricity Generation Capacity*
(1995, 1997 and Plants under construction)

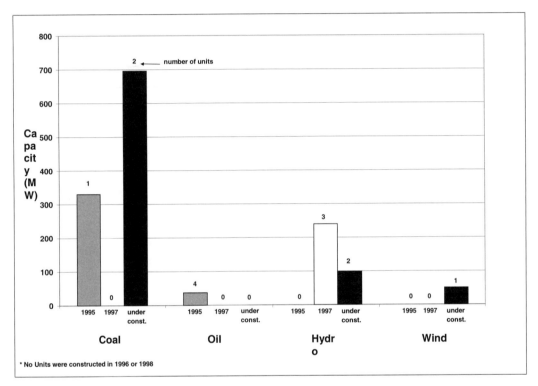

Source: UDI/McGraw-Hill, 1999

* No units were constructed in 1996 or 1998

155

ANNEX C

Table C3-1

Recent (operation started after 1994) electricity generation plants and plants under construction: Assumptions for load factors and efficiencies

	Brazil	**India**	**Morocco**
Steam turbine (boiler)			
- Efficiency**	35%	32*%	35%
- Load	75%	70*%	75%
Hydro[1]			
- Load	50%**	40%	32%***
Nuclear			
- Load**	69%	46*%	n.a.
Gas turbine in combined cycle			
- Efficiency**	50%	50%	50%
- Load	75%	75%	75%
Internal combustion (reciprocating engine or diesel engine)			
- Efficiency	33%	33%	33%
- Load	50%[2]	35%	35%
Gas/combustion turbine (peak load)			
- Efficiency**	35%	35%	35%
- Load	50%[2]	35%	35%
Wind turbine generator			
- Load	25%**	25%	25%

* Lower values for India are due to poor maintenance and low quality coal in India.

** Based on IEA (1998a) assumptions.

***African average, as per IEA (1998a)

[1] Hydro performance is site specific, but to facilitate calculations, an average figure is used here, based on IEA (1998a) assumptions.

Other figures based on recommendations from electricity experts at the IEA.

[2] A load of 50% is assumed for the North Isolated region (all internal combustion engine plants are located in that region and 10 out of the 12 gas/combustion plants are located in the North Isolated region). The load factor is assumed to be 0.35% for these types of plants located in other regions.

ANNEX D

Table D3-1

Baselines based on entire existing generation capacity in 1997 (t CO_2/GWh)

	All existing electricity generation capacity (fossil fuel only)	All existing electricity generation capacity (all sources)
Brazil	894	49
India	1117	912
Morocco	884	745

Sources: IEA 1999b, IEA 1999a

157

ANNEX E

National baselines based on recent capacity additions (after 1994) and those currently under construction

Table E3-1

Brazil

Electricity source	No. of plants	Total capacity (MW)	Electricity output (GWh)	Percentage of total electricity output	GHG emissions (tCO$_2$/GWh) *Weighted average*
All sources	229	19,040.80	87,912.72	100%	108.03
Fossil fuel only	123	2,034.30	11,754.79	13.4%	807.93
Hydro	99	15,487.80	67,182.96	76.4%	0.00
Nuclear	1	1,325.00	7,926.55	9%	0.00
Oil	116	632.90	2,642.18	3%	761.2
Natural Gas	4	351.40	2,284.98	2.6%	426.4
Coal	3	1,050.00	6,827.63	7.8%	953.7
Wind	5	33.70	73.04	0.1%	0.00
Waste heat	1	150.00	975.38	1.1%	0.00

N.B. OIL includes diesel oil, heavy fuel oil and distillate oil; COAL includes bituminous coal.

Table E3-2

India

Electricity source	No. of plants	Total capacity (MW)	Electricity output (GWh)	Percentage of total electricity output	GHG emissions (tCO$_2$/GWh) *weighted average*
All sources	617	35770	168,710	100%	565
Fossil fuel only	273	17286	99,352	58.9%	960
Nuclear	7	2,160	8,615	5.1%	0.00
Waste heat	14	1,475	9,592	5.7%	0.00
Biomass	2	49	295	0.2%	0.00
Hydro	190	14,437	50,069	29.7%	0.00
Natural Gas	35	1,774	10,493	6.2%	418
Oil	170	2,990	12,842	7.6%	661
Coal	68	12,523	76,017	45.1%	1,085
Wind	131	363	787	0.5%	0.00

N.B. 'Oil' includes diesel oil, heavy fuel oil, distillate oil and naphtha; COAL includes bituminous coal, sub-bituminous coal, lignite, coke-oven-gas, blast furnace gas and coal gas from coal gasification; BIOMASS includes bagasse.

Table E3-3

Morocco

Electricity source	No. of plants	Total capacity (MW)	Electricity output (GWh)	Percentage of total electricity output	GHG emissions (tCO$_2$/GWh) *weighted average*
All sources	13	1,452	7,834	100%	824
Fossil fuel only	7	1,064	6,786	86.6%	951
Hydro	5	338	939	12%	0.00
Oil	4	38	114	1.5%	791
Coal	3	1,026	6,672	85.2%	954
Wind	1	50	109	1.4%	0.00

ANNEX F

Disaggregated baselines based on recent capacity additions (after 1994) and those under construction

Table F3-1

Brazilian sub-national baselines based on recent capacity additions (after 1994) and those under construction

Region	Electricity sample	No. of plants	Total capacity (MW)	Electricity output (GWh)	% of total Brazilian electricity output	GHG emissions (tCO$_2$/GWh)
Brazil	All sources	229	19,041	87,913	100%	108
Brazil	Fossil fuel only	123	2,034	11,755	13.4%	808
North Isolated	All sources	116	628	2,724	3.1%	677
North Isolated	Fossil fuel only	114	555	2,405	2.7%	764
North-Northeast	All sources	14	3,435	14,850	16.9%	0.60
North-Northeast	Fossil fuel only	1	3.40	22	0.03%	403
South/South-east/Midwest	All sources	99	14,978	70,338	80.0%	109
South/South-east/Midwest	Fossil fuel only	8	1,476	9,327	10.6%	820

Table F3-2

Indian baselines for peak and baseload based on recent capacity additions (after 1994) and those under construction

Type of plants	No. of plants	Total capacity (MW)	Electricity output (GWh)	% of total Indian electricity output	GHG emissions (tCO$_2$/GWh)
Peaking	177	2,199	6,674	3.96%	789
Baseload	440	33,571	162,036	96.04%	556

N.B. Peaking plants are assumed to be gas/combustion turbine plants and internal combustion engine plants. Baseload plants are assumed to be all other types of power plants.

3.9 References

Bernstein, M., P. Bromley, J. Hagen, S. Hassell, R. Lempert, J. Muñoz, D. Robalino, RAND, June 1999. *Developing Countries and Global Climate Change: Electric Power Options for Growth*, prepared for the Pew Center on Global Climate Change, US.

CCAP, 2000. Submission to UNFCCC on Mechanisms.

Electrobrás and the Brazilian Ministry of Mines and Energy, 1999. *Ten-Year Expansion Plan: 1999/2008*, produced by the GCPS Electric Systems Planning Coordination Group, Brazil.

Ellis, Jane, 1999. *Experience with Emission Baselines Under the AIJ Pilot Phase*, OECD/IEA Information Paper, Paris (www.oecd.org/env.cc/freedocs.htm).

Ellis, Jane and Martina Bosi, 1999. *Options for Project Emission Baselines*, OECD Information Paper, Paris (www.oecd.org/env.cc/freedocs.htm).

European Commission, 1995. Directorate-General XII, Science, Research and Development, *Externe: Externalities of Energy*, Belgium.

Government of India, 1997. Ninth Five-Year Plan (1997-2002) (www.nic.in/ninthplan).

Hagler Bailly, 1998. *Evaluation of Using Benchmarks to Satisfy the Additionality Criterion for Joint Implementation Projects*, prepared for US Environmental Protection Agency, US.

Hargrave, Tim, Ned Helme and Ingo Puhl, 1998. *Options for Simplifying Baseline Setting for Joint Implementation and Clean Development Mechanism Projects*, Center for Clean Air Policy.

IEA, 1998b and 1999b editions. *CO_2 Emissions from Fuel Combustion*, Paris.

IEA, 1999. *Emissions Trading and the Clean Development Mechanism: Resource Transfers, Project Costs and Investment Incentives*, paper released at COP5 (www.iea.org/climat.htm).

IEA, 1999a. *Energy Balances of Non-OECD Countries: 1996-1997*, Paris.

IEA, 1998a. *World Energy Outlook*, Paris.

IEA, 2000 forthcoming. *Energy Capital Stock Turnover: A Critical Element in Reducing Future Greenhouse Gas Emissions*, Paris.

IEA, March 2000. *India - A Growing International Oil and Gas Player*, Note by the Secretariat (Pierre Audinet), IEA/SOM/SEQ/NMC(2000)1.

Herold Anke, Uwe Fritsche, Martin Cames and Sabine Poetzsch (Oeko-Institut), February 2000. *Wood Waste Power Plants in Zimbabwe as Options for CDM*, Draft Final Report, prepared for GTZ, Germany.

Intergovernmental Panel on Climate Change (IPCC), 1995. *IPCC Guidelines for National Greenhouse Gas Inventories*, prepared by UNEP, OECD, IEA and IPCC.

Joint Implementation Registration Centre (JIRC), February 2000. *Setting a Standard for JI and CDM: Recommendation on baselines and certification based on AIJ experience*, commissioned by the Dutch Ministries of Economic Affairs, Foreign Affairs and Housing, Spacial Planning and Environment, The Hague.

Leining, Catherine and Ned Helme, January 2000. *Recommendations for the Development of Baseline Guidelines for Article 12 of the Kyoto Protocol -* Submission to the UNFCCC Secretariat, Center for Clean Air Policy, US

Nuclear Energy Agency (NEA) and the International Energy Agency (IEA), 1998. *Projected Costs of Generating Electricity - Update 1998*, Paris.

OECD, 1998. *Status of Research on project Baselines Under the UNFCCC and the Kyoto Protocol* (www.oecd.org/env.cc/freedocs.htm).

Pew Center on Global Climate Change, 1999, Developing Countries and Global Climate Change: Electric Power Options for Growth, US

Resource Publications (PTY) Ltd., 1999. African Energy, Volume 1 No.3, *New Wind, Hydro and Gas-Fired Power for Morocco* (www.africanenergy.co.za./magazines/evol1no3/story08.htm)

Royaumc du Maroc, 1998, *Annuaire Statistique du Maroc - 1998*.

Shukla, P.R., D. Ghosh (Indian Institute of Management, Ahmedabad) and W. Chandler, J. Logan (Battelle, Advanced International Studies Unit), October 1999, *Developing Countries and Global Climate Change: Electric Power Options in India*, prepared for the Pew Center on Global Climate Change, US.

Tellus Institute, Stockholm Environment Institute and Stratus Consulting, 1999, Boston. *Evaluation of Benchmarking as an Approach for Establishing Clean Development Mechanism Baselines*, prepared for US EPA.

UNIDO, 2000, *Generating Guideline Options to Support Decision-Making on Baseline Setting and Additionality Assessment for Industrial Projects*, Draft report (www.unido.org).

Utility Data Institute (UDI)/McGraw-Hill, 1999, *World Electric Power Plants Data Base*.

4. ENERGY EFFICIENCY CASE STUDY

4. ENERGY EFFICIENCY CASE STUDY[101]

4.1   Executive Summary

Extending previous OECD and IEA work on emission baselines (Ellis and Bosi, 1999), this case study provides an initial view on the potential for standardising the construction methods for greenhouse gas emissions baselines for JI and CDM energy efficiency projects. The focus is on baselines in the lighting and motors sectors.

This analysis is largely based on the experience gained through energy efficiency projects and programmes in industrialised countries - which may provide valuable lessons for the construction of baselines for JI and CDM projects in developing countries, as well as in economies in transitions. It is also based on the examination of seven examples of energy efficiency projects and programmes undertaken in four developing countries[102] (*i.e.* Mexico, Morocco, Pakistan and Thailand).

Three key factors point towards a possibly large potential for energy efficiency projects in the context of the Clean Development Mechanism:

- High growth in energy demand is forecast for developing countries, with electricity use expected to increase significantly by 2015.

- The most cost-effective energy efficiency projects tend to be those implemented as part of new construction or major facility modification efforts and these types of projects are projected to be significant in developing countries.

---

[101] This paper was prepared by Daniel Violette, Christina Mudd (Hagler Bailly Services Inc.) and Marshall Keneipp (Summit Blue Ventures) for the IEA and OECD Secretariats. The authors thank Martina Bosi (IEA) for her comments and oversight of this project. The authors are also grateful for useful comments and suggestions received from Jonathan Pershing and Benoît Lebot (IEA), Jan Corfee Morlot, Jane Ellis, Thomas Martinsen and Stéphane Willems (OECD), as well as from the delegations to the Annex I Expert Group.

[102] This case study focuses on energy efficiency projects in the context of developing countries and thus the Clean Development Mechanism. However, many issues and insights from this study are likely to be applicable in the context of JI energy efficiency projects, although this may merit further examination.

- Most developing countries did not participate in the wave of energy efficiency investment that occurred (mostly in OECD countries) after the oil price shocks of the 1970s and 1980s. Consequently, there are still numerous opportunities to increase energy efficiency in developing countries (as well as in countries with economies in transition).

Energy efficiency projects tend to have particularities that need to be taken into account when developing baselines. In contrast to other sector projects, energy efficiency projects often comprise bundles of smaller projects. For example, one AIJ pilot phase energy efficiency project in Mexico (see Annex A) involved the replacement of existing lights with higher-efficiency compact fluorescent lamps. While there are some single-site, large-scale energy efficiency projects that have been implemented (*e.g.* a large district heating system or a single large industrial facility), energy efficiency projects are more likely to be characterised by two factors:

- They span a large number of sites or locations.

- There is a specified target market area, although multiple sites may be targeted (*e.g.* the AIJ lighting project in Mexico spanned many households in a target market covering two cities).

The development of GHG emission baselines for energy efficiency projects can be divided into two main steps: (1) the development of the energy use baseline; and (2) the translation of this baseline into GHG emissions.

There are essentially three options, or levels, for the standardisation of energy use baselines for energy efficiency projects. These are: *standardising baseline calculation methods; standardising operating and performance parameters*; and *standardising energy use indices*. Each is discussed below:

Standardising baseline calculation methods and data collection protocols (*i.e.* the algorithms and models used to compute energy use and the data that provide inputs to the algorithms).

In traditional energy efficiency projects and programmes undertaken to date, relatively little attention has been paid to the development of baselines (or reference scenarios). JI and CDM energy efficiency projects will clearly demand a greater focus on these.

Standardising calculation algorithms, data requirements supporting those algorithms and data collection protocols would promote the application of appropriate procedures and reduce project developer's uncertainty. Such standardisation could be reasonably done for a variety of energy efficiency projects, including equipment replacement (*e.g.* lighting, motors and appliances). Simplified calculation algorithms for the construction of baselines for lighting and motors energy efficiency projects are developed in this case study.

168

It is important to keep in mind that data are key in the development of baseline. In fact, most debates over the quality of the baseline revolve around concerns about whether the sample selected for the baseline development is indeed representative of the project participants and their energy use. As a result, the selection of a sample is often a crucial determinant of "good" baseline. The use of sampling is important in that it keeps the costs of establishing a baseline using project-specific information manageable.

In the particular context of energy efficiency projects in the lighting sector, baseline calculation methodology (algorithms) and data collection protocols appear suitable to standardisation. A review of lighting sector projects across three countries indicated that differences in the technologies, targeted participants and in-field operating conditions in each country make it inappropriate to share baseline data (*i.e.* use identical baselines across countries). However, a common approach to collecting the required data using state-of-the-practice techniques could be shared across countries.

Similarly, in the case of the development of baselines in electric motors, the calculation methodology used for estimating the energy use for a population could be standardised across countries. Data on the number of motors categorised by horsepower can be collected at either the site or the population level. The data for the efficiency and operating hours can be obtained through estimation from technical data, engineering methods or field observations.

However, not all energy efficiency projects are amenable to the same level of standardisation; some require project-specific data to establish baselines. Some simplification is still possible; methods exist whereby national or regional sector baselines can be used as starting points and then adjusted according to in-field data collected from participants in the project. These methods use statistical procedures (*e.g.* energy-use realisation rates, ratio estimation methods) and can significantly lower the cost of baseline construction below that incurred using methods where each project developer has to start *de novo*, *i.e.* without a "prior" estimate of the baseline from aggregate data. Such a method essentially combines standardisation with project-specific elements to produce a cost-effective hybrid approach.

Standardising operating (e.g. number of hours) and performance (e.g. motor efficiency) parameters necessary for the baseline calculation (*i.e.* the values that describe the energy use characteristics of a given technology or end-use)

The standardisation of baseline operating and performance parameters brings greater uniformity and consistency to the CDM/JI baseline development process. It would also reduce the time and cost of estimating the energy use baselines for project developers - although it does not, of itself, establish baseline energy use for energy efficiency projects.

In the lighting sector, it is likely that the standardisation of operating and performance parameters would be possible for most common types of lighting devices. This seems to be particularly appropriate in the residential and commercial sectors, where lighting operating hours tend to be relatively consistent. The operating hours parameters would need to be differentiated according to market sector/segment and developed and standardised on a country-by-country basis (or on a regional basis if circumstances are sufficiently similar), in order to take into account differences in domestic markets and the mix of technologies. Similarly, performance parameters such as input wattage for the most common lighting fixture types could be standardised. For example, it would be possible to establish baseline data on wattages for common types of incandescent and fluorescent residential and commercial fixtures.

In the motors sector, it would be possible to standardise motor efficiency parameters, as equipment performance tends to be more uniform across market segments than other operating characteristics. Such standardisation seems particularly applicable for certain motor types and size ranges that are most common in the commercial sector and industrial application. In fact, it would seem useful to further examine, in the context of developing countries, the possibility of standardising motor efficiencies for the most common types, sizes, classes and applications, based on manufacturers' data.

In addition to motor efficiencies, energy use baselines in the motors sector requires data on operating hours, load factors and "diversity" factors. These latter parameters lend themselves to standardisation (albeit with certain limitations). As operating hours tend to be relatively consistent within specific market segments, particularly in the commercial sector, this parameter could be conservatively standardised by market sector/segment. These baseline values would need to be derived from end-use load information on a country-by-country, or possibly regional, basis.

Standardising energy use indices (EUI) by sector, market segment and/or end-use (i.e. indices that are representative of the energy use of a population of technologies or segment of the population, such as lighting kWh per square metre for certain commercial building types).

With respect to lighting projects, it seems possible to standardise indoor lighting EUIs (*e.g.* lighting kWh/square metre) for certain market segments of the commercial sector (*e.g.* offices, schools and hospitals). In the residential sector, it may be possible to standardise EUIs for certain appliances (*e.g.* refrigerators). Standardised lighting EUIs are probably less applicable in the industrial sector, where a hybrid approach combining standardised and project specific elements is likely more appropriate.

Standardisation of motor energy use indices (*e.g.* kWh/square metre) for the commercial sector does not seem appropriate, as motor energy use is often tabulated or subsumed in other end-uses, particularly space heating and cooling. However, in the industrial sector, where motors are often the primary energy-consuming devices, it may be possible to develop baseline motor energy use indices related to the unit of production (motor kWh/unit of production) for selected industries.

170

Other energy efficiency baseline issues

The environmental risks associated with accepting an "incorrect" baseline varies significantly by type of energy efficiency project. The potential negative environmental consequences of using an "incorrect" baseline are probably highest if an energy efficiency project includes only one or two very large facilities (*e.g.* district heating systems, large industrial applications). Projects that embody a portfolio concept where several energy efficiency measures are installed across a large number sites may pose less environmental risk (as the baseline would probably be "correct" for the project as a whole, even though some individual components may not be "additional" on their own).

The methodologies examined to estimate energy use baselines for energy efficiency projects normally only consider direct energy use. However, energy efficiency projects may lead to two indirect energy use (and GHG) effects: free riders and spillover effects. These two indirect effects work in opposite directions and both are difficult to quantify. Until better information is available, it may be practical to assume (as have some regulatory jurisdictions in the case of traditional energy efficiency projects and programmes) that these two effects cancel each other out.

Project developers need a framework that allows them to assess the economics of a project. Several actions can be taken that help ensure environmental integrity and help project developers better and more efficiently, evaluate potential JI/CDM projects, including:

- Setting an emissions rate per kWh reduced for a pre-determined period of time. This is likely to be the most important standardisation action that can be taken, as it would apply equally to all projects across all sectors in a given country/region and thereby would help encourage all energy efficiency projects.

- Setting the crediting lifetime associated with an energy use baseline. This paper proposes a five-year crediting lifetime, arguing it provides project developers with enough time to recover costs and earn a return on a wide range of energy efficiency projects and stimulate investments in JI/CDM energy efficiency projects. (Such a baseline could be set in such a way that energy efficiency would be required to increase at a given rate over the five-year period; project confidence would be possible only if such a dynamic rate were agreed at the outset of the project).

In terms of the level of stringency of the energy efficiency baseline level, the key criteria should be what most reasonably reflects the likely "business-as-usual" scenario.

Setting the baseline level based on what investments should theoretically take place using traditional financial assessment criteria (*e.g.* pay-back period), is not likely to be a good proxy for "business-as-usual", as such theoretical financial criteria do not take into account the various (*e.g.* non-monetary) barriers to energy efficiency investments (*e.g.*

information cost, attention cost, market distortion cost, public policy costs, cultural barrier costs, *etc.*).

The other two main approaches of determining an appropriate baseline stringency level are based on: existing stock of equipment in the field; and "best practice", using either highest rated equipment found in the field or equipment for sale. The most appropriate choice would depend on what is reasonable to assume under a business-as-usual scenario. In a case where all new sales are for equipment that has a higher efficiency level than older equipment, then the new equipment efficiency level should be used for developing the baseline. On the other hand, if the technology is entirely new and only a small fraction (*e.g.* less than 30%) of new sales represent this technology, then the average efficiency level (or potentially a reasonable "better-than-average" efficiency level) of the stock of equipment in the field may be more appropriate.

Finally, it is important to recognise that some energy efficiency JI or CDM projects will probably "beat the system" and receive more emissions credits than they deserve. No process will be perfect and any energy efficiency baseline construction process is likely to have defects. However, as search for perfection is likely to result in no process being judged as acceptable, the goal instead should be to strike both a reasonable balance among various risks: among environmental objectives; among the interests of project developers and among those of potential host countries.

4.2   Introduction

This chapter extends previous IEA and OECD work on greenhouse gas emissions baselines for the Kyoto Protocol's project based mechanisms: Joint Implementation (JI) and the Clean Development Mechanism (CDM). Specifically, Ellis and Bosi (1999) examine issues in developing greenhouse gas (GHG) emission baselines, including the possibility of standardising them (*i.e.* multi-project baselines). This paper examines issues surrounding the potential standardisation of baselines for JI and CDM energy efficiency projects, focusing on approaches that have been used to establish baselines in conjunction with planning, implementing and evaluating energy efficiency projects in selected developing countries.[103] Energy efficiency projects from Thailand, Mexico, Morocco and Pakistan are used as examples.

Establishing emission baselines for energy efficiency projects is a two-step process. First, an energy use baseline must be established for the energy efficiency project. Second, this baseline must be translated into a GHG emissions baseline. This paper focuses on the first step - establishing baselines for energy use, *i.e.* what would the energy consumption have

---

[103] This chapter focuses on baselines for energy efficiency projects in the context of developing countries and thus the Clean Development Mechanism. However, many issues and insights from this report are also likely applicable in the context of JI energy efficiency projects, although this may warrant further examination.

been if the demand-side energy efficiency project had not been installed. The second step - translating the change in energy use into a change in GHG emissions, which requires emission values associated with electricity use - is being addressed separately (see Electricity Case Study).

The accomplishments of energy efficiency programmes to date imply that using energy efficiency as a way to reduce GHG emissions within both Annex I and non-Annex I countries has the potential to greatly reduce the costs of GHG mitigation. Further, these benefits extend beyond GHG emissions reductions by providing host countries with other environmental benefits associated with reduced energy use (local air, water and land use impacts), the installation of current technology in important sectors and the development of a sustainable infrastructure. In addition, there are likely to be spillover economic and environmental benefits for all parties.

Given the magnitude of the environmental and economic benefits that can be expected, the challenge is how to set up a reasonable process for constructing baselines. A number of suggestions regarding the baseline-setting process are offered below. Issues addressed include: areas were the process might be standardised, trade-offs in baseline complexity, balancing risks, baseline stringency and potential biases in the baselines and their impact on the selection of potential energy efficiency projects.

4.3   Sector Overview

Energy efficiency projects may be found in a wide variety of initiatives in the residential, commercial and industrial sectors. This diversity makes it difficult to determine the exact size of the market and opportunities for GHG mitigation through energy efficiency projects. However, a handbook on climate change mitigation options for developing countries prepared by the USEA/USAID estimated that current world-wide energy demand could be by reduced 3-7% by year 2010, with corresponding reductions in GHG emissions through Demand-side management (DSM).[104]

Three factors make developing countries strong candidates for energy efficiency projects:

- High growth in energy demand is forecast for developing countries, with electricity use expected to increase nearly eight-fold by 2015.
- The most cost-effective energy efficiency projects tend to be those implemented as part of new construction or major facility modifications,[105] and these types of projects are projected to be significant in developing countries.

---

[104] *USEA/USAID Handbook*, 1999, pp. 7-3.

[105] Many energy efficiency advocates argue that it is of critical importance to implement projects in new construction, since once a facility is built, it will not be cost-effective to go back and retrofit it for some time. These missed or "lost opportunities" can reduce the overall potential for energy savings in a country.

- Most developing countries did not participate in the wave of energy efficiency investment that occurred (mostly in OECD countries) after the OPEC oil embargo and the resulting high energy prices of the 1970s and 1980s. Consequently, there are still numerous opportunities to increase energy efficiency in developing countries, as well as in countries with economies in transition.

As a result of these factors, a significant fraction of the GHG emissions reductions achieved via the Kyoto Protocol's project-based mechanisms could potentially result from successful energy efficiency projects implemented in developing countries.

4.3.1   Energy efficiency sector trends

On average, the residential sector typically accounts for 20 to 35% of a country's energy use.[106] Candidate residential sector projects can be directed at: 1) improving the energy efficiency of residential lighting and appliances; 2) improving the energy efficiency of new and existing construction; and 3) improving the energy efficiency of space heating and cooling systems. Efficient residential construction and high-efficiency appliances can reduce household energy use by 33% using available technologies.

Commercial sector energy use typically accounts for 10 to 30% of a country's energy use. Candidate commercial sector projects are likely to be designed to address: 1) building envelopes; 2) efficient equipment (*e.g.* lighting, motors, variable speed drives, heating, ventilation and air conditioning (HVAC) equipment); and 3) community energy systems such as district heating in commercial areas. Some energy efficiency programmes have lead to reductions in energy use of up to 50% with the installation of efficient lighting, space conditioning and building controls.[107]

---

[106] According to the IEA's *Energy Statistics of OECD Countries (1999a),* the residential sector, on average, makes up 30% of total electricity consumption (kWh) in a country. Mexico's residential electricity consumption accounts for 22% of that nation's total. Developing countries tend to have a wider range in the share of energy devoted to electricity in the residential sector with, for example, Thailand at 22% and Pakistan at 41% (*Energy Statistics of Non-OECD Countries* (IEA, 1999b); statistics for non-electric energy use are not available).

[107] *Energy Statistics of OECD Countrie*s (IEA, 1999a) shows that in OECD countries, the commercial sector makes up 27% of electricity consumed (kWh) on average (Note: Mexico has a commercial sector share of 18%). Again the range is broader for non-OECD countries but, in general, the share of electricity use in the commercial sector is lower in non-OECD countries than in OECD countries (*e.g.* Thailand at a 10% share and Pakistan at a 14% share for commercial sector electricity use).

174

The industrial sector is typically the largest energy using sector, often accounting for more than 40% of a country's electricity use.[108] The industrial sector accounts for almost one half of global energy-related CO_2 emissions. With industry-specific energy intensities in developing countries often being two to four times greater than the average in OECD countries, energy efficiency and process improvements in the industrial sectors can produce substantial reductions in GHG emissions. These energy efficiency projects can be focused (*e.g.* they might address a single industrial process such as aluminium smelting) or diffuse (*e.g.* an industrial sector motors replacement project spanning hundreds of facilities).

Large-scale energy efficiency projects can produce substantial GHG emissions reductions in all three sectors. In addition, these projects are likely to provide various economic spin-off benefits through, for example, the education and training of regional workers, operational improvements, enhanced technology transfer, localised environmental improvements, enhanced competitiveness of regional industries and an overall improvement in regional economies.

Only a few developing countries have undergone the end-use profiling of energy demand that allows for the successful planning of energy efficiency projects. Independent of the value this information might have for establishing baselines, national end-use energy analyses will be critical to the identification of cost-effective, high-impact energy efficiency projects that might be implemented in developing countries.

As discussed later in this case study, it is likely that the estimated baselines for most JI and CDM energy efficiency projects will rely on some data that are unique to that project, rather than relying entirely on national or standardised data. However, the project developer's screening of and planning for candidate energy efficiency projects will have to be based in large part on end-use data for major sectors that are collected on a national basis. National data are critical for these planning applications since, in the planning phases, there are no identified project participants. The quality of these national data will affect the realisation rates for baseline estimation, *i.e.* the ratio of planned or expected baseline energy use to the in-field[109] estimated baseline energy use for the actual project

---

[108] *Energy Statistics of OECD Countries* (IEA, 1999a) shows, on average, the industrial sector comprising 40% of electricity consumed (kWh) and 32% of heat energy (TJ) consumed. Average shares for industrial energy use in the countries analysed in the examples included in Annex A: Mexico - 60% of total electricity consumed, Thailand - 42% of electricity consumed and Pakistan - 28% of electricity consumed (statistics for non-electric/heat energy use are not available).

[109] In-field estimates are based on measurements taken at specific facilities. In-field estimates for a specific set of facilities are used to verify and modify energy use baselines from more aggregate national databases constructed using sector averages to make them more representative of the actual sites that are participating in a specific energy efficiency project. A realisation rate of 1.1 would indicate that the baseline obtained from in-field data from project participants is 10% greater than a baseline estimated using aggregated national data. The in-field estimate is assumed

participants once the project is rolled out. In addition, countries with high-quality national data (*e.g.* on sectoral and end-use energy consumption) that allow for good project planning would likely attract more JI/CDM energy efficiency projects.

Table 4-1

Vietnam's changing sectoral and end-use electrical energy shares

(Based on GWh Sales Projections)

Sector/End-Use	1994 End-Use Share	1994 Sectoral Share of Sales	2010 End-Use Share	2010 Sectoral Share of Sales
Industrial		42%		62%
Motors	76%		76%	
Lighting	4%		4%	
Process	20%		20%	
Commercial		9%		12%
Lighting	56%		34%	
HVAC	23%		49%	
Other	21%		17%	
Residential		34%		22%
Lighting	45%		28%	
Refrigeration	5%		7%	
Cooking	20%		9%	
Other	30%		56%	
Other		15%		4%
Sectoral Total		100%		100%

Source: Hagler Bailly Consulting, Inc., 1996.

As an example of the current status of one developing country, Table 4-1 illustrates end-use and sector projections of electricity use for Vietnam. These data indicate that motor drives will account for 76% of the electricity use in the industrial sector in 2010 and that the industrial sector as a whole will increase its share of national electricity use from 42 to 62%. Lighting makes up a large fraction of commercial and residential sector energy use, but HVAC (*i.e.* mechanical heating, ventilating and air conditioning of buildings) shows the largest growth and will surpass lighting in electric use in residential and commercial buildings by 2010. These general end-use trends are not uncommon for developing countries located in warm climate zones.

---

to be more accurate since it takes into account information specific to that subset or sector of facilities that are participating in a given energy efficiency project.

4.3.2   Energy efficiency market trends

Nearly all OECD countries have seen substantial improvements in the efficiency of their energy using equipment in the past two decades. As a result, they have established markets for energy-efficient products and services with personnel trained in the installation and maintenance of high-efficiency equipment. The oil price shocks of the 1970s highlighted the economic benefits of energy efficiency and developed countries had the capital resources required to make energy efficiency investments. In contrast, the energy efficiency wave of the 1970s largely bypassed developing countries, where national governments lacked the institutional capabilities to implement and promote energy efficiency policies. Today (in the foreseeable future), new market drivers are expanding the energy efficiency sector in developing countries. Some key trends in the energy efficiency sector include:

- Subsidy removal. In recent years, many developing countries have begun to decrease or remove energy subsidies. This makes the true cost of energy more apparent to end-users and increases the incentives for efficiency;

- Restructuring and privatisation. Restructuring of the electricity sector is typically undertaken to open the power sector to competition and encourage outside investment. In the course of restructuring, many countries are privatising their state-owned utilities and major industries, which generally increases the pressure on companies to cut costs and increase efficiency;

- Demand-side management (DSM). Governments struggling with power supply problems, brown outs, black outs and increasing electricity demand, often encourage energy efficiency through DSM. DSM is viewed as a means of implementing load management and energy conservation initiatives to mitigate these problems;

- Construction boom. Economic growth in developing countries has led to a construction boom, expanding the demand for greenfield energy efficiency projects, specifically those related to building envelope and control technologies;

- Environmental concerns. A growing interest in energy efficiency is coming from the threat local and global environmental problems, including global climate change and concerns for resource scarcity.

4.3.3   Barriers to investments in energy efficiency

Traditional benefit-cost assessments of energy efficiency investments typically show many projects to be very cost-effective. It is not uncommon to see study-based benefit-cost ratios exceed 10 to 1. Still, large-scale investment in these projects has not generally been undertaken by developing countries. Various barriers to implementation are typically cited as the reason why these potentially cost-effective investments are not undertaken. Another view is that traditional benefit-cost analyses do not fully account for all the costs involved in implementing energy efficiency projects in developing countries. To the extent that barriers exist and represent costs of implementing energy efficiency projects, they need to be addressed as part of the baseline (*i.e.* they are part of the business-as-usual case). A list of barriers might include the following:

- An information cost - a lack of awareness and general misinformation about the benefits of energy efficiency projects;

- An attention cost - managers and households have limited time and attention to devote to the manifold aspects of their business and lives. Energy efficiency projects may have a high rate of return, but still be too small and too complicated to justify the expenditure of attention;

- A technical cost - lack of technical specifications required to select the most appropriate technology;

- A market distortion cost - pricing policies that under-price the true value of the resources being consumed makes conservation less economic for participants;

- Capital allocation costs - the capital pool in the country may not be adequate for incremental/discretionary investments in energy-efficient technologies, which drives up the cost of capital and allocates it to the highest risk-adjusted return projects;

- Public policy costs - taxes and tariffs that discourage the import of foreign-manufactured energy-efficient equipment;

- Cost of cultural barriers - local customs and inertial behaviour can work to maintain the status quo in the design, selection and operation of energy-using equipment.

This partial list of factors might explain different propensities to invest in what may be viewed, in some circumstances, as "economic" energy efficiency projects. Traditional financial analyses may not appropriately address the costs of these barriers. Some of these costs can be overcome by JI/CDM investments (*e.g.* the availability of capital and technical specifications). Other costs (*e.g.* those related to cultural barriers) may remain for JI/CDM project developers.

4.3.4   *Trends in energy efficiency projects and baseline implications*

In contrast to other sector projects, energy efficiency projects often comprise bundles of smaller projects. For example, one AIJ pilot phase energy efficiency project in Mexico (see Annex A) involved the replacement of existing lights with higher-efficiency compact fluorescent lamps. This project targeted residential energy use and in two geographic areas - the cities of Guadalajara and Monterrey. While there are some single-site, large-scale energy efficiency projects that have been implemented (*e.g.* a large district heating system or a single large industrial facility), energy efficiency projects are more likely to be characterised by two factors:

- They will span a large number of sites or locations;
- While targeting multiple sites, there still is a specified target market area (*e.g.* the AIJ Pilot Phase lighting project in Mexico spanned many households in a target market covering two cities).

For example, a candidate CDM energy efficiency project might involve retrofitting lighting fixtures in existing commercial buildings larger than 1,000 square metres in that country's four largest cities, *i.e.* the specified target market. The logistics of project implementation have a significant impact on project design. Commercial buildings larger than 1,000 square metres might be targeted since the project developer will want to ensure that, if an engineering team is sent to a site, there will be enough savings at that site to justify the set-up costs of the installation. The target market is limited to the four largest cities in a country due to the costs of shipping and warehousing the lamps and ballasts. Logistics related to the timing of a lighting replacement at a specified site often determines whether an energy efficiency project turns out to be cost-effective in practice as opposed to theory.

The fact that many energy efficiency projects are "targeted" due to implementation challenges can pose problems for establishing baselines. Unadjusted national and even sector-specific energy-use data may not be appropriate for baselines where energy efficiency project developers target a narrow set of facility types in specific regions. Highly tailored energy efficiency projects that focus on only certain types of facilities, with pre-specified energy consumption characteristics, in select markets may not lend themselves to the general application of national or even regional baseline data. The risk that actual project participants will be substantively different in their baseline energy use than those used to create aggregate sector data may be unacceptably high for many energy efficiency projects.

As mentioned earlier, project planning, the screening of energy efficiency measures and final project design, will require national and regional aggregate data. However, for project baselines, some information specific to the facilities and energy users that choose to participate will need to be collected to augment or adjust more aggregate sector baselines. Thus, standardised baseline data for project types and sectors are critical for project planning. However, project baselines likely will need to be more precise and require some information specific to the energy efficiency project participants that can augment or adjust aggregate sector baselines.

Adjustments to standardised energy use baselines to better reflect the particular participants and markets addressed by a specific energy efficiency project can be one component of a standard baseline setting process using project-specific data (see section 4.5.5). A starting-point energy use baseline subject to adjustment using in-field data on project participants is an established approach and is expected to be much less expensive than having each project develop its own baseline *de novo*. The types of building block information for use in baseline construction that can be developed at a national or regional level are discussed in section 4.5.5.

4.4   Baseline Construction

This section presents a simplified example of the typical construction of a baseline for an energy efficiency project. All of the examples of energy efficiency projects and programmes in Annex used variants of this simple case. This approach begins with an algorithm that calculates energy use; then, data are gathered as inputs to this algorithm. In most cases, cost-effective data collection requires the use of a sample from the target population. This sample is used to provide "average value" baseline inputs to the standard algorithm (or calculation).

4.4.1   Baseline calculation: data needs, quality and availability

Energy efficiency baseline construction requires information on the energy consumption characteristics of the energy end use/application targeted by the project. The following equation provides a simple generic formulation of energy use for a population of electrical technologies:

Equation 1, Baseline energy use:

Energy Use = Quantity x *Power* x *Operating Hours* x *Diversity Factor*

Where:

Quantity is the number of devices in each type and size category.

Power is the electrical[110] input to the device. This is typically reported as Watts for lighting fixtures. For other technologies, this value is often estimated from other performance parameters. For example, motor power can be estimated from horsepower, efficiency and load factor.

Operating hours is the annual hours of during which the device operates.

Diversity factor is a measure that account for the fact that in a population of devices, some fraction of the units will either be off or out of service at any point in time due to burnout, modernisation or repairs/maintenance; this factor is related to the quantity.

---

[110] "Power" could also represent other fuels.

This formula is important because it defines which data need to be collected, which factors have to be estimated and which factors lend themselves to standardisation. This generic formula is adaptable to most end-use and technology categories. Energy efficiency projects are typically directed at influencing some combination of power and/or operating hours, through equipment control, repair, retrofit or replacement.

The diversity factor accounts for the real-world operating conditions of a population of devices and has the net effect of discounting estimates that are based only on gross equipment counts and/or rated conditions. This is an important factor in assuring that the energy use and savings attributable to energy efficiency projects are not overestimated.

While energy-use analyses typically begin with an algorithm, these algorithms can be part of a model that incorporates many energy uses and therefore many algorithms (*e.g.* energy audit software for buildings or industrial processes). They can also be made more complex by incorporating multiple pieces of equipment and interactions across end-uses (*e.g.* installing energy-efficient lights reduces the amount of heat given off by the light fixtures and thereby reduces energy required for space cooling during hot weather). However, these algorithms use the same basic parameters regardless of the equipment or end-use they are meant to address. Issues in the construction of the baseline often stem from the way in which data are collected for use in an algorithm, rather than the algorithm itself.

Simplified application - a lighting equipment example

Energy efficiency projects in lighting are a good example of potential JI/CDM projects since they are relatively simple and lighting is an energy application where large gains in efficiency often can be obtained at relatively low cost.[111]

The basic algorithm used to calculate baseline energy use (kWh) for a lighting fixture may be constructed as follows:

Equation 2, Calculation for baseline energy use for a lighting fixture:

Lighting Fixture Energy Use (kWh) = Power (kW) x *Hours of Operation*

---

[111] Energy-efficient lighting is one of the largest market segments in the energy efficiency market. Lighting accounts for over 25% of CO2 emissions in the commercial and residential sectors and offers, perhaps, the largest and most cost-effective opportunity for reducing energy use in these sectors. Fluorescent (tubes and compact fluorescent lamps/CFLs) and incandescent lamps are widely used in the commercial and residential sectors. Fluorescent lamps generate less heat than incandescent lamps and are much more energy efficient, reducing energy by as much as 75% through a simple replacement programme. Since incandescent lamps dominate the residential market in both industrialised and developing countries a lighting replacement project represents a significant opportunity for energy savings and potential emissions reductions.

For a specific existing lighting fixture in a building, the baseline annual energy use (kWh) is the measured (or estimated) kW, multiplied times the hours of operation. Issues in determining the baseline energy use for this fixture involve different ways of obtaining the data that are input to the algorithm and used to calculate annual energy consumption.

The first term in the equation (power) is measured in kW and can be obtained using several different methods.

Methods for estimating power (kW) for lighting fixtures

1. *Nameplate ratings* can be used where the manufacturer of the lamp and the ballast is identified. The manufacturer's ratings can be used as the estimate of the in-field power draw (kW).

2. *Bench tests* can be made using different lamp and ballast[112] combinations to determine the actual kW draw for each combination. Bench test results are used rather than the manufacturers' nameplate ratings.

3. *In-field spot-watt measurements* can be taken. An energy efficiency analyst can take a measurement from a specific fixture, or set of fixtures, on a lighting electric circuit. The kW draw for that circuit or fixture is measured using a watt metre that provides a kW measurement for a single point in time. Watt metres are inexpensive and often used in lighting applications since the kW draw for lighting fixtures is not expected to vary much across time, *i.e.* the light is either on or off. Other equipment such as motors and air conditioners can run at "part loads" and the kW draw may vary over time.

4. *Interval metering* of lighting equipment can be performed. The three options listed above provide only instantaneous kW measurements. Operating hours to determine energy use (kWh) must be obtained from some other source. Interval metering provides both kW and hours of operation. A metre is installed at a lighting fixture or on a lighting circuit and left in place for a period of time. This provides a measure of kW on 5-minute or 15-minute intervals and it also provides data on operating hours. Thus, it can provide an estimate of kWh for the time period in which the metre is installed, including any variations in kW from hour to hour, should such variations occur. Short-term metering refers to a metre installation that lasts for a period of weeks. Long-term metering refers to periods of nine months or more and could be for periods of up to several years. Long-term metering can

---

[112] Fluorescent lighting fixtures are comprised of different lamp/ballast combinations - one to four lamps, one or two ballasts. Energy efficiency improvements in lighting can be made by replacing existing lamps with high-efficiency lamps, replacing existing ballasts with high-efficiency ballasts, or by installing a combination of these actions. In general, different lamp and ballast combinations have different power draws.

capture changes in operating hours that occur seasonally.[113] There is a significant cost trade-off between short- and long-term metering. If the meter interval is only two weeks, then the metres can be re-used at different sites. In long term metering, a larger inventory of metres is needed, resulting in higher costs for baseline data collection.

5. *Most efficient replacement equipment* is also used in some instances as the appropriate baseline value for kW. The argument is that the average kW power draw of existing equipment does not represent what would have been installed in a facility if the energy efficiency project did not exist. In this case, the baseline assumption is that, instead of replacing the existing lamp with another lamp that has the same level of efficiency, a more efficient lamp would have been installed. In this case, lamps in stock at suppliers would be examined and the nameplate rating of the most often sold equipment would be used as the baseline data input.

Nameplate ratings are the simplest and least-costly data source and are reasonably accurate for most lighting applications. Bench tests and spot-watt measurements also are cost-effective methods of establishing baseline power and performance characteristics, particularly for technologies with relatively constant performance characteristics such as most lighting applications. Interval metering is typically not necessary or justifiable on a cost basis for lighting, whereas it can be a valuable tool for technologies that exhibit variable performance characteristics.

The three lighting project examples shown in Annex A used the kW of existing in-field equipment as the basis for constructing the baseline. The use of the "most-efficient replacement" kW value is not a common method for determining energy use baselines in developing countries. A more efficient piece of equipment may have a lower lifetime cost, but capital constraints in developing countries make it likely that the lowest initial cost equipment will be selected. There is also an educational component to this decision.[114]

---

[113] The appropriate interval for metering is an issue of debate among energy efficiency engineers and statisticians. In general, the state-of-the-practice has been the use of short-term metering for lighting projects, with an adjustment factor estimated to account for seasonal effects (*e.g.* less hours of daylight in the winter). Often, the compromise has been to do mixed metering. A small number of installations have been metered for nine months to capture both the summer and winter seasons. A larger number of installations have short-term interval metering (*e.g.* two weeks). A ratio that shows the relationship between hours of operation in the summer, between summer and the shoulder seasons (spring and autumn) and between summer and winter. This ratio is then applied as an adjustment factor to energy use estimates from the sample that only has short-term metering available. In some regions, there has been extensive metering on lighting use from earlier studies where results from previous projects are used to calculate adjustment factors for new energy efficiency projects. This is one example of how field data can be used across projects.

[114] Studies have shown that many purchasers are sceptical about the energy efficiency claims made by manufacturers and consumers may select the lower initial-cost equipment because they are

For lighting baselines, it has been common even in developed countries to use the average in-field efficiency of lighting fixtures for projects aimed at replacing existing equipment, as was done in the three developing country case studies. In contrast, most developed countries use "most efficient replacement equipment" for other end uses such as air conditioning and refrigeration, which have shown steady efficiency improvements over time and where replacements typically only occur at the time of equipment failure or a major renovation project. The justification for using different approaches is that lighting has generally represented a "change in technology" and the new technology would not have been available without the programme. Appliances such as refrigerators have not seen the step-change in technology but, instead, have shown steady improvement over time and, therefore, would have been available in the business-as-usual case as replacement technology.

After estimating the power (kW) for a lighting fixture, it is necessary to estimate the operating hours to determine electricity use. Just as there are several options for estimating power for lighting fixtures, there are several methods for estimating baseline operating hours.

Methods for estimating operating hours for a lighting fixture

1. *Occupant estimated* hours of use can be obtained. This approach simply surveys the building occupants to obtain their estimates of the hours a lighting fixture is on.

2. *Runtime metres* can be installed. Runtime metres measure the number of hours a piece of equipment is on or off. These metres are relatively inexpensive and easy to use and they can measure the number of on/off hours in more than one time period, *e.g.* they can measure the number of hours of operation during a peak period and the number of hours of operation in an off-peak period.

3. *Interval metering* can also be used, as discussed above. An interval metre is installed for a period of time and measures both kW and operating hours, as well as the load curve. A load curve provides the kW loads for each 5- to 15-minute interval during a day. These data can be used to calculate contributions to peak demand (*i.e.* peak coincident factors) and diversity factors (*i.e.* what fraction of the participating lighting fixtures are on at any point in time). If information on peak demand and peak period energy use is important for calculating reductions in emissions, then interval metering provides the information necessary to make these calculations.

The most common approach, in the context of traditional energy efficiency programmes, calculates energy use baselines for lighting fixtures using either occupant surveys or runtime metres to obtain estimates of operating hours. Interval metering has generally

---

uncertain about whether the savings in terms of higher equipment efficiency will, in fact, be realised.

been viewed as cost prohibitive[115] for most lighting projects in developing countries. For kW estimates, the most common approaches are to obtain estimates from nameplate ratings, bench tests or watt metres. Occasionally, short-term interval metering has been used for lighting equipment. While the appropriate estimation approach may depend upon the specifics of the lighting project, it is generally becoming recognised that run-time metres combined with spot-watt measurements provide accurate information at a relatively low cost.

The lighting example discussed above generally applies to other energy using equipment as well. All the methods for estimating kW and operating hours discussed above were used in one or more of the project examples presented in the Annex A, with the exception that no example used the kW of "most efficient replacement equipment" for either lighting or motor baseline.

Simplified application - estimating the energy use baseline for a lighting project

The discussion above focused on how an energy efficiency baseline can be established for a specific piece of energy using equipment. Energy efficiency projects typically involve large numbers of equipment at many different sites. For example, the Mexico AIJ energy efficiency project, Ilumex, targeted lighting across many residences. Most energy efficiency projects target a specific sector and end-use (*e.g.* residential lighting, industrial sector motor drive, commercial sector lighting and refrigeration in food service applications). As a result, the baseline must address energy consumption across many pieces of equipment in a selected sector.

While the details of energy use baseline assessment vary, the general approach in most applications is composed of a common set of elements. The basic steps in developing a baseline for an energy efficiency project again start with the standard engineering algorithm. Continuing to use lighting as the example, the algorithm for the project energy use baseline becomes:

---

[115] While interval metering has not been common for use in energy use baseline development in developing countries, it has been used after the installation of the energy efficiency equipment to monitor how well the equipment is working. Extending this post-installation interval metering to pre-/post-metering that also provides baseline estimates is not difficult and the costs of metering equipment are rapidly declining with more variants of equipment available.

Equation 3, Calculation of energy use baseline for energy efficiency project:

Baseline for Lighting Energy Use (kWh)   = *Average Power (kW)*
                                              x *Average Hours of Operation*
                                              x Number of Sites

The energy use baseline needs to represent the average[116] equipment energy use as determined in the data collection. This is done by selecting a sample of project participants, collecting data on kW and hours of operation for the sample (as discussed above) and using the mean values of these sample data as estimates for average use for all project participants.[117] Note that there is no need to establish the total energy used for lighting since the role of the energy use baseline is to assist in estimating the change in energy use due to the sites participating in the project. This change equation is shown below:

Equation 4: calculation of energy savings from energy efficiency CDM projects

Energy Savings at Site (i)   = *[(Baseline Lighting Use) - (New More*
                                  Efficient Lighting Use)]
                                  x *[No. of Fixtures at Site (i)]*

Total project energy savings is the sum of the site energy savings across all project participants.

Simplified application - converting energy use to GHG emissions

Once baseline electricity use has been established, it still is necessary to translate the electricity use into GHG emissions. The conversion of electricity use into GHG emissions is the subject of a separate case study on methodologies for emission baselines in the electricity sector (see Electricity Case Study).

---

[116] It may also be useful to consider developing energy use baselines based on a "better than average" equipment energy use. This may warrant further examination.

[117] As discussed earlier, instead of using the average efficiency level of existing equipment in the field, another option is to use the average or even the highest efficiency level of equipment being sold as replacements. Compromises can also be made where replacement equipment is estimated to have an efficiency between that of the in-field equipment and highest available efficiency. This assumes that a fraction of the participants would have purchased the most-efficient equipment. In such cases, "better than average" efficiency might be appropriate.

186

4.4.2   Essential steps in baseline construction

This section summarises the basic steps constructing baselines for energy efficiency projects. The baseline setting approach comprises six steps, namely:

1. *Define project participation criteria.* One of the most important steps is to develop criteria for participation in the energy efficiency project. This sets the initial project boundaries and defines the population whose energy use is to be represented by the estimated baseline. For example, the population of potential project participants might include all residences in a geographic area, or all commercial buildings over 1,000 square metres in five major cities.

2. *Determine sample size.* The sample size is determined using appropriate techniques; however, for lighting projects, sample sizes of between 60 and 100 participants have been adequate.

3. *Draw baseline sample.* Once criteria are established for participation and the sample size is determined, the next step is to draw the sample from the population of eligible participants. Data are collected on these sample participants and used to develop the energy use baseline.

4. *Determine method for estimating power and operational and performance factors for the baseline sample.* For the sample, power (kW) and operating hours are estimated using the methods presented in section 4.4.1.

5. *Establish energy use baseline.* Using the operational and performance data collected in Step 4, the project energy use baseline is estimated from the baseline energy use calculated for the sample.

6. *Calculate corresponding GHG emissions baseline.* Here, the baseline energy use is translated into GHG emissions.

The data collection and analysis for estimating the energy use for a lighting fixture or piece of equipment can be approached in a number of ways, depending on time and cost constraints. In developing countries, the survey- and field-intensive data collection methods are often preferable to installing measurement equipment since the cost of capital and technology is often well above the cost of labour. In countries without privatised electricity markets, there can be high amounts of unmetred electricity use both from direct theft and equipment failure. Information in developing countries may also be more difficult to find, for example, public records listing building size and use may not always be available. This poses as many problems for project planning and implementation as it does for baseline construction. Countries with better information and more accurate energy billing will likely be more attractive to host JI and CDM energy efficiency projects.

The use of sampling is important in that it keeps the costs of establishing a baseline using project-specific information manageable. Now, information is required on only a sample of project participants. Since the baseline is based on energy use for the sample, the baseline for a specific site may be, in some cases, inaccurate individually. However, if a large number of sites participate in the energy efficiency project, the baseline aggregate energy savings will be accurate in general. This approach assumes that the sample selected to calculate average consumption is representative of the sites that actually participate in the programme.

Most debates over the quality of the baseline revolve around concerns about whether the sample selected is indeed representative of the project participants and their energy use going forward. As a result, the selection of a sample is often a crucial determinant of a "good" baseline.

As a summary, Figure 4-1 illustrates the baseline energy use estimation challenge.

The line segment AB shows the business-as-usual trend in average energy consumption (per unit of energy service) for a group of customers prior to their participation in an energy efficiency project. The segment B' - C' shows the new trend in energy consumption after participating in the project. The line segment BC shows the business-as-usual energy consumption trend that the participating customers would have been on had they not participated in the project. Project impacts, in terms of reduced energy use, occur after the measures are installed, *i.e.* at time $T = T_{part}$ and are equal to the difference between C and C', *i.e.* the difference between the necessarily estimated baseline consumption C and C', current energy use which can be measured through monitoring the energy efficiency project.

Segment AC represents the energy use per unit of energy service baseline and it needs to account for projected increases in efficiency, technological change, economic growth and other exogenous factors that affect the level of energy use (or emissions) at a facility or region targeted by the CDM project. The basic approach outlined in this section uses the in-field experience of representative project participants and compares that experience to the energy use of project participants after participating in the project. In certain cases, it will be important to review the baseline over time via a participant or comparison group to obtain an estimate of the time trend in baseline energy use. This is represented by line segments AB and BC in Figure 4-1. Additional information on energy use baseline estimation issues - such as free riders, free drivers and self-selection, in the context of energy efficiency programmes, can be found in IEA (1996).

Figure 4-1

Illustration of an energy use (per unit of energy service) baseline estimation

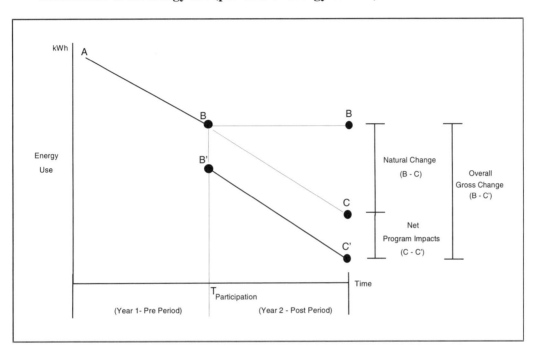

4.4.3   Energy use baseline construction - application to energy efficiency projects and programmes implemented in developing countries

All of the examples of energy efficiency project baselines presented in Annex A used the basic approach discussed above. Two general types of energy efficiency activities are addressed in Annex A: (1) targeted equipment replacement projects (*e.g.* lighting, motors) and (2) audit-based evaluation and installation programmes.

Examples of data collection protocols, which are necessary for the construction of energy use baselines, can be found in the energy efficiency projects and programmes in Annex A. In addition, a number of industrialised countries have created national data sets that are used both in project planning and energy use baseline development. Such data sets could also be created in developing countries and countries with economies in transition. It may be difficult, however, to standardise all of the data inputs required by the algorithms used to set baselines for energy efficiency projects due to project and site diversity. Nonetheless, the baseline-setting process for energy efficiency projects does appear to lend itself to a high degree of standardisation in the general method used as well as guidelines and standards for project-specific data collection (this is further discussed below).

Audit-based programmes as a means of constructing baselines

Several of the energy efficiency examples presented in Annex A involve audit-based programmes where participating facilities underwent an energy audit to determine which energy efficiency measures were the most cost-effective, *i.e.* which achieve the greatest reduction in energy use per dollar expenditure. Significant energy savings can occur when a project combines audits with the implementation of identified energy efficiency measures. This has resulted in a number of combined "audit/implementation" programmes being undertaken in developed countries and several of the Annex A examples represent programmes of this type.

Audits typically examine a comprehensive set of measures spanning a wide range of end-use applications. One advantage of these programmes is their comprehensiveness. Since audits are designed to examine all major energy end-uses, there are few lost opportunities at a site (*i.e.* few cost-effective measures not identified). In addition to equipment replacement options, audits will generally examine thermal shell measures such as wall and ceiling insulation, high-efficiency windows and using light-coloured roofing materials to reflect heat from the building. A second advantage is that audits are more likely to examine interactions among installed energy efficiency measures. For example, reducing lighting wattage will also reduce the cooling requirements of a commercial space.

The audit process uses the same algorithms discussed above and the process can be standardised, even to the extent of having common software packages developed for specific types of assessments. One difference is that the population of participants undergoes an audit. In some cases, a sample of participants will be given a more detailed audit, supported by run-time and kWh metering, to calibrate less rigorous audits that may borrow data from other similar audits (*e.g.* an audit of one commercial building may borrow data on lighting intensity per square metre from an earlier audit of a similar building). In this instance, all the basic steps for baseline construction discussed above, including sampling, still apply. However, the baseline estimation problem is simplified because all participants undergo an energy audit, which establishes the baseline energy use at that site. The energy use baseline for the project is then the sum of each project participant's audit baseline.

One concern might be that the auditor would have an incentive to overstate current energy consumption, thereby inflating the estimated energy savings from measures installed at that site. However, there are a number of controls that can be implemented to reduce the likelihood that this will occur. Three such controls are:

- Audit standards and protocols can be established. For example, several professional associations offer training and certify energy professionals as "energy auditors". Several universities also have programmes that provide similar credentials.

190

- Audits are designed such that the sum of energy used in all end-uses equals the total measured consumption as shown on bills or as metre reads. This helps prevent egregious errors in energy baseline assessment.

- The auditors themselves can be audited. A number of audit-based programmes have had provisions where outside professionals would re-audit a sample of facilities to assess the quality of the work.

4.5   Standardising Baseline Assumptions

This section employs the energy-use baseline construction methods from the Annex A examples to develop several options for preparing energy use baselines and standardised protocols. Lighting and motor replacement programmes are the focus of this section to allow specific options to be developed, but the general conclusions can be applied to any equipment replacement project or audit programme.

Several of the examples in Annex A estimate a reference case or baseline for energy use as part of a larger impact evaluation or market assessment study. These examples did not focus on baseline construction per se, but instead concentrated on estimating and monitoring the post-installation energy use of the energy-efficient technologies promoted by the project. For many energy efficiency projects in developing countries (and even in developed countries), it is generally assumed that the project is cost-effective. After all, older less-efficient equipment is being replaced by more efficient equipment.

As a result, the primary concern in many studies of energy efficiency projects in developing countries was not energy use baseline estimation but, instead, the focus was on the appropriate installation, operation and maintenance of the new energy efficient equipment. In many cases, there was limited experience with the new equipment in developing countries and there was concern over how to install and operate the equipment to obtain maximum benefits. Consequently, the methods of constructing energy use baselines for a number of the energy efficiency projects in Annex A were generally not well documented and were supported by relatively little data.

In the case of JI and CDM energy efficiency projects, there will clearly need to be a greater focus on the baselines. CDM or JI project developers (and the international community) will be concerned about the actual magnitude of energy saved (not just whether the programme exceeds a cost-effectiveness threshold) and the corresponding GHG emission reductions. For this reason, historically-applied energy use baseline methods in developing countries may not be an appropriate roadmap for future JI and CDM baselines.

191

Table 4-2

Summary of implications for standardisation from energy efficiency case studies

(See Annex A for further details)

Sector/End Use	Energy Use Baseline Development Approach	Implications for Baseline Standardisation for Energy Efficiency Projects
Residential and non-residential lighting (Thailand)	▪ A sampling protocol was developed to collect on-site data for estimating typical operating parameters for all project participants. ▪ Calibrated engineering algorithms were used to compute baseline energy usage. ▪ Performance parameters were verified via on-site spot measurements and data logging.	▪ Develop standardised calculation procedures using algorithms similar to those used in this project. Build "efficiency timeline" considerations (e.g. persistence) into algorithms. ▪ Develop standardised performance parameters (e.g. operating hours) in the residential and commercial sectors. ▪ Develop standardised sampling and data collection protocols in order to allow data collected from a sample of sites to be representative of all project sites.
Residential and non-residential lighting (Pakistan)	▪ A sampling protocol was developed to collect on-site data for compiling building and energy system features that characterise the entire population. ▪ Detailed on-site audits were conducted for a sample of buildings for all major end uses.	▪ Develop standardised sampling and data collection protocols in order to allow data collected from a sample of sites to be representative of all potential project sites.
Residential lighting (Mexico)	▪ A sampling protocol was developed to leverage information across sites. ▪ Surveys were used to estimate the number and wattage of lamps installed. ▪ Actual watt savings and operating hours were verified via on-site spot measurements and data logging.	▪ Develop standardised performance parameters (e.g. operating hours) in the residential sector. ▪ Develop standardised sampling and data collection protocols in order to allow data collected from a sample of sites to be representative of all project sites.

(continued)

Table 4-2

Sector/End Use	Energy Use Baseline Development Approach	Implications for Baseline Standardisation for Energy Efficiency Projects
All major end uses in residential, commercial and industrial sectors (national assessment) and residential lighting (pilot study) (Morocco)	■ A sampling protocol was developed to collect on-site data for estimating typical operating parameters for all programme participants. ■ Surveys and interviews with samples of end-users to collect detailed information on all major end uses. ■ Baseline energy used initially estimated with engineering algorithms. ■ Energy savings estimated via a statistically-adjusted engineering approach using billing data and samples of end-use metered sites.	■ Develop standardised calculation procedures using algorithms similar to those used in this project. ■ Build "efficiency timeline" considerations (e.g. persistence) into algorithms. ■ Develop standardised performance parameters (e.g. operating hours) in residential and commercial sectors. ■ Develop standardised sampling and data collection protocols in order to allow data collected from a sample of sites to be representative of all project sites.
Commercial and industrial electric motors (Mexico)	■ A sampling protocol was developed to facilitate data collection. ■ Detailed on-site audits were conducted for a sample of sites to collect data on technical performance and operating characteristics.	■ Develop standardised sampling and data collection protocols. Sampling and in-field data collection protocols could be developed to follow standardised guidelines for use in developing baselines using project-specific data.
Agricultural tubewell water pumping (Pakistan)	■ Detailed on-site audits were conducted to collect data on technical performance and operating characteristics. ■ Baseline pre-retrofit operating data and energy usage were determined from the on-site data.	■ This project indicates that sampling and in-field data collection protocols could be developed that follow standardised guidelines. ■ In general, operational and performance parameters were determined from site-specific audits.
Commercial and industrial boilers (Pakistan)	■ A sampling plan and protocol were developed. ■ Detailed on-site audits were conducted for a sample of sites to collect data on technical performance and operating characteristics.	■ This project indicates that sampling and in-field data collection protocols that follow standardised guidelines could be developed. ■ Site-specific operational and performance parameters were determined by energy audits.

Table 4-2 presents an overview and summary of seven examples of energy efficiency projects and programmes in developing countries. A full discussion of the examples is found in Annex A. For the reasons cited above, these examples were generally weak in their documentation of energy use baseline assumptions and reporting of statistical information. This may indicate a need to develop reporting guidelines for JI and CDM energy efficiency projects explicitly requesting this type of information.

4.5.1   Determining standard baseline performance

This section assesses the different options for constructing energy baselines in the lighting and electric motors sectors, with emphasis on how standard approaches might be used to simplify energy use baseline construction. In each instance, examples are drawn from Annex A to show how these options have already been - and are currently being - adapted to a certain extent in the examination of energy efficiency projects in developing countries.

Factors that tend to support or limit standardisation possibilities include:

- Energy use characteristics of the market segment. Constructing energy use baselines requires information on the particular consumption patterns of market segments. Energy consumption patterns may be more uniform in one segment than another and this supports the standardisation of consumption values and indices. In addition, equipment performance (*e.g.* efficiency) for certain technologies may be relatively uniform across segments, but operating characteristics (*e.g.* operating hours) may vary and each may have characteristics that are unique to, or typical of, that sector/segment.

- Homogeneity of markets. Residential applications tend to be more homogenous than industrial, for example. Thus, more opportunities exist to standardise energy use characteristics in the residential sector. As a general rule, moving across the market segment spectrum from residential to industrial, energy markets are increasingly heterogeneous and less subject to overall standardisation.

- Technology performance variability. End uses that tend to have more constant performance characteristics lend themselves to greater standardisation of baseline performance. For example, residential refrigerator energy use tends to be relatively uniform within certain categories and lighting systems tend to show more constant performance characteristics (they are either on or off and may have well defined operating hours). Space heating and cooling, on the other hand, are very weather dependent and have variable output and efficiency characteristics. Energy use baseline construction needs to account for this variability.

There are essentially three options available for energy use baseline standardisation for energy efficiency projects. They are:

- Standardising baseline calculation methods and data collection protocols. The algorithms and models used to compute energy use and the data that provide inputs to the algorithms.

- Standardising operating and performance parameters. The values that describe the energy use characteristics of a given technology or end use, such as lamp wattage for lighting and motor efficiency for electric motors.

- Standardising energy use indices. Indices that are representative of the energy use of a population of technologies or segment of the population, such as lighting kWh per square metre for certain commercial building types.

Each of these options is discussed below along with insights from the examples presented in Annex A.

4.5.2   Standard calculation and data protocols - lighting and motors

One option is to standardise baseline calculation methods (*i.e.* algorithms and models), baseline data requirements and collection methods for different energy efficiency applications. To a certain extent, this has already been done through and EPRI impact analysis literature (EPRI, 1991, 1995a, 1995b, 1996) and the IPMVP protocols (US DOE, 1997). This body of work has universal applications for energy use assessment and could provide a sound theoretical and methodological basis for the development of energy use baselines for CDM projects in developing countries.

Standard calculation and data collection protocols for lighting

As noted in Equation 3, the annual energy consumption for a population of lighting devices is a function of power draw (input wattage to the fixture) and operating hours. Data for each of the parameters need to be collected or estimated.

Standardisation of the calculation algorithms, data requirements to support those algorithms and data collection protocols would help promote the application of appropriate procedures and reduce the uncertainty in baseline construction faced by JI or CDM project developers. Wattage and operating hours could be estimated from technical data tables, engineering methods, or a sample of field observations. Standardised guidelines could be prepared to lend uniformity and consistency to these data collection tasks for energy efficiency projects. Three of the energy efficiency examples in Annex A provide some insights on the application of this approach:

- The Thailand CFL lighting replacement project (in progress) has planned to employ a uniform calculation methodology similar in format to Equation 3 for estimating programme impacts and systematic data collection methods supplemented by in-field and bench test spot-watt measurements. Calculation algorithms and spot-watt measurements for estimating input wattage similar to those used in Thailand could be standardised for similar lighting projects.

- The Mexico Ilumex project used the wattage of the incandescent lamps replaced by the programme as the baseline. Compact fluorescent lamp wattages were determined from spot-watt measurements and operating hours were estimated from a sample of on-site, run-time measurements. Spot-watt measurements and run-time data collection protocols and sampling techniques similar to those used in this project could be standardised to estimate operating hour assumptions for other residential sector lighting projects. In the commercial sector, a similar process could be used to standardise lighting operating hours, although it would be necessary to disaggregate the results by market segment.

- The Morocco residential Lighting Pilot Project employed standard engineering algorithms with well-developed and fundamentally sound data collection techniques. Engineering estimates of savings were developed using the following algorithm:

$$
\begin{aligned}
\textit{Energy Savings} \quad &= \textit{(Watts}_{incandescent} - \textit{Watts}_{CFL}\textit{)} \\
&\quad x \textit{ Operating Hours} \\
&\quad x \textit{ (1 + Take Back Factor)}
\end{aligned}
$$

The approach used in this project provides an example of methods that could be standardised for cross-sector baseline development that accounts for factors such as urban and rural energy use variation.

All three examples of lighting projects employed a similar approach to baseline energy use construction using a general energy use algorithm similar to Equation 1. Differences in data collection methods were found in the examples examined; however, no information is available from these examples on how the different data collection techniques might have influenced the baselines. In general, it is believed that it would not have been appropriate to use a standardised set of data across countries. Data on the technologies deployed and their operating conditions unique to each country would most likely be required to develop appropriate baselines. However, a common (standardised) approach to collecting the data, using state-of-the-practice techniques, could be shared across all three countries.

Standard calculation and data collection protocols for motors

Annual energy consumption for a population of motors can also be characterised by an algorithm similar to Equation 1. Energy use is then characterised by motor size, efficiency and operating hours. While the basic energy algorithm is simple, energy use baseline development depends on values for each of these parameters. Data for each of the parameters need to be collected or estimated. As a general guide, the number of motors by horsepower category is collected and tabulated at either the site or population level (population of motors within a market or market segment to which the efficiency project will apply). Efficiency and operating hours, on the other hand, must be estimated from technical data, engineering methods or a limited sample of field observations.

For example, the Mexico industrial motors efficiency project discussed in Annex A used a standard engineering algorithm to compute energy use for both standard and energy-efficient motors. This is a typical approach for motor applications and is well suited to a standardised methodology.

4.5.3   *Standardising operating and performance parameters - lighting and motors*

Equation 1 identified the generic types of operating and performance parameters that need to be known or estimated in order to develop baseline energy use for an end-use or sector. For many common energy efficiency applications, it is possible to define typical baseline values for operating and performance parameters. Parameters such as operating hours, efficiency and power draw lend themselves to standardisation within certain sectors and applications. For example, experience with demand-side management programmes in developed countries has shown that it is possible to tabulate baseline efficiencies for common types and sizes of electric motors. This would be a reasonable option to undertake for a country or for selected regions. While the authors are not aware of a study that has been conducted to validate any specific regional delineation, it is likely that areas such as Central America could share a common data set and possibly portions of Asia and Africa. However, the homogeneity of any region can only be known after the data are collected and analysed in a variance/co-variance analysis.

The standardisation of baseline operating and performance parameters does not, of itself, establish the baseline energy use for energy efficiency projects. However, it reduces the time and cost of estimating the energy use baseline for project developers and brings greater uniformity and consistency to the CDM/JI baseline development process. Developing parameter values that err on the conservative side could minimise uncertainty and opportunities for gaming the system, while maintaining reasonable incentives for investors. Examples of "conservative" parameter values are presented below for lighting and motors projects.

Standardised operating and performance parameters for lighting

Performance parameters such as fixture input wattages could be standardised for typical fixture types. The average input wattage for common types of fixtures, lamps and ballasts can be estimated from manufacturers' data and verified with a sample of in-situ spot measurements or bench tests. Variations in manufacturers' products in different countries could complicate this process, although there are typically only a few dominant manufacturers in each country. The standardisation of operating and performance parameters would be applicable to the most common types of devices, particularly in residential and commercial applications. For example, baseline data on wattages for common types of incandescent and fluorescent residential and commercial lighting fixtures could be established, whereas large industrial projects such as stadium lighting would most likely be based on specific site data. Even though it would be difficult to standardise operating and performance parameters for these types of industrial projects, analytic and data collection methodologies could still be standardised.

Operating hours and the diversity factor are examples of parameters needed to compute energy use for a population of lighting devices and lend themselves to standardisation within certain limitations. Operating hours tend to be relatively consistent within specific market segments (particularly in the residential and commercial sectors) and could be conservatively standardised. Operating hours, however, are variable by market sector/segment. Establishing these baseline values would require end-use load research on a country-by-country, or possibly regional, basis. For example, residential lighting operating hours are typically 1000-1100 annually and commercial office lighting applications are in the 3500-4000 range. With a reasonable sample of observations, these could be conservatively estimated across a sector or segment by selecting the lower end of this range. This would still provide a reasonable incentive to potential project developers, while assuring that energy savings are not overestimated. The same reasoning applies to other performance factors. For example, fluorescent ballast input wattages for different lamp/ballast combinations vary by manufacturer. By selecting a set of input wattages for the most common/standard fixture types that tend toward the lower end of the range, a conservative baseline condition is established. This approach has been applied in North American DSM projects. Baseline development for a lighting energy efficiency project applied across a broad market in a country may require an estimate of the quantity of lighting devices by type and input wattage.

Examples from Annex A showing how operating and performance parameters can be estimated include:

- The Thailand CFL lighting replacement project has planned to estimate average input wattages for each lamp type promoted by the programme and average operating hours for the participant population. A similar approach could be taken for common lamp, ballast and fixture configurations and for lighting operating hours. In order to support realistic incentives to project sponsors, it would be desirable and possible to differentiate operational parameters such as operating hours by market segments.

- The Mexico Ilumex project estimated input wattages from a sample of spot-watt measurements and operating hours from a sample of on-site, run-time tests. Wattages and operating hours are summarised in Table 4-3. Average run-time hours were applied to all project participants in this project. This was a residential sector project and, since operating hours tend to be relatively uniform across the residential sector, this represents a reasonable approach to standardising a key performance parameter. Again, in the commercial sector (*e.g.* office buildings, convenience stores and schools) lighting operating hours could be standardised by market segment.

Table 4-3

Lamp performance data (Mexico Ilumex project)

Baseline Incandescent (Watts)	CFL Watts		Daily Hours of Operation
	Nominal	**Measured**	
100	23	21.1	3
75	20	17.8	3
60	15	16.1	3

- The Morocco DSM market research study and the residential lighting pilot produced a valuable dataset of energy use characteristics. This project provides an excellent example of an approach that could be employed to develop standardised performance and operating parameters in selected market sectors. Examples of operating and performance parameters from this study that could potentially be standardised include:

    – Residential sector: average number of lamps per household, average baseline lamp wattages and average lamp operating hours for both urban and rural customers. Table 4-4 summarises the lighting characteristics determined by the market research study.

Table 4-4

Summary of lighting characteristics by urban and rural areas

	Urban	Rural
Average Number of Lamps per Household	9	6
Average Wattage of Lamps	93	87
Average Daily Hours of Use	2	2

Source: USAID, 1997

    – Commercial sector: input wattages by lighting type (incandescent, fluorescent, halogen and compact fluorescent) and average daily operating

199

hours by facility type. Table 4-5 summarises commercial indoor lighting characteristics found by the market research study.

Table 4-5

Summary of commercial indoor lighting (Morocco DSM research study)

Type of Lighting	Average Number of Units Per Facility	Average Wattage	Average Daily Hours of Use
Fluorescent Lamps	263	53	10
Incandescent Lamps	269	93	6.5
Halogen Lamps	39	262	9.2
Compact Fluorescent Lamps	47	22	6.6

Source: USAID, 1997

These lighting examples and the wide range of experience in developed countries show that it would be possible to develop a set of standardised operating and performance parameters for energy efficiency projects in the lighting sector. Table 4-6 gives an example of a framework for organising lighting performance data that has been successfully employed in North American DSM projects. These parameters would be used in Equation 1 to build up an estimate of the energy use baseline for the given market or market segment to which the project may apply. It is important to note that the actual datasets would most likely need to be developed on a country-by-country (or at least regional) basis to account for the particularities of the local market and the mix of technologies deployed in each market segment.

Table 4-6

Framework example of standardised baseline parameters for lighting efficiency projects

Efficiency Project	Lamp/Ballast/ Fixture Type	Baseline Equipment Performance Parameters		Baseline Operating Parameters	
		Lighting Type	Input Watts/ Lamp/Ballast/ Fixture	Sector/ Segment	Operating Hours
High-Efficiency	Type 1	Standard	w_1	Sector 1	h_1
Lamp/Ballast/Fixture	Type 2	fluorescent	w_2	Sector 2	h_2
Replacements	...	lamps/	...	...	...
	Type n	ballasts	w_n	Sector n	h_n
Compact Fluorescent	Type 1	Incandescent	w_1	Sector 1	h_1
Lamp Replacements	Type 2	lamps	w_2	Sector 2	h_2
	...		...	...	...
	Type n		w_n	Sector n	h_n

200

Standardised operating and performance parameters for motors

Performance parameters such as motor efficiencies could be standardised. This is particularly true for certain types of motors. The average efficiency for each horsepower can be estimated from manufacturers' data. Standardisation would be most applicable for certain motor types and size ranges that are most common in the commercial sector and certain industrial applications. For example, DSM applications in North America have typically developed baseline efficiencies for motors in two frame types (open drip-proof and totally enclosed fan-cooled), four speeds (900, 1200, 1800 and 3600 RPM) and horsepowers ranging from 1 to 200. Similarly, it may be possible to standardise assumptions for these types, sizes, classes and applications of motors in developing countries.

Operating hours, load factor and diversity factor are parameters needed to compute energy use for a population of motors and lend themselves to standardisation within certain limitations. Operating hours tend to be relatively consistent within specific market segments - particularly in the commercial sector - and could be conservatively standardised. Operating hours, however, are variable by market sector/segment. Establishing these baseline values would require end-use load research on a country-by-country, or possibly regional, basis. For example, operating hours for 3-shift industrial plants may well be over 8000 per year, whereas commercial ventilation fans might be only 3500 - 4000. A reasonable sample of these could be analysed and a conservative estimate selected from the lower end of this range. For example, motor efficiencies for different types and sizes of standard-efficiency motors vary by manufacturer. By selecting a set of efficiencies that tend toward the upper end of the range in each category, a conservative baseline condition is established.

Insights on the potential standardisation of parameters in motors projects from the examples presented in Annex A include:

- The Mexico motor efficiency project examined motors that ranged in size from 15 to 600 hp with 70% of the motors in the range of 1-20 hp. Figure 4-2 presents a distribution of motors by horsepower. This type of information and data organisation is necessary to quantify baseline energy use for an end use such as electric motors. Typically, certain types of common motors under 200 hp fall into fairly consistent efficiency ranges, whereas larger motors and motors of custom or specialised construction are evaluated on a unit-by-unit basis. The largest fraction of the motors in this study would then be likely candidates for the standardisation of at least baseline efficiencies.

Figure 4-2

Distribution of motors by horsepower (Mexico Motors Replacement Project)

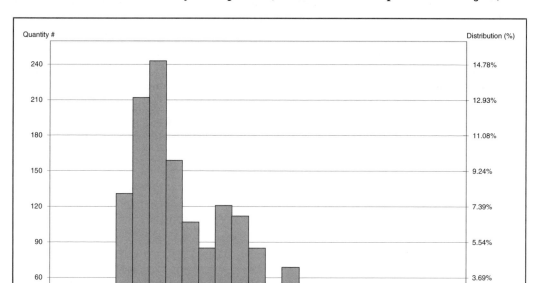

- The Pakistan ENERCON project tabulated data on over 350 electric motors in buildings. Data were recorded on maximum rated demand (kW) and operating hours. It does not appear that efficiency information was either available or recorded for the project. However, for a sample of this size, it would be possible with a carefully constructed study to develop standardised values for certain operating parameters such as operating hours for certain motor applications (*e.g.* HVAC fan motors) in selected market segments. Table 4-7 presents a distribution of motors by application and maximum rated demand determined by the project.

Table 4-7

Distribution of electric motors by application and demand

Motor Application	Number of Motors by Maximum Rated Demand (kW)					
	<1	1-2	2-5	5-10	10-20	>20
Air Compressors	2	-	-	-	-	-
Air Movement	12	-	3	24	24	5
Boiler Systems	-	2	12	-	-	-
Chiller Systems	-	-	25	-	-	5
Cooling Towers	-	6	-	12	19	2
Lifts	-	-	5	9	6	6
Water Pumping	9	7	18	4	19	10
Other	-	-	43	22	31	2

Source: Hagler Bailly Services Inc., 1990

An example of a framework for organising baseline efficiency data for motor efficiency projects that has been used in North American DSM projects is shown in Table 4-8.

Table 4-8

**Framework example for standardised energy use
baseline motor efficiencies for energy efficiency projects**

Motor HP	Open Drip-Proof RPM				Totally Enclosed Fan-Cooled RPM			
	900	1200	1800	3600	900	1200	1800	3600
1	e_1	e_1	E_1	e_1	e_1	e_1	e_1	e_1
2	e_2	e_2	E_2	e_2	e_2	e_2	e_2	e_2
...	...	...	...	...	...	...	...	...
200	e_{200}	e_{200}	e_{200}	e_{200}	e_{200}	e_{200}	e_{200}	e_{200}

4.5.4 Energy use indices - lighting and motors

Another level of standardisation for energy use baselines, in the context of energy efficiency projects, involves the development of unit energy use indices by sector, segment and/or end use. Energy use indices such as kWh/square metre can be useful for characterising energy use within a market segment or end use and in some cases could serve as baseline values. For example, commercial lighting end-use intensities could be defined by market segment and used as baseline values, particularly for new building construction projects. In the residential sector, it would be possible to construct energy use baseline consumption values such as annual kWh/appliance. Similarly, in the industrial sector, it may be possible to develop annual kWh/unit of production values within a country for selected industries.

Standardised energy use indices (EUI) for lighting

For the commercial sector, indoor lighting EUIs (*e.g.* lighting kWh/square metre) could be developed by market segment. While EUIs are useful for general comparison purposes, they could also serve as commercial sector baselines in certain market segments such as offices, schools and hospitals. For example, energy efficiency efforts following the energy crisis of the 1970s were successful in reducing lighting power densities in US commercial office buildings from 38-43 watts/square metre to 27-32 watts/square metre and progressive standards and DSM efforts were successful in further reducing this value (particularly in new construction) to 15-22 watts/square metre by the 1990s. EUIs are probably less useful in the industrial sector, where a hybrid baseline approach (*i.e.* combining standardisation with project-specific elements) would be more generally applicable. In this case, performance parameters such as input wattages for each common fixture type could be standardised and operating parameters would be site/project-specific. The examples from Annex A include:

- The ENERCON project in Pakistan collected detailed information from on-site audits for a sample of 50 buildings. These data could be used to support the development of baseline values for a wide range of energy indices for both the residential and non-residential sectors. In lighting, it appears that the necessary data were collected to develop baseline lighting power densities (*i.e.* watts/square metre) for a sample of building types. This is useful in characterising baseline energy use.

- The EGAT lighting replacement project in Thailand has planned to develop average load shape profiles for both residential and non-residential lighting from the on-site runtime data collection effort.

- The Moroccan DSM potential and market assessment study produced a valuable set of information on energy use characteristics within all major customer sectors. Among the results of the study were end-use energy breakdowns and load shapes. These data form useful benchmarks for understanding energy use within a county and market sector and, while not explicitly included in this study, these types of data could be used to produce useful indices such as annual lighting energy use per household in the residential sector and lighting energy use per square metre for key segments of the commercial sector.

These examples from the case studies demonstrate the potential for standardising selected energy use indices and per-unit values. As a further example, baseline office lighting energy use for new construction could be defined for a given country as follows:

Baseline lighting intensity = 27 watts/square metre
Standardised operating hours for office buildings = 3500 hours per year
Baseline energy use intensity = 27 watts/sq. metre. x 3500 hours per year
= 94.5 kWh/sq. metre

Table 4-9 provides another framework example of EUI development for the commercial sector.

Table 4-9

Framework example for lighting energy use indices

Segment	Lighting Energy Use (MWh/yr)	Floor Stock (Sq. metre	Lighting EUI (kWh/Sq. metre
Office	MWh_o	sf_o	eui_o
Retail	MWh_r	sf_r	eui_r
...	...	...	...
Misc.	MWh_m	sf_m	eui_m

Standardised energy use indices for motors

For the commercial sector, motor energy use indices such as kWh/square metre tend to be less useful because motor energy use is often tabulated or subsumed in other end uses, primarily space heating and cooling. In the industrial sector however, since motors are often the primary energy-consuming devices, it may be useful to develop baseline motor energy consumption indices related to unit of production (motor kWh/unit of production) for selected industries. Table 4-10 presents a framework example of how this type of index could be formulated.

Table 4-10

Framework example for electric motor energy use intensities

Sector Segment	Motor Energy Use (kWh/yr)	Production Units	Motor EUI (kWh/Unit)
Segment 1	KWh_1	u_1	eui_1
Segment 2	KWh_2	u_2	eui_2
...	...	...	...
Segment n	KWh_n	u_n	eui_n

4.5.5 Data issues

The challenges to implementing standardisation opportunities should not be understated. Given that much of the methodology, approach and data structure has already been established in the energy efficiency industries in industrialised nations and that this infrastructure could be transferred to developing nations, the primary challenge lies in the data themselves. From the perspective of setting baselines for common energy efficiency measures, key data challenges include:

- *Cost and time of collection.* Data collection can be expensive and time consuming. Skilled labour in the form of trained energy analysts and auditors is also required.

- *Management and maintenance.* End-use data systems require management and maintenance. That is, data need to be systematically organised so that relevant data can be accessed and manipulated for the needs of different projects.

- *The need for supplemental sources.* The data sets available for the assessment of efficiency opportunities are rarely a perfect fit for a given project. Each project invariably has somewhat unique data needs. This typically requires that the analyst developing the baseline supplement the data on hand from other sources. This is not to diminish the value of the initial data, however, because a foundation dataset, often at the country level, invariably reduces the time and cost of developing a unique dataset for the project at hand, by allowing existing data to be leveraged with new data specifically designed to make the existing data set more representative of project participants.

- *The need to periodically refresh the data.* End-use data sets age over time with advances in energy technology and changes in the energy consuming market. As such, these data need to be periodically refreshed with additional data collection and analysis. The actual time periods at which these data need to be revisited depend on technology advancements, market dynamics and the degree to which

206

energy efficiency initiatives are stimulating the entrance of more-efficient products into the market. However, North American DSM experience suggests that it would be reasonable to refresh baseline energy use datasets every three to five years. The existence of a foundation dataset and protocols that are established from the first phases of developing the data infrastructure make this a much less daunting and costly task.

Several of the examples examined in this case study demonstrate the type of sampling and data collection approach necessary to develop foundation data for energy efficiency analysis and project assessment. Most notably, the Morocco and Pakistan projects provide examples of how this type of information infrastructure project can be executed. In this regard, it is clear that the foundation has been laid (at least in part) for establishing data collection methods to support standardised baseline development for CDM and JI projects in developing countries.

4.6   Issues in constructing baselines

This section discusses a number of issues surrounding baseline estimation. These issues may be of particular importance given the magnitude of the potential benefits that can be expected from the use of energy efficiency projects as an approach for mitigating GHG emissions. Practical baseline estimation methods should seek to balance the interests of the various parties. The issues discussed below address balancing risks in baseline construction, assumptions affecting baseline stringency and potential biases in baseline construction.

4.6.1   *Baseline construction and the potential volume of energy efficiency projects*

The volume of projects undertaken under JI/CDM is a crucial factor in determining the environmental effectiveness of the project-based mechanisms. Several factors could influence potential JI/CDM project developers' willingness to undertake energy efficiency projects. Two important factors are: 1) the balance of risks in the construction of the baseline and 2) how the business deal is determined for project sponsors, *i.e.* is it framed in a manner that will allow project developers to assess the economics of the project?

Balancing risks in energy efficiency projects

For JI and CDM to be successful overall, a large number of projects will have to be implemented. This means that the risks of under-stating baselines (*i.e.* being overly conservative) and thereby understating project benefits should not be so great as to overly discourage potential project developers. At the same time, there must be some assurances

207

that the expected environmental improvements are, in fact, occurring. Different methods or measures could be used to balance these risks. Each is discussed below.[118]

- *Establish the burden of proof that has to be met.* For example, a burden of proof could be set based on a one-tailed 75% confidence interval. As long as the baseline is estimated so that there is only a 75% probability that the "true"[119] baseline would be equal to or lower than the estimated baseline, the baseline is judged to be estimated with the necessary degree of confidence. This is a reasonably high burden of proof. It means that there can be no more than a 25% likelihood that the actual baseline is higher that the baseline estimated for the project. This burden of proof results in the discounting of impacts down to a level that might be judged as a reasonable assurance against over-estimating environmental improvements. The highest discount rates will likely be for projects that focus on only one large site, because reasonable sensitivity analyses around the selected energy use baseline will have large impacts on the estimated emissions reductions at a single site. The process of constructing the 75% confidence interval around a given baseline can be statistical where sampling approaches are used; it can be based on simulation analyses with judgementally assigned probabilities to alternative scenarios; or it can be determined with Bayesian approaches using subjective probability assessment techniques.[120] Regardless of whether the confidence interval is based on sampling and statistics, sensitivity analyses, or expert judgements; the final confidence interval will have to be assessed judgementally, *i.e.* does it span a reasonable range of possible outcomes?

- *Less rigorous baseline estimation approaches can be allowed and the resulting baseline would be discounted.* This provides the project developers with a choice. On the one hand, they could use a simpler estimation method and have a lower energy use baseline, resulting in lower GHG reductions and thus fewer GHG emission credits. On the other, they could use a more sophisticated estimation

---

[118] The US EPA has employed these general methods of balancing risks in awarding SO_2 emission credits to electric utilities as part of its Acid Rain programme and emissions trading process. This is documented in US EPA (1995).

[119] While the "true" baseline will never be known, statistical inference can be used to develop interval estimates around values that cannot be observed. The application of statistical methods requires an accurate definition of the participant population and the use of appropriate sampling methods. In general, statistical methods focus on estimating the pre-project baseline energy use of energy efficiency project participants. Assumptions are required to determine how this initial baseline might change over time in the business-as-usual case. However, establishing a sound estimate of pre-project baseline energy use ensures that benefits in the initial years of the project (*e.g.* five years) will be estimated quite accurately, since it is likely that there would have been little change in energy use patterns over the short term.

[120] There are formal methods for dimensioning the uncertainty around judgements. These are discussed in EPRI (1991).

approach with larger number of in-field measurements and potentially obtain a greater number of emissions reduction credits (*i.e.* less or no discounting of emissions would be done).

- *The rate at which energy reductions are translated into GHG emissions could be fixed.* A key uncertainty for JI and CDM energy efficiency project developers is the rate at which energy reductions are translated into GHG emissions. This rate can be set in advance to remove this uncertainty for project sponsors. It is important that the project developers have some certainty over time with respect to the emissions reduction credits they receive for each kWh of electricity conserved. Setting an emissions rate awarded per kWh for a period of time through electricity multi-project baselines (which would be fixed for given period of time) is probably the most significant standardisation action that could be taken, since it would encourage all forms of energy efficiency projects across all sectors. It is possible that the difference in electrical system emissions rates per kWh could vary across peak and off-peak periods.

- *A fixed baseline crediting lifetime could be set for energy efficiency projects.* The length of time during which a baseline is considered valid for calculating a particular energy efficiency CDM project's GHG emission reductions (and thus emission credits) could be limited. After that period of time, it would be equivalent to assuming that the baseline is no longer valid. The authors recommend a five-year crediting lifetime. This is based on a subjective assessment, but one factor influencing the choice of this term is the payback periods seen for most energy efficiency projects. Holding the baseline set for five years would provide project sponsors with a planning period long enough to recover their costs and earn a return on a wide variety of energy efficiency projects, *i.e.* it is a timeframe that would not unduly reduce the number of economically viable projects available to developers.[121] While the recommendation is that the baseline be set for five years, that is not the same as holding the baseline constant. The baseline could be set such that energy efficiency is assumed to increase at a given rate over the five-year period. However, once the baseline terms are set, they should be kept in place so that they provide project sponsors with a five-year planning horizon.

These methods[122] have been undertaken in North America in the case of traditional energy efficiency projects and programmes, but may require further examination with respect to their application in the context of CDM/JI.

---

[121] No specific decision is likely to be appropriate in all circumstances. Where a fast moving energy-efficient technology can be identified that is expected to change the market in less than five years, then it may be appropriate to hold the baseline constant for a period of less than five years. The five-year recommendation for holding the baseline constant is a subjective decision.

[122] These types of risk balancing measures have been taken by agencies in North America responsible for overseeing energy efficiency projects of US$100 million or more, with potential for monetary incentives to be paid to project sponsors that are in the tens of millions of dollars. In

4.6.2 Potential biases in baseline construction: free riders and spillover effects

Two main issues that arise in estimating an energy efficiency project's contribution to GHG emissions reductions based on a baseline are the potential for free riders and project spillover:

Free riders. Free riders are defined as those that would obtain emission credits for whole projects that would have gone ahead in the absence of CDM/JI projects (for more information see Ellis and Bosi, 1999). The concern is that a large number of free riders could inflate the number of projects and resulting emission credits. The free-rider issue is a baseline estimation problem that stems from a systematic bias in the construction of the baseline.

There are many types of free riders. A full free rider is an entity that would have installed the same set of energy efficiency measures at the same point in time as they did under the offered energy efficiency project. A partial free rider is an entity that would have installed some, but not all of the energy efficiency measures offered by the project or would have installed the measures, but at a later time. In most instances, there are likely to be more partial free riders than full free riders.

Spillover effects[123]. These are additional energy efficiency impacts that result from the project, but are viewed as indirect rather than direct impacts. These can occur through a variety of channels including 1) an energy-using facility hearing about an energy efficiency project-sponsored measure from a participant and deciding to pursue it on his or her own (the so-called free-driver effect); 2) project participants who undertake additional, but unaided (*e.g.* without CDM emission credits), energy efficiency actions based on positive experience with the project; 3) equipment manufacturers changing the efficiency of their products and/or retailers and wholesalers changing the composition of their inventories to reflect the demand for more efficient goods created by the project; and 4) governments adopting new building codes or appliance standards because of improvements to equipment resulting from energy efficiency projects (*e.g.* the US DOE's Energy Star Programme). Together, these effects can transform the market for energy-related equipment in a positive manner and they are a consequence of a project developer's energy efficiency project offerings.

Theoretically, spillover impacts should be identified and measured as benefits to energy efficiency projects. Practically, they are difficult to identify and measure. However, some

---

this context, a survey of twelve US states viewed to be leaders in the promotion of energy efficiency found that each state believed it was able to design oversight procedures that meet the baseline estimation challenges, *i.e.* provide assurances that impacts were accurately estimated and that any financial incentives paid were warranted. See NARUC (1994).

[123] Good discussions of spillover and market transformation can be found in Violette (1996) and EPRI (1995A, chapter 6).

of the attempts to measure spillover in areas that have had an energy efficiency project in place for a period of time has shown that these impacts can be large.

When spillover and free riders are taken together, the end result is that there are two difficult-to-quantify baseline estimation biases that work in opposite directions. Some regulatory jurisdictions have decided that, in the absence of better information, they will assume these two effects cancel each other out for projects that reach a large number of facilities, unless substantive evidence is produced to indicate otherwise[124].

4.6.3   Baseline stringency

It is important that baseline assumptions provide reasonable assurances that the expected environmental benefits from the energy efficiency projects are, in fact, occurring. Baseline stringency is influenced by the assumptions used to define the "business-as-usual" case. Depending upon the assumptions made, the baseline can be set at a low energy use level, leaving little room for incremental contributions to emissions reductions from potential energy efficiency projects; or they can be set to produce a high energy use baseline that will result in higher estimated emissions reductions, all else being equal. Key factors that influence the stringency of the business-as-usual case, which include the assumptions about the energy efficiency of energy-using equipment, the assumptions about what energy efficiency investments would have occurred in the business-as-usual case and the variability across projects, are discussed below:

In-field efficiency levels in the business-as-usual case

There are two basic methods for setting the baseline efficiency levels of energy-using equipment. The first involves examining the existing stock of equipment in the field. The average efficiency of in-place equipment would be used as the baseline level. This value can be ascertained by selecting a sample of facilities and determining the efficiency of the equipment present in that sample using the methods discussed earlier. The second method takes a "best practice" approach and either uses the highest rated equipment found in the field, or looks at the equipment for sale that could replace existing equipment. New equipment may have higher efficiency levels that the average for equipment currently installed at facilities. Further, it could be argued that energy efficiency projects that install new equipment should use the efficiency levels of the likely replacement equipment, had their project not been offered.

One approach to determining which method to use is to examine the technology involved and the trend over time in the efficiency levels of that equipment. In general, it would seem appropriate to use the efficiency levels of new equipment rather than the average in-

---

[124] See NARUC (1994) for a discussion of how free riders and spillover have been addressed in North America.

field level when there has been a steady improvement in efficiency over time. This has occurred in refrigerators, air conditioners and other types of equipment. However, it may be appropriate to use the average in-field efficiency levels for equipment that represent new technology breakthroughs. The move toward T-8 lamps and electronic ballasts represents a new technology. In some developing countries, there is virtually no penetration of these efficient lighting technologies. As a result, it may be appropriate to use the average in-field efficiency for the lighting baseline when such projects span a large number of participants.

In summary, the selection of "best practice" efficiency levels or the use of average efficiency levels of in-field equipment should be made on the basis of which will more accurately represent the business-as-usual baseline. If all new sales are for equipment that has a higher efficiency level than older equipment, then the new equipment efficiency level should be used. However, if the technology is new and only a small fraction of new sales represent that technology, then the average efficiency level (or potentially a reasonable "better-than-average" efficiency level) of the stock of equipment in the field may be more appropriate. In this case, 70% of participants in a project might have purchased the lower efficiency level equipment and only 30% would have purchased the new, more efficient technology. Even today, the penetration of highly efficient CFLs in OECD countries is only a small fraction of conventional 60 watt and 100 watt incandescent light bulbs. It would be inaccurate to assume as the baseline that all lighting purchases are for the most efficient CFL. Simply stated, that is not the current baseline and it would penalise project developers for JI and CDM projects with the potential to greatly discourage the design of cost-effective energy efficiency projects.

Assumptions about business-as-usual investments in energy efficiency

One baseline issue commonly raised concerns what types of energy efficiency investments should be assumed to take place in the business-as-usual case and, therefore, be included in the baseline. Some have proposed that energy efficiency investments currently judged as economic should automatically be included in the baseline. For example, should all projects with an estimated payback of less than two years be considered projects that would have been undertaken anyway? The answer to this question revolves around what is appropriate to assume for the baseline. It is important to remember that the baseline is supposed to be representative of energy efficiency project participants. If none of the participants are currently implementing these energy-efficient measures (even though they are, in theory, viewed as very cost-effective), what is going to change in the future? If a specific factor cannot be identified that will eliminate a barrier to implementation, the past is probably the best predictor of the future.

Potential barriers to energy efficiency investments were presented in section 4.3.3. These barriers can, in many cases, be viewed as costs that are frequently omitted from traditional economic analyses of projects. It would thus be inappropriate to ignore them in setting baselines for energy efficiency in developing countries. In summary, if certain theoretically economically energy efficiency actions are not currently being undertaken, it would seem to be inappropriate to assume that, under a BAU scenario, these investments would be made in the absence of an identified factor that would change this behaviour, *e.g.* remove the barriers to investment in energy efficiency.

4.7   Insights and conclusions

Significant energy efficiency opportunities are generally believed to exist in developing countries (as well as in economies in transition), particularly as these countries did not experience the wave of energy efficiency improvements experienced in industrialised countries after the oil price shocks of the 1970s. Although many of these potential opportunities appear "economic" according to traditional cost-benefit assessments, there are barriers (*e.g.* in the form of information costs, technical costs, market distortion costs, public policy costs, *etc.*) that impede their implementation. The Kyoto Protocol's project-based mechanisms (*i.e.* CDM and JI) could help overcome some of these barriers, particularly if the development and use of baselines is made transparent and consistent.

The development of GHG emission baselines for energy efficiency projects can be divided into two main steps: (1) the development of the energy use baseline; and (2) the translation of this baselines into GHG emissions.

There are essentially three options, or levels, for the standardisation of energy use baselines for energy efficiency projects. Extensive experience with energy efficiency projects and programmes in industrialised countries, as well as some developing country experience in energy efficiency projects and programmes (in the lighting and motors sector) examined in the context of this case study, allow to draw some initial insights on the different baseline standardisation possibilities:

a) Standardising baseline calculation methods and data collection protocols

There is likely to be significant scope for the standardisation of baseline calculation methods and data collection protocols.

Insights on the potential for baseline standardisation can be drawn from the lighting and motors project examples in developing countries examined in this case study. Standardisation of baseline calculation methodologies could contribute to consistency, rigor and reproducibility of analytic methods and data systems for future JI and CDM energy efficiency projects.

The baseline calculation methodology (algorithms) and data collection protocols necessary for the construction of baselines for energy efficiency projects in the lighting sector appears suitable to standardisation. Such standardisation could apply across countries.

Similarly, in the case of the development of energy use baselines in the motors sector, the calculation methodology used for estimating the energy use for a population of motors could be standardised across countries. The data on the number of motors by horsepower category can be collected at either the site or the population level. The data for the efficiency and operating hours would need to be obtained through estimation from technical data, engineering methods or field observations.

Standardising operating (e.g. number of hours) and performance (e.g. motor efficiency) parameters necessary for the baseline calculation

The standardisation of baseline operating and performance parameters would bring greater uniformity and consistency to the CDM/JI baseline development process.

In the lighting sector, it is likely that the standardisation of operating and performance parameters that are necessary for the development of energy use baselines for energy efficiency projects would be possible for the most common types of lighting devices. This seems to be particularly appropriate for in the residential and commercial sectors, where lighting operating hours tend to be relatively consistent. For example, it would be possible to establish baseline data on wattages for common types of incandescent and fluorescent residential and commercial fixtures. The operating hours parameters would need to be differentiated according to market sector/segment. In addition, it would be necessary to develop and standardise these baseline values on a country-by-country basis (or on a regional basis if circumstances are sufficiently similar), in order to take into account differences in domestic markets and the mix of technologies. The standardisation of operating hours could be done through conservative estimates based on a reasonable sample of observations. Similarly, performance parameters such as input wattage for the most common lighting fixture types could be standardised. In the case of large industrial lighting projects, site-specific data would be more appropriate.

In the motors sector, it would be possible to standardise motor efficiency parameters, as equipment performance tends to be more uniform across market segments than operating characteristics. Such standardisation seems applicable particularly for certain motor types and size ranges that are most common in the commercial sector and industrial application. In fact, it would seem useful to further examine the possibility of standardising motor efficiencies for the most common types, sizes, classes and applications, based on manufacturers' data, in developing countries.

In addition to parameter values for motor efficiencies, the calculation of energy use baselines for energy efficiency projects in the motors sector requires parameter values for operating hours, load factors and "diversity" factors. These latter parameters lend themselves to standardisation with certain limitations. As operating hours tend to be relatively consistent within specific market segments, particularly in the commercial sector, this parameter could be conservatively standardised by market sector/segment. These baseline values would need to be based on end-use load information on a country-by country, or possibly regional, basis.

b) Standardising energy use indices by sector, market segment and/or end-use (e.g. lighting kWh per square metre for certain commercial building types)

With respect to the potential for standardising energy use indices (EUI) for lighting projects, it would seem possible to standardise indoor lighting EUIs (*e.g.* lighting kWh/square metre) for certain market segments of the commercial sector (*e.g.* offices, schools and hospitals). Such EUIs could be used as the baseline values for energy use related to lighting in those commercial sector market segments.

In the residential sector, it may be useful to consider the potential standardisation of EUIs for certain appliances (*e.g.* refrigerators).

Standardised lighting EUIs are probably less applicable in the industrial sector, where a hybrid approach combining standardised and project specific elements is likely more appropriate.

Motor energy use indices (*e.g.* kWh/square metre) for the commercial sector do not seem appropriate, as motor energy use is often tabulated or subsumed in other end-uses, particularly space heating and cooling. However, in the industrial sector, where motors are often the primary energy-consuming devices, it may be possible to develop baseline motor energy use indices related to the unit of production (motor kWh/unit of production) for selected industries.

Other baseline issues

Translating energy saved to GHGs: The rate at which reductions in energy use are translated into GHG emissions is one of the key elements of developing an emission baseline for energy efficiency projects. Setting an emission rate per kWh (which could be differentiated for peaking and baseload electricity use, for example) for a fixed period of time through electricity multi-project baselines is probably one of the most significant baseline standardisation elements for CDM/JI energy efficiency projects.

Crediting lifetime: Another important baseline standardisation element is the crediting lifetime associated with a particular baseline. The authors recommend fixing, at the start of an energy efficiency CDM/JI project, the length of time during which a baseline is considered valid for calculating that project's GHG emission reductions (and thus emission credits). A baseline crediting lifetime of about five years would seem adequate to balance environmental and project developers' interests. This would not preclude the possibility that the baseline be set such that energy efficiency is assumed to increase at a given rate over the five-year period. However, this would need to be determined at the outset.

Free riders and spillover effects: The methodologies examined to estimate energy use baselines for energy efficiency projects normally only consider direct energy use. However, energy efficiency projects may lead to two indirect energy use and GHG effects: free riders and spillover effects. These two indirect effects work in opposite directions and both are difficult to quantify. Until better information is available, it may be practical to assume, as have assumed some regulatory jurisdictions in the case of traditional energy efficiency projects and programmes, that these two effects cancel each other out.

Determining stringency: In terms of the appropriate stringency level for energy efficiency projects, it is important that the level provide a reasonable reflection of the "business-as-usual" case. Basing the baseline level on what investments should, theoretically, take place, such as through a traditional economic assessment criteria (e.g. pay-back period), is likely not a good proxy for "business-as-usual", as they do not take into account the various (non-purely economic) barriers to energy efficiency investments.

The other two main approaches of determining an appropriate baseline stringency level are based on: 1) existing stock of equipment in the field; and 2) "best practice", using either highest rated equipment found in the field or equipment for sale. The most appropriate choice would depend on what is reasonable to assume under a business-as-usual scenario. In a case where all new sales are for equipment that has a higher efficiency level than older equipment, then the new equipment efficiency level should be used for developing the baseline. On the other hand, if the technology is brand new and only a small fraction (e.g. less than 30%) of new sales represent this technology, then the average efficiency level (or potentially a reasonable "better-than-average" efficiency level) of the stock of equipment in the field may be more appropriate.

Finally, it is important to recognise that some of energy efficiency JI or CDM projects will probably "beat the system" and receive more emissions credits than they deserve. No process will be perfect and any energy efficiency baseline construction process will likely have defects. A search for perfection will likely result in no process being judged as acceptable. The goal is to strike both a reasonable balance among various risks including among the interests of project developers, those of potential host countries and the environmental objectives of the project-based mechanisms.

ANNEX A

EXAMPLES OF BASELINE DEVELOPMENT FOR ENERGY EFFICIENCY PROJECTS AND ENERGY EFFICIENCY MARKET ASSESSMENT

This section presents selected examples where baseline energy use and/or market characteristics were developed as part of an energy efficiency project evaluation or market assessment to determine the cost-effective potential for an energy efficiency project. None of the examples focused on stand-alone energy use baseline assessments, nor did they deal with the issue of forecasting baseline conditions into the future. For the project examples that developed a reference case (or baseline) for energy use, the baseline was part of a larger study or project to estimate actual energy savings or the market potential for savings. In those cases where estimates of energy savings were the objective, the studies were less focused on baseline construction than on estimating the energy use of the newly installed or proposed energy-efficient technologies.

Although the purpose of these examples was generally not to help evaluate GHG emission reductions resulting from energy efficiency projects (with the exception of the Mexican Ilumex project), they nonetheless may provide useful insights for the development of baselines for energy efficiency projects undertaken in the context of JI and CDM.

Seven case studies of lighting, motors and audit-based energy efficiency projects in developing countries follow.

Fluorescent lamp and compact fluorescent lamp market transformation project[125] - Thailand

This project is a national DSM programme intended to transform the indoor lighting market. The existing standard fluorescent lamps installed in commercial buildings are 40 watt and 20 watt "fat tube" (T12) fluorescent lamps. An agreement was reached between the national government and manufacturers of lamps sold in Thailand. This agreement called for manufacturers to stop making the 40 and 20 watt fat tube T12 lamps and replace them with 36 and 18-watt thin tube (T8) lamps. The project also encouraged the replacement of incandescent lamps with more efficient compact fluorescent lamps (CFL) in both residential and non-residential applications.

---

[125] EGAT reports (1997a and 1997b) contain information on the lighting programme plans and evaluation plans.

The energy use baselines required by these two projects focused on the typical performance and operational factors (*i.e.* wattage and operating hours) of 40 and 20 watt tubular fluorescent and the older incandescent lamps (to be replaced by the CFLs), maximum peak coincident demand and baseline annual energy consumption.

The data used to construct the energy baselines were based on the following sources:

- Spot-watt measurements of a sample of fixtures using fat tubes to estimate the average kW per lamp.

- Calibration of these spot-watt measurements by bench tests of different lamp and ballast combinations for fluorescent lamps.

- Estimation of operating hours from customer self-reports for all participants, as well as run-time data from a sample of installations. The customer estimates of operating hours are compared to the run-time logger data and an adjustment factor is calculated using the ratio between the two numbers. This ratio is then used to "calibrate" estimated operating hours as reported by building or residence occupants.

Baseline energy use is to be estimated by taking the product of estimated lamp wattage (kW) multiplied by estimates of operating hours to obtain kWh. The actual data used in the analysis, the results of the bench tests and field monitoring and the final evaluation findings are not public information at this time and thus cannot be reported here. The evaluation will utilise a calibrated engineering algorithm[126] approach that accounts for the number of units installed lamp wattage and average annual lamp operating hours for both the fat tube and CFL projects.

There are several notable aspects of the baseline constructed for this application. First, a sample of older lamps had to be identified and spot-watt measurements taken on these lamps, along with the use of run-time data loggers to obtain accurate estimates of operating hours for the baseline technologies. Occupant self-reports of operating hours are also obtained from customer surveys. These self-reported estimates are adjusted by the estimates from the more accurate run-time loggers, resulting in an adjustment factor or ratio. This approach of using a ratio comprising a more accurate estimate divided by a less accurate estimate and then applying that ratio to the larger number of self-reported operating hours is an example of data leveraging. Data leveraging procedures are increasing in use and can be expected to become standard in baseline development in the context of energy efficiency projects.[127]

---

[126] The report describes this approach as a "calibrated engineering approach." This approach is described in section 4.5.2 in Violette (1996).

[127] A data leveraging approach uses two methods of data collection. A small sample is selected for which extremely high-quality data are obtained. A larger sample is also selected and a less expensive, less accurate estimation is approach is applied to this larger sample. A ratio estimate is used to leverage the small amount of highly accurate data within the larger sample of data. This is described in Violette (1991).

Ilumex compact fluorescent lamp replacement project[128] - *Mexico (AIJ Pilot Phase)*

This AIJ pilot phase energy efficiency project provided rebates for the purchase of compact fluorescent lamps (CFLs) sold through retail outlets. The project was intended to encourage the widespread use of CFLs and was restricted to residential applications in two metropolitan areas, Guadalajara and Monterrey.

The energy use baseline developed in this project is a performance and operational baseline (*i.e.* wattage and operating hours) of existing incandescent lamps resulting in a baseline annual energy consumption of a population of lamp replacement projects. The data used to construct the baseline included vendor surveys of lamp sales and stocks used to estimate the number and type of units sold and participant surveys used to estimate the number and type of CFLs installed and characteristics of the incandescent lamps they replaced. The project baseline assumes that participants would have continued to use ordinary incandescent lamps and that the replacements would not have occurred in the absence of the project.

Initial planning assumptions specified that each wattage of CFL would replace an equivalent incandescent lamp (*e.g.* a 15-watt CFL would replace a 60-watt incandescent bulb). The wattage values used for the baseline incandescent lamps and the CFLs are presented in Table A4-1. The preliminary results of the spot-watt measurements [129] showed that the average energy savings per lamp were 50 watts compared to the planned 54 watts. While these data allow the quantification of baselines for typical programme participants, the project report clearly states that "... data do not exist for Mexico which would allow us to define a meaningful detailed national baseline projection."

The baseline operating hours were assumed to be 4 hours per day. However, the monitoring and evaluation plan called for baselines for impact assessment to be developed from post-implementation surveys and follow-up runtime hour data logging on a sample of lamps. The results of the runtime metering at a sample of sites (as of 1997) showed that the average operating hours for the lamps was about 3 hours per day compared to the 4 hours in the planning assumptions.

While the study indicates the need to adjust the baseline over time to account for natural change and market transformation effects and the challenges associated with doing so, it does not provide a specific forecast of the baseline into the future. It was assumed that the energy savings benefits of the project would extend for eight years; the anticipated life of a CFL.

---

[128] World Bank (1997) and related updates and descriptions.

[129] The detailed evaluation of the programme by CFE is not public information. World Bank and FCCC reports provide only aggregate data.

Table A4-1

Lamp performance data

Baseline Incandescent Watts	CFL Watts		Watt Savings
	Nominal	**Measured**	
100	23	21.1	78.9
75	20	17.8	57.2
60	15	16.1	43.9

The GHG emissions reductions of the project were estimated as follows:

1.   The kilowatt hours of electricity use avoided from replacing 1.7 million incandescent bulbs with the more efficient CFLs. These estimations were based on the following parameter values:

- number and type of bulbs installed by month;

- an average bulb use of three hours per day (based on preliminary results of on-site metering of bulb use in participants' homes) and 30 days per month;

- a bulb lifetime of 8,760 hours (12.4% less than the technical specifications of the CFLs);

- an average savings of 50 watts per bulb (taken from the difference between the average incandescent bulb wattage and the average wattage of the CFLs used as replacements);

- assuming transmission and other losses of 18% on the CFE system.

2.   The kilowatt hours not generated are converted to emissions saved using:

- standard emissions factors for each fuel type, expressed in tons per Tera Joule;

- fuel mix actually used at the Monterrey and Manzanillo plants in 1995 and 1996;

- heat rate, or efficiency, of the plants.

Table A4-2 summarises the results of the GHG reduction estimates.

Table A4-2

AIJ component baseline and estimated GHG reductions

	Units	1995	1996	1997	1998	1999	2000	2001	2002	2003	2004	2005	2006
A) Baseline Scenario	MWh	1,748	7,016	12,918	15,763	15,763	15,763	15,763	15,763	14,346	9,257	3,272	36
B) Project Scenario	MWh	499	2,004	3,694	4,504	4,504	4,504	4,504	4,504	4,099	2,645	935	10
C) Effect (B-A) MWh not consumed	MWh	1,249	5,011	9,224	11,259	11,259	11,259	11,259	11,259	10,247	6,612	2,337	26
D) MWh not generated	MWh	1,523	6,111	11,261	13,731	13,731	13,731	13,731	13,731	12,496	8,064	2,850	31
GHG Reductions	Metric tonnes												
E) Effect of (D)	CO_2	1,176	4,721	8,700	10,608	10,608	10,608	10,608	10,608	9,654	6,230	2,202	24
	CH_4	0.03	0.12	0.22	0.27	0.27	0.27	0.27	0.27	0.25	0.16	0.06	0.00
F) Cumulative Effect of (D)	CO_2	1,176	5,897	14,597	25,205	35,813	46,421	57,029	67,637	77,291	83,521	85,723	85,748
	CH_4	0.03	0.15	0.37	0.64	0.91	1.18	1.45	1.72	1.97	2.13	2.19	2.19

Source: World Bank (1997)

Demand-side management assessment[130] - Morocco

The Morocco DSM study included three components: 1) a national assessment of DSM potential, 2) a national market research study of energy use patterns, equipment distribution channels and customer attitudes and preferences and 3) a pilot residential lighting demonstration project.

Growth in lighting energy use constitutes a large fraction of growth in residential electricity demand in Morocco. Most residential lighting is incandescent, with the majority of lamps being either 75 watt or 100 watt. The residential lighting pilot project installed 2,147 compact fluorescent lamps in 1,412 households.

All major end uses in the residential, commercial and industrial sectors were examined for the National Assessment of DSM Potential and the National Market Research Study. The data used to construct the energy use baseline came from a national market research study. This study included of surveys of 2000 residential customers, 61 commercial sector interviews, 52 industrial sector interviews and 50 interviews with trade allies (*e.g.* architects, engineers and installers). These data were compiled and analysed to characterise energy use and energy use parameters in each market sector and to produce the estimate of DSM potential.

For the residential lighting pilot project, baseline consumption was estimated using a standard engineering algorithm that accounted for lamp wattage and operating hours. It was found from the field research that 50% of incandescent lamps were 100 watt and 28% were 75 watt. Operating hours were determined from runtime metering at a sample of sites. For the hours of operation, only one time period was taken into account.[131] The average usage per lamp across the retrofit and control groups was 3.5 hours/day. Hours of operation did not show any significant changes after the retrofit, demonstrating that there is no short-term take back. The actual operating hours averaged only 75% of the operating hours estimated by the resident.

For the residential lighting pilot project, the following categories of data and data collection activities were used for the energy analysis:

- Customer survey data, including both the participant group and a control group.
- Programme tracking data for the lighting programme.
- Utility billing data for both the participant group and the control group.
- On-site metered data for a sample of sites.

---

[130] Hagler Bailly Services, Inc. (1997).

[131] The second time period would have conflicted with Ramadan.

- Post-installation survey data for a sample of the customers receiving the CFL retrofits.

The baseline was used to produce estimates of energy savings using an engineering estimation procedure with final estimates calibrated through a statistically adjusted engineering analysis (SAE)[132] of utility billing records. The "realisation rate" of the engineering estimate based on the SAE analysis was 75%.[133] A number of other useful and informative factors influencing energy savings (and energy use) were also identified in this study including:

- Estimated incandescent lamp wattages for each equivalent CFL (Table A4-3).

- Typical seasonal weekday and weekend lamp operating hours.

- Operating hour estimates were also adjusted to account for the Ramadan holiday (this is an instructive example of the need to examine the in-country particularities that might effect a standardised baseline).

- Load shapes were developed and coincident diversity factors were estimated.

- The "takeback" effect (taking back savings in terms of greater lighting use) was estimated.

Table A4-3

Incandescent and CFL wattages

Existing Incandescent Wattage	CFL Wattage
100	23
75	20
60	15

The baseline stemming from this national assessment of DSM potential produced a useful characterisation of electricity use in Morocco, including breakdowns by market sector and subsector, end-use breakdowns for major markets, sector and end-use load shape profiles and average wattage ratings and operating hours for a variety of lighting uses. These data form an excellent foundation for baseline construction for energy efficiency projects. The national market research took the analysis a step further to develop a

---

[132] Descriptions of statistically adjusted engineering estimates are presented in Violette (1993 and 1996).

[133] "Realisation rate" is defined as the percentage of the engineering estimate of energy savings that is realised, on average, according to an analysis of actual consumption records.

detailed baseline profile of energy use by major end use. The study employed surveys of and interviews with customers that examined all aspects of energy use.

For residential lighting, the market research survey produced energy use and performance and operating data for both rural and urban customers, including:

- A profile of the number of lamps and average number of lamps per household (Table A4-4).

- Average lamp wattages and a breakdown of wattages by wattage category (Table A4-5).

- Average lamp operating hours.

Table A4-4

Summary of lighting characteristics by urban and rural areas

	Urban	Rural
Average Number of Lamps per Household	9	6
Average Wattage of Lamps	93	87
Average Daily Hours of Use	2	2

Table A4-5

Distribution of indoor incandescent lamps by wattage

<60 W	60 W	75 W	100 W	>100 W
2%	14%	37%	42%	4%

For commercial lighting, the study produced energy use and performance and operating parameters for both indoor and outdoor lighting, including:

- A breakdown of lighting by type (incandescent, fluorescent, halogen and compact fluorescent).

- Average number of lamps per facility by lamp type.

- Average daily operating hours by lighting type.

A summary of commercial indoor lighting characteristics is presented in Table A4-6.

Table A4-6
Summary of commercial indoor lighting

Type of Lighting	Average Number of Units Per Facility	Average Wattage	Average Daily Hours of Use
Fluorescent Lamps	263	53	10
Incandescent Lamps	269	93	6.5
Halogen Lamps	39	262	9.2
Compact Fluorescent Lamps	47	22	6.6

The industrial lighting assessment produced a similar dataset to the commercial sector data.

High-efficiency motors replacement project[134] - Mexico

In this pilot project, 1,624 standard efficiency motors at 20 customer sites were analysed for replacement with high-efficiency motors. The participating customers included industries in the manufacturing, food processing, chemical, rubber processing, steel production, mining, pharmaceutical and paper industries. The programme included a detailed audit of the existing motor systems with recommendations for replacement motors. To encourage implementation, the audit was free for companies that implemented the recommended measures, including motor replacement.

The motor system audit included the following information/data for each motor in the facility:

- Information on the existing motor: brand, body-type (open, closed, *etc.*), capacity/power in horsepower, speed (revolutions per minute), voltage, current, efficiency (if available), power factor, service factor, country of origin.
- Type and characteristics of the power transmission system.
- Operating characteristics of the driven equipment.
- Operation including hours and production loads.

---

[134] Hagler Bailly Services, Inc. (1998).

- Spot-watt measurements.

- Power logging of some motors with particularly variable loads.

While all motor systems were audited, with spot measurements of load on the different motors, a sample of the motors to be replaced was actually measured before replacement and measured again once the higher-efficiency motor was installed. The energy use baseline described by this project is the baseline performance and operational factors (*i.e.* horsepower, efficiency, load factor and operating hours) for the standard efficiency motors. Results of the data collection are summarised in Table A4-7 and Figures A4-1 and A4-2.

Table A4-7

Distribution of motors by brand

BRAND	SHARE
ABB	4%
General Electric	4%
IEM Westinghouse	21%
Lincoln	1%
Reliance-Remsa	7%
Siemens	20%
Magnetek	2%
US Motors	17%
Sin Placa	15%
Others	9%

The energy use baseline was constructed through detailed audits with complete data logging for every motor replaced, including:

- Measurement of the electric parameters (*e.g.* kW, power factor, current, rpm) under baseline conditions of typical load, noting the exact process conditions at the time and logging over a 48-hour period.

- Evaluation of the installed motors in terms of operational efficiency to meet load demands.

- The characteristics of a proposed new higher-efficiency motor (the highest efficiency motor available to meet the required load).

- Measurement of the electric parameters (*e.g.* kW, power factor, current, rpm) of the replaced motor, noting the exact process conditions at the time and logging over a 48-hour period.

- Evaluation of the actual savings, based on post-implementation logging results compared to baseline logging results.

Although measurements were carried out during the audits, the energy use baselines developed as part of the evaluation effort required additional logging. In this project, every motor to be replaced was measured and logged prior to replacement under careful monitoring of process conditions, whether or not the motor had been measured as part of the audit. Project staff felt that the only sure way to obtain the "real" energy savings was to provide coherent measurement before and after installation. This is a luxury that few energy efficiency evaluation programmes have been able to afford. The results showed a wide disparity of savings, often differing from the engineering calculations. However, upon averaging 40-50 motors, the energy savings were only slightly higher than engineering calculations predicted. Although not conclusive, this may imply that in motor applications, a project consisting of a large enough sample of replaced motors may be able to rely on an average energy use baseline developed from sectoral efficiency and measured load data.

Figure A4-1

Distribution of motors by horsepower

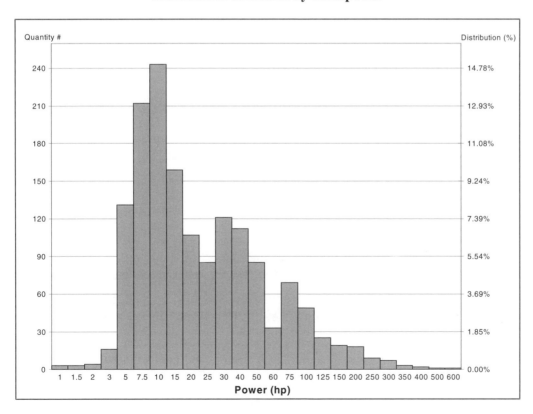

Figure A4-2

Distribution of motors by percentage of load

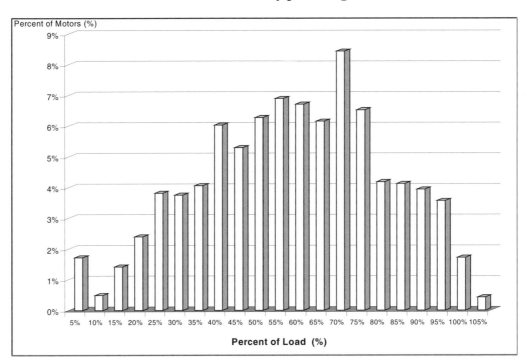

ENERCON technical energy efficiency assistance programme[135] - Pakistan

The ENERCON Technical Assistance Project was a detailed end-use market assessment and energy efficiency demonstration programme sponsored by USAID. The project included:

- Detailed energy audits at 248 industrial sites.

- Over 600 boiler/furnace tune-ups.

- Energy audits and consumption monitoring at 50 buildings, followed by the installation of energy conservation measures and subsequent monitoring and analysis.

- Energy audits at 256 agricultural tubewells followed by energy efficiency upgrades at 115 sites.

- Audits and tune-ups for 50 agricultural tractors and audits/tune-ups of over 3000 automobiles.

---

[135] Hagler Bailly, Inc. (1987).

228

While this project covered a wide range of sectors and end-use applications (see below), the discussion that follows in this case study applies only to the buildings components of the project. Baseline data were collected on the full range of building equipment/systems including HVAC, motors, appliances and lighting. However, for the purposes of this case study, we have focused on lighting and motors only. The baseline described by this study is the development of baseline energy consuming equipment/systems performance and operational characteristics.

The energy use baseline was constructed from data collected as part of a series of walk-through audits of a sample of buildings. The audits identified:

- Historical energy consumption patterns.

- Occupancy patterns of buildings.

- Data on energy consuming equipment and systems.

Data were collected on generators, boilers, chillers, air conditioners, pumps and motors, gas and electric appliances and lighting. The information presented here is limited to motors and lighting.

In the case of electric motors, information was collected on over 350 motors of different types, in a wide range of sizes and a variety of applications. The data collected and tabulated for each motor included:

- manufacturer;

- motor type;

- use or application of motor;

- size in kW;

- operating hours.

Table A4-8 presents a distribution of motors by application and maximum rated demand.

For lighting, data were collected on 36,680 fixtures in 43 buildings. The data collected and tabulated for each building included:

- lamp type;

- no. of lamps and fixtures per site;

- Watts per fixture;

- function of the space where the fixtures were installed;

- square footage of floor space served by the fixture;

- operating hours.

Table A4-8

Distribution of electric motors by application and demand

Motor Application	Number of Motors by Maximum Rated Demand (kW)					
	<1	1-2	2-5	5-10	10-20	>20
Air Compressors	2	-	-	-	-	-
Air Movement	12	-	3	24	24	5
Boiler Systems	-	2	12	-	-	-
Chiller Systems	-	-	25	-	-	5
Cooling Towers	-	6	-	12	19	2
Lifts	-	-	5	9	6	6
Water Pumping	9	7	18	4	19	10
Other	-	-	43	22	31	2

Table A4-9 presents a distribution of lighting fixtures by wattage and type.

Table A4-9

Distribution of lighting fixtures by wattage and type

Fixture Type	Number of Fixtures by Wattage								
	20-30	30-40	40-50	50-60	60-80	80-100	100-200	200-300	300+
Fluorescent	665	1231	22227	-	-	1368	-	-	-
HPS	-	-	-	-	-	-	-	-	2
Incandescent	220	691	410	3604	82	3387	2478	7	203
Mercury vapour	-	-	-			-	100	5	-

The walk-through audits included visual inspection and data collection of equipment/systems and interviews with building operators. The results of the surveys were compiled in an energy conservation database for the buildings sector and tabulations were compiled for each end use/equipment type.

Tubewell audit and retrofit project (Hagler Bailly, Inc. 1987 and 1990) - Pakistan

Electric tubewell water pumping accounts for nearly 20% of electricity use in Pakistan and is the single-largest end use of electricity. Detailed field audits of 132 electric tubewells were conducted to collect data on operating characteristics, efficiencies and causes of low energy efficiency, to collect pre- and post-retrofit energy consumption data and to identify potential energy efficiency improvements. Of the tubewells that received audits, 43 received energy efficiency retrofits that yielded an estimated average energy efficiency improvement of 24%.

The tubewell audit and retrofit project provides an example of an approach to sampling and field data collection for a specialised and unique energy efficiency project. While it is unlikely that standardised baseline consumption values or operational/performance parameters could be developed for this particular end-use application, the approach to sampling indicates that standardised data collection protocols could be developed that would apply across a broad range of end-use applications and would help to establish uniformity, consistency and replicability in the energy use baseline construction process.

A detailed countrywide sampling strategy was developed for the tubewell pumping sector. In order to identify tubewell sites that were candidates for audits, farmers were invited to participate in the programme. Three hundred and ninety five farmers representing 622 tubewells responded and indicated an interest in the project. Of those, 381 tubewells were identified as audit candidates (*e.g.* operational, electrically driven, geographically distributed, accessible and within the travel range of the auditors). Candidate sites were grouped into 55 geographic clusters in 20 districts of the country. One hundred and twelve tubewells were selected for audits conducted by field engineers. Data were collected on technical characteristics, operating conditions and pre- and post-retrofit energy consumption. The pre-retrofit data were used to describe baseline performance. Baseline pumpset efficiency was estimated to be about 21.5%.

The audits performed on the sites contained in the sample collected detailed information on pump technical and operating data including:

- Pump functionality and condition.
- Year of installation.
- Pump performance specifications and installation details.
- Estimated daily hours of use.
- Pre- and post-retrofit energy consumption.

Summaries of these data were not included in the documents available to the authors. The size and energy consumption of tubewells varied from 3 hp (2.2 kW) to 50 hp (37.3 kW) in both electric and diesel powered pumps.

231

Boiler/furnace tune-up energy efficiency assessment program (Hagler Bailly, Inc., 1990) - Pakistan

Under the ENERCON Project, a boiler/furnace tune-up programme was designed and implemented to go beyond the audit and ensure energy savings from implementation. The boiler/furnace tune-up energy efficiency assessment programme was initially offered for about one year at no cost to participants. After the start-up period, audits and tune-ups were offered at cost. In total, over 600 audits and tune-ups were completed. Energy efficiency measures included low-cost measures such as combustion control retrofits and fuel/air tune-ups based on combustion analyser measurements. Average combustion efficiency was measured before and after the work; on average, the efficiency improved by about 8%.

The boiler/furnace tune-up project produced a dataset on the baseline energy efficiency and performance/operational characteristics of a sample of over 600 boilers and furnaces. Data included monthly energy consumption, production, inventories of major energy consuming equipment (including boilers and furnaces) and technical specifications and specific fuel consumption of major energy consuming equipment. Databases were developed for profiling the consumption characteristics in major end uses, including boiler/furnace heating applications.

4.8   References

AGRA Monenco Inc., 1998. *DSM Program Evaluation Plan - Conservation Program Impact Evaluation*, prepared for Electricity Generating Authority of Thailand, prepared by AGRA Monenco, Inc., Oakville, Ontario.

Begg, Katie *et. al.*, 1999. *Overall Issues for Accounting for Emissions Reductions of JI Projects*, Centre for Environmental Strategy, University of Surrey, UK.

Chomitz, K., 1998. *Baselines for Greenhouse Gas Reductions: Problems, Precedents and Solutions,* World Bank.

EGAT, 1997a. *High Efficiency Fluorescent Tube Program - Program Plan Evaluation Plan*, Demand-Side Management Office, Planning and Evaluation Department, January.

EGAT, 1997b. *Compact Fluorescent Lamp Program - Program Plan Evaluation Plan,* Demand-Side Management Office, Planning and Evaluation Department, January.

Ellis, Jane, 1999. *"Experience with Emission Baselines Under the AIJ Pilot Phase,"* OECD Information Paper, ENV/EPOC(99)23/FINAL, May.

Ellis, Jane and Martina Bosi, 1999, *"Options for Project Emission Baselines,"* OECD and IEA Information Paper, Paris, October.

EPRI, 1991, *Impact Evaluation of Demand-Side Management Programs, Volume 1: A Guide to Current Practice*, EPRI Research Project 2548-11, CU-7179. Prepared by RCG/Hagler, Bailly. Palo Alto, California: Electric Power Research Institute.

EPRI, 1995a, *Performance Impacts: Evaluation Methods for the Nonresidential Sector*. EPRI Research Project 3269, TR-105845. Edited by D. Violette, M. Keneipp and I. Obstfeld. Prepared by Xenergy, Inc. Palo Alto, California: Electric Power Research Institute.

EPRI, 1995b, *Evaluation of Commercial-Sector Lighting Retrofit Programs*, EPRI RP 3823-02. Palo Alto, California: Electric Power Research Institute.

EPRI. 1996. *End-Use Performance Monitoring Handbook*, Research Project 3269-19, TR-106960. Edited by D. Violette and M. Keneipp, Hagler Bailly. Palo Alto, California: Electric Power Research Institute.

Hirst, E. and Reed, J. eds., 1991, *Handbook of Evaluation of DSM Programs*, Oak Ridge National Laboratories, ORNL/Con-336, December.

Hagler Bailly, Inc., 1987, *Preliminary Energy Surveys in Buildings, Summary Report, ENERCON,* prepared for US Agency for International Development, Washington, DC.

Hagler Bailly, Inc., 1988, *Tubewell Pre-Audit Survey Report, Technical Assistance Project Summary Report*, ENERCON, prepared for US Agency for International Development, Washington, DC.

Hagler Bailly, Inc., 1990, *Pakistan ENERCON Technical Assistance Project Summary Report*, prepared for US Agency for International Development, Washington, DC.

Hagler Bailly Consulting, Inc., 1996, *Demand-Side Management Assessment for Vietnam, Phase 1 Final Report,* prepared for the World Bank.

Hagler Bailly Services, Inc., 2000a, *Análisis de la Base de Datos del Proyecto Piloto para la Substitución de Motores Estándar por Motores de Alta Eficiencia* (Mexico Motors Project), prepared for US Agency for International Development, Arlington, VA.

Hagler Bailly Services, Inc., 2000b, *Impacto de Los Evaluaciones* (Mexico Motors Project), prepared for US Agency for International Development, Arlington, VA.

International Energy Agency (IEA), 1996, *Evaluation, Verification and Performance Measurement of Energy Efficiency Programs,* prepared by D. Violette, Hagler Bailly Consulting, Inc., 1996.

Hagler Bailly Services, Inc., 1997, *Demand-Side Management in Morocco, Volumes 1, 2 and 3*, prepared for US Agency for International Development, Washington, DC.

Hagler Bailly Services, Inc., 1998, *Pilot Project for the Substitution of Standard Motors with High-Efficiency Motors*, prepared for US Agency for International Development, Washington, DC.

IEA, 1999a, *Energy Statistics of OECD Countries: 1996-1997.* Paris.

IEA, 1999b, *Energy Statistics of non-OECD Countries: 1996-1997.* Paris.

NARUC, 1994, *Regulating DSM Program Evaluation: Policy and Administrative Issues for Public Utility Commissions,* ORNL/Sub/95X-SH985C. Co-authors: J. Raab and D. Violette. Washington, D.C.: National Association of Regulatory Utility Commissioners.

Oak Ridge National Laboratories, 1996. *A DSM Manual for the APEC Economies*, prepared for Douglas Bauer, ORNL, prepared by Ahmad Faruqui and Kathleen McElroy, Hagler Bailly Services, Inc.

US Agency for International Development (USAID), 1997. *Demand-Side Management in Morocco: Volume II - National Market Research, Final Report*," prepared for USAID Office of Energy, Environment and Technology, Washington, DC, prepared by Hagler Bailly Consulting, Arlington, VA, March.

US Agency for International Development/Hagler Bailly Services, Inc., 1997, *The Energy Efficiency Market in Developing Countries: Trends and Policy Implications.*

US Department of Energy, 1997, *International Performance Measurement and Verification Protocols.*

US Energy Association/US Agency for International Development, 1999, *Handbook of Climate Change Mitigation Options for Developing Country Utilities and Regulatory Agencies.*

US Environmental Protection Agency, *1995, US EPA Conservation Verification Protocols: Version 2.0,* EPA Publication 430/B-95-012, Governmental Printing Office.

US Environmental Protection Agency, 1999, *Clean Development Mechanism Baselines: An Evaluation of the Benchmarking Approach*, prepared for US EPA Contract No. 68-W6-0055 (Contact: Shari Friedman), prepared by Stratus Consulting, Boulder, CO and Tellus Institute, Boston, January, 1999.

Vine, E. and J. Sathaye, J., 1997, *The Monitoring, Evaluation, Reporting and Verification of Climate Change Mitigation Projects*, prepared for US Environmental Protection Agency.

Vine, E. *et. al.*, 1999, "Project Monitoring, Reporting and Verification," chapter 13 in *The U.N. Framework Convention on Climate Change Activities Implemented Jointly (AIJ) Pilot: Experiences and Lessons Learned*, R. Dixon (Ed.). Kluwer Academic Publishers.

Violette, D. *et. al.*, 1991, *Handbook of Evaluation of Utility DSM Programs, Volumes I and II: A Guide to Current Practice*, Electric Power Research Institute.

Violette, D., 1993, "Statistically Adjusted Engineering Estimates," in *Proceedings of the 1993 International Energy Program Evaluation Conference*, IEA.

Violette, D., 1995, *Performance Impacts: Evaluation Methods for the Non-Residential Sectors*, Electric Power Research Institute, EPRI RP-3269, TR-105845.

Violette, D., 1996, *Evaluation, Verification and Performance Measurement of Energy Efficiency Programmes,* prepared for the IEA by Hagler Bailly Consulting, Inc.

Violette, D. *et. al.*, 1998, *Evaluating Greenhouse Gas Mitigation through DSM Projects: Lessons Learned from DSM Evaluation in the United States*, World Bank.

World Bank, 1996. *Demand-Side Management Assessment for Vietnam: Phase I Final Report*, prepared by Hagler Bailly Consulting, Inc., August.

World Bank, 1997, *Mexico High Efficiency Lighting Pilot Project, AIJ Pilot Phase.*

World Bank, 1998. *Evaluating Greenhouse Gas Mitigation Through DSM Programs*, Prepared for Carbon Offsets Unit, Environment Department (Contact: Kenneth Chomitz), prepared by D. Violette *et. al.*, Hagler Bailly Services, Inc.

5. IRON AND STEEL CASE STUDY

———— 5. IRON AND STEEL CASE STUDY[136]————

5.1 Executive summary

The iron and steel industry is the largest energy consuming manufacturing sector in the world. In 1990, its global energy consumption was estimated to be 18-19 exajoules (EJ), or 10-15% of total annual industrial energy consumption. The associated CO_2 emissions are estimated to be 1425 Mt. In 1995 this amount increased to 1442 Mt CO_2, equalling about 7% of global anthropogenic CO_2 emissions.

Before an international regime for Joint Implementation (JI) or the Clean Development Mechanism (CDM) can be implemented, the problem of setting baselines needs to be solved in a satisfactory way.

This report examines the possibilities for establishing multi-project baselines in the iron and steel sector and is based on a general assessment of the iron and steel sector with examples from India, Brazil and Poland. The report concludes that it is possible to define multi-project baselines in the iron and steel sector using standardised energy intensities for different production routes. The standardised baselines would apply to the production of crude steel (the intermediate product in steel making), as final products differ in energy intensity. Baselines may also need to take the product mix and quality of coal and iron ore inputs into account when determining the credits available for potential projects in the sector. Given the international homogeneity of the sector, it is suggested that standardised energy intensities could apply to similar projects across countries.

---

[136] This paper was prepared by Jan-Willem Bode, Jeroen de Beer, Kornelis Blok (Ecofys) and Jane Ellis (OECD). The authors are grateful for useful comments and suggestions received from Jan Corfee Morlot, Thomas Martinsen, Gene McGlynn, Stéphane Willems (OECD), Jonathan Pershing, Martina Bosi (IEA), as well as from delegations to the Annex I Expert Group.

5.1.1   The iron and steel process and potential for emission savings

The iron and steel making process may be divided into five different steps:

1. treatment of raw materials;

2. iron making;

3. steel making;

4. casting; and

5. rolling and finishing.

Emissions (predominantly CO_2) from iron and steel production are caused by the combustion of fossil fuels, the use of electrical energy and the use of coal and lime as feedstock.

There are different production routes with substantially different energy intensities in which steel can be manufactured from iron ore or scrap. However, as step 2 (iron making) is the most energy intensive, steel production from minimills is generally much less energy and GHG intensive than steel production from an integrated steel mill.

Production is primarily undertaken through three different processes:

• Integrated Steel Plants (ISPs);

• Scrap based Electric Arc Furnaces (scrap-EAF); and

• Direct Reduced Iron Electric Arc Furnaces (DRI-EAF).

The dominant steel production processes are the integrated steel mill (where steel is produced from iron ore by following steps 1 - 5 above) and the minimill (where steel is produced from scrap steel or substitutes by following steps 3 - 5 above).

The greenhouse gas emissions associated with iron and steel production depend on how much energy is used and the greenhouse gas intensity of that energy. Energy intensities are used as the standardised component of emission baselines instead of CO_2 intensities because there is lower variation in the former. Using energy intensities avoids having to effectively proscribe which fuel should be used, the relative proportions of fuel and electricity and the GHG-intensity of electricity used in the steel production process.

There are a number of potential energy-related JI/CDM project types in the iron and steel sector. These include:

• increasing the energy efficiency of steel production (*e.g.* by installing more efficient equipment and/or implementing good housekeeping measures);

- changing the manufacturing process (*e.g.* by installing new equipment); or

- changing the fuel used for the direct reduction of iron (*e.g.* from coal to gas).

5.1.2 *Benchmarking versus technology matrix*

Several methods for multi-project baseline development have been described in the literature. This analysis considers two: benchmarking (setting a standardised value for energy use for a particular process) and technology matrix (setting a standardised value for energy use for a particular technology).

The differences in the environmental credibility (additionality requirement) between the two baseline types are relatively small. However, the data requirements for the latter are large, particularly for the inclusion of technologies that do not cause step change difference in performance. Such data requirements translate into substantially higher costs for development. Given the increased transparency possible with a benchmarking approach and the difficult data demands of the matrix approach, a baseline based on standardised energy values for different production processes ("benchmarks") is recommended.

5.1.3 *Stringency of baselines*

This report proposes setting different standardised energy intensities for the different major steel production routes, *i.e.*:

- Integrated Steel Plants (ISPs);

- Scrap based Electric Arc Furnaces (scrap-EAF); and

- Direct Reduced Iron Electric Arc Furnaces (DRI-EAF).

The benchmark value in the benchmarking approach, or the standard set of technologies in a technology matrix, can be determined based on various assumptions. These different assumptions result in baselines that are more or less stringent.

The levels of stringency studied are:

1. best practice world wide level;

2. world wide average level (with and without an autonomous energy efficiency improvement);

3. country level (average and "better than average"); and

4. a "graduated crediting" level, which takes into account both technological best practice and country average levels.

This analysis evaluates the stringency options against a set of selected criteria, including environmental additionality, potential volume of projects, transparency and verifiability and baseline costs (Table 5ES). This analysis indicates that any particular baseline approach involves trade-offs between factors, with no single option emerging as a unique "best" solution in all cases.

However, for refurbishment of existing plants, a benchmark on the world-wide average is considered to be a good trade-off between environmental credibility and the potential volume of projects.

For new capacity, a benchmark based on the world-wide best practice (which is equal to marginal technology addition) is considered the most suitable.

5.1.4   Potential for JI/CDM projects

Potential project volumes under each level of stringency are quantified in three case study countries. The analysis suggests that the likely number of that would meet minimum standards is not high, whichever approach is used.

One potential method to increase the potential volume of projects while still preserving the environmental credibility may be to provide credit in a progressive way. For example, refurbishing plants so that they perform better than the country or production process average may result in these projects being eligible for some credits even if the refurbished performance does not reach BAT standards. Shortening the emissions timeline for such "intermediate level" projects would have a similar effect on the number of credits they generate.

5.1.5   Data availability and other issues

In general, data availability is limited with respect to the iron and steel sectors. However, the detailed research undertaken for the India case study suggests that the necessary data may be available, but that their collection may require additional research (and cost).

It is difficult to give general rules regarding emission timelines, mainly because the average lifetime of an industrial technology is very difficult to determine, as it can vary substantially from site to site (depending on its operation, maintenance and thus, indirectly, on the availability of funds). This also means that the current age of the stock is therefore not considered to be a useful indicator for determining the additionality of CDM/JI projects.

Table 5ES

Scoring the proposed baselines for refurbishment projects in the iron and steel sector against selected criteria

Criteria	Benchmarking[1]					Technology matrix[2]		
	World-wide best practice	World-wide average	World-wide average with AEEI	Country average	Graduated crediting	World-wide best practice	World-wide mode	Country mode
Environmental Additionality[3]	++	- to +[5]	-- to +	-- to ++[6]	- to +	++	++[5]	-- to ++[6]
Potential volume of projects	--	+	+	0 to ++[7]	0 to +	--	+	0 to ++[7]
Transparency and verifiability	++	++	++	+	-/+	++	+	+
Costs to draw up the baseline system[4]	++ [low cost]	+	+	+	+/-	-	-- [high cost]	-

5.2   Introduction

This analysis proposes methodologies for developing multi-project baselines in the iron and steel industry and suggests potentially appropriate values for these baselines. The potential volume of projects under these different baselines is also estimated. Based on these inputs, conclusions and recommendations with regard to the possibilities for multi-project baselines in the iron and steel industry are given.

This section gives an overview of the global iron and steel sector, including the important players and the different processes and production routes. Also, an overview of energy consumption, carbon dioxide emissions and regional distribution thereof is discussed. This section ends with a description of the iron and steel sector in India, Brazil and Poland.

5.2.1   Iron and steel production processes

The iron and steel industry is the largest energy consuming manufacturing sector in the world. In 1990, its global energy consumption was estimated to be 18-19 exajoules (EJ), or 10-15% of the annual world industrial energy consumption (WEC, 1995). The associated CO_2 emissions are estimated to be 1425 Mt (De Beer *et. al.*, 1999). In 1995 this amount increased to 1442 Mt CO_2, equalling about 7% of global anthropogenic CO_2 emissions[137]. When mining and transportation of ore and coal are included, this share is near 10% of total emissions. Fossil fuel combustion is the primary source of GHG emissions from iron and steel production and energy costs represent 15-20% of steel manufacturing costs.

Currently, two processes dominate the global steel production. These may be generally be described as:

(a) the integrated steel mill, where steel is made by reducing iron ore in a blast furnace to make pig iron which is subsequently processed in an oxy-steel plant; and

(b) the minimill, in which steel is made by melting scrap or scrap substitutes in an electric arc furnace (EAF).

Other processes that are in use are either outdated, *e.g.* the open-hearth furnace, or so new that their share in the world steel production is still small, *e.g.* smelt reduction processes and direct reduction processes (*e.g.* Corex).

---

[137] These include energy related emissions as well as process emissions (Olivier *et. al.*, 1996).

The iron and steel making process may be divided into 5 different steps (see Figure 5-1):

1. treatment of raw materials;

2. iron making;

3. steel making;

4. casting; and

5. rolling and finishing.

At the end of step 3, an intermediate product (molten steel) is common to all production routes. The technologies and fuels used in the two main steel production processes can be used to further disaggregate steel production. This report examines how emission baselines could be standardised for four "process routes" to produce molten steel:

1. Blast Furnace - Basic Oxygen Furnace (BF-BOF);

2. Blast Furnace - Open Hearth Furnace (BF-OHF);

3. Scrap-based Electric Arc Furnace; and

4. Direct Reduced Iron - Electric Arc Furnace (either coal based or gas based).

The energy intensity of final steel products can vary substantially, but adjustments to emission baselines to take into account product differences are beyond the scope of this analysis.

The GHG emissions from iron and steel production in integrated steel mills are mainly from the combustion of fossil fuels for energy (heat), electrical energy and the use of coal and lime as feedstock. These emissions are primarily of CO_2, although very small amounts of CH_4 and N_2O may also be emitted. Only emissions of CO_2 are assessed in this case study. Emissions from feedstock use is mainly from step 2 and 3 and some from step 1.

The blast furnace is the most energy-intensive step in an integrated steel mill and requires about 11-15 GJ per tonne of pig iron produced. Of this amount approximately 7 GJ is used for the chemical reduction of iron ore to pig iron. In addition, energy input is required to raise the temperature to a level at which the chemical reduction can thermodynamically proceed at a sufficient rate. Carbon (from energy sources such as coal or coke) is used both as the reducing agent and as the energy input. The reducing agent (feedstock energy use) may constitute up to 50% of the total energy demand of an integrated steel mill. Accounting for which proportion of energy input results in energy-related emissions and which results in process-related emissions is ongoing.

Description of the steel production process

The integrated steel mill process starts with the production of coke (step 1) by heating metallurgical coal in the absence of air in coke ovens*. The coke oven gas is fed into the blast furnace (step 2) and the energy in the gas is used for the iron making. In some cases coke is (partially) purchased. Iron ore is agglomerated in sinter plants or pellets plants[138]. Coke, ore and lime are fed alternately in the blast furnace (step 2). A hot compressed stream of air, the blast, is blown from the bottom into the furnace. A gas is produced that reduces iron ore. Molten pig iron, rich in carbon, is tapped from the bottom and transferred in isolated vessels to the oxy-steel plant (step 3). Here carbon and other impurities are removed by oxygen blowing. Usually part of the input into the oxy-steel plant is scrap or other iron-bearing materials. The characteristics of the crude steel are adjusted in a series of ladle treatment processes. The casting of steel can either be continuous or batch (ingot casting) (step 4). The cast steel is reheated, rolled and sent to a number of finishing operations. These final operations depend largely on the type of steel that is produced. Integrated steel mills may use the Open Heart (OHF) furnace or the Basic Oxygen Furnace (BOF). The electric arc furnace mainly uses electrical energy. The largest part of the world steel production is made in integrated steel mills.

* This step and associated capital expenditure, energy use and GHG emissions, are avoided in the Corex process.

The ranges in energy use to produce molten steel for a given technology type are influenced by the quality of fuel and iron/scrap inputs, but also by variations in the relative proportion of fuel input used. The share of electricity in the total energy demand varies from plant to plant but is not reported separately. Based on statistics published by IISI (IISI, 1996) this share is estimated to range from 2.5 to 7% of the final energy use in an integrated steel plant. Integrated steel mills may generate (part of) their electricity use and purchase the remainder. Electricity can account for between 50-85% of total energy inputs to an EAF[139]. The GHG-intensity of steel produced by the same production route in different plants will vary according to the fuel used and to differences in GHG-intensity of electricity.

---

[138] Pellet plants are more frequently located near the ore mine than at the site of the integrated mill.

[139] Jeremy Jones, *Electric Arc Furnace Steelmaking,* (www.steel.org/learning/howmade/eaf.htm)

The lay-out of the energy system varies considerably from plant to plant. The potential to recover energy contained in process gases, heat and pressure energy will also vary from site to site, depending on its layout.

A minimill uses scrap (or scrap substitutes) rather than iron ore as its material input. The scrap is melted in an electric arc furnace to produce crude steel, which is cast, rolled and given a final treatment. However, due to contaminants in the scrap the quality of the steel produced in an EAF may be lower than that of oxy-steel. The demand for high-quality scrap, *i.e.* low in contaminants, has increased significantly and has pushed up the market prices for such scrap. Therefore, minimill steel producers also use other iron-bearing materials as raw material. These materials are usually sponge iron, produced in direct reduction plants, or (hot) pig iron, produced in a blast furnace. The electricity consumption from an electric arc furnace has come down from about 550 kWh/tonne liquid steel in 1970 to 350 kWh/tonne liquid steel in the late 1990s. The theoretical minimum is 300 kWh/t. Obviously, the CO_2 emissions associated with such energy use depends on the way the electricity is produced. The range of products produced by minimills used to be limited to long products only, because the quality of the scrap was not high enough to produce flat products[140]. Moreover, the investment costs for a hot strip mill are high. However, with the availability of scrap substitutes and, more important, with the introduction of new casting techniques, minimills have entered the market of flat products.

The energy demand for direct reduction varies from 13 to 18 GJ per tonne of sponge iron. Energy in the form of natural gas or coal is used. Scrap preparation requires different amounts of energy, depending on the quality of the scrap.

5.2.2 *Production and expected growth*

The iron and steel industry has an annual global production of 775 Mt of crude steel in 1998 (IISI, 1999). Table 5-1 gives a listing of the 20 largest steel producing countries in 1999, which combined account for 87% of global steel production.

Demand for steel is growing at a moderate pace (+2% in 1998/99 and projected to average 1.6% p.a. to 2005 - IISI 1999). However, steel demand can vary widely from country to country and year to year, depending on economic conditions. Demand for steel is linked to demand in construction and for automobiles. The growth in EU and NAFTA countries is expected to be small, whereas in South America a large growth is expected. The development in China is hard to predict, but in general a large growth is expected. A recovery of production (with levels returning to pre-1990 volumes) is expected in the former Soviet Union.

---

[140] Flat products are used in the production of automobiles and appliances, such as refrigerators. Long products are used in infrastructure

247

Figure 5-1

Processes for steel production

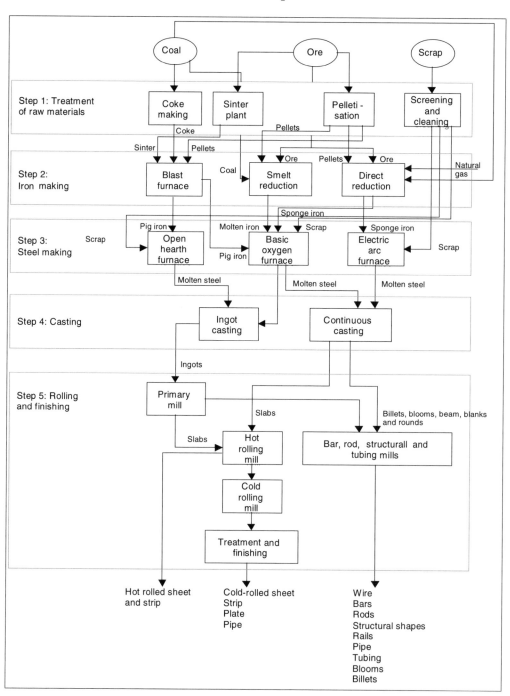

Table 5-1

The 20 largest steel producing countries and their change in production in 1999 relative to 1992

	Production 1999 (provisional) (Mt crude steel)	Production 1992 (Mt crude steel)	Change 92/99 (%)		Production 1999 (provisional) (Mt crude steel)	Production 1992 (Mt crude steel)	Change 92/99 (%)
China	123.3	80.9	52	France	20.2	18.2	11
US	97.2	84.3	15	UK	16.3	16.2	1
Japan	94.2	98.1	-4	Canada	16.3	13.9	17
Russia	49.8	67	-26	Chinese Taipei	15.4	10.7	44
Germany	42.1	39.7	6	Mexico	15.3	8.5	80
S. Korea	41	28.1	46	Spain	14.6	12.3	19
Ukraine	27	41.8	-35	Turkey	14.4	10.3	40
Italy	25	24.8	1	Belgium	11	10.3	7
BRAZIL	**25**	**23.9**	**5**	**POLAND**	**8.8**	**9.9**	**-11**
INDIA	**24.3**	**18.1**	**34**	Australia	8.2	6.8	21

Source: IISI, 2000

N.B. The countries written in bold capital letters are those which have been selected as cases in this study.

The three countries that are selected as cases in this study, *i.e.* Brazil, India and Poland, are all among the world's top 20 steel producers. Since 1992, the largest growth in steel production has been in Mexico, Taiwan, Republic of Korea and China, where production jumped more than 40% between 1992 and 1999. In the former Soviet Union and Japan the steel production declined over the same period.

5.2.3   Major players

The 20 largest steel companies world wide produced about a third of global steel production in 1998 (Table 5-2). The largest producers are in Asia and Europe. However, market share is susceptible to changes. For example, the recent merger between British Steel and Hoogovens brings the new company Corus at the third place of largest producers.

Table 5-2

The twenty largest steel producing companies in the world in 1998

Rank	Production (Mt)	Company	Country	Rank	Production (Mt)	Company	Country
1	28.1	Nippon Steel	JAP	11	10.9	SAIL	IND
2	26.4	POSCO	ROK	12	10.9	Kawasaki	JAP
3	18.8	Arbed	LUX	13	10.6	Sumitomo	JAP
4	17.4	Thyssen Krupp[1]		14	9.6	Bethlehem Steel	USA
5	17.0	British Steel	GBR	15	8.9	BHP	AUS
6	16.1	Usinor	FRA	16	8.9	Cherepovets	RUS
7	14.8	Riva[2]	ITA	17	8.8	Nucor	USA
8	12.0	NKK	JAP	18	8.7	China Steel	TAI
9	12.0	USX	USA	19	8.6	Baoshan	PRC
10	11.4	LNM	GBR	20	8.3	Anshan	PRC

Source: IISI, 1999

[1] includes 50% of HKM
[2] includes ILVA LP

5.2.4   Regional production trends

Over the 1990s, the distribution of the CO_2 emissions from the iron and steel industry shifted considerably over the world regions. This is due to a decline in production and emissions in the countries of the former Soviet Union and Eastern Europe on the one hand and to a rapid increase of production and emissions in China and other developing countries on the other hand.

The energy consumption per ton steel produced is typically 19 to 40 GJ/tcs for an integrated steel mill using a BOF and 30-45 GJ/tcs for an integrated steel mill using open hearth furnaces (De Beer *et. al.*, 1999). A scrap based minimill uses typically 7.7-12.5 GJ/tcs, a DRI (gas)-EAF typically 22-30 GJ/tcs and a DRI (coal)-EAF typically 30-40 GJ/tcs (De Beer *et. al.*, 1999; IISI, 1998).

Iron and steel plants (especially integrated steel plants) often generate part of their own electricity consumption. Fuel input data (*e.g.* as given in the following sections for each of the countries) do not give an indication about the fraction of electricity generated within the plants, nor how these fuels are used within the plant.

There are large regional differences between energy performance of steel making. This is due to differences in operation and maintenance of the processes, the fuel input and the different use of new technologies. The outdated open-hearth furnace has been completely replaced by the oxy-steel process (first introduced in the 1950s) in the developed countries. In the former Soviet Union, however, this process is still in operation. India also operates open hearth furnaces. China also still operates open hearth furnaces, but intends to have them all closed in 2000.

A new process, Corex, has been developed that avoids the need for the coke processing step (and a coke plant). This means that the Corex process is less energy, emission (and capital) intensive than traditional steel-making routes. It also allows lower grade coals and ores to be used, which are more readily available worldwide. Corex plants are currently installed in only a few countries (*e.g.* US, India, Japan and South Africa), although are planned in more (*e.g.* Thailand). Because of its limited use to date, this production route is not taken into account on a detailed level here. Future analysis of the uptake of this process will need to assess to what extent its lower GHG emissions should influence the suggested standardised energy values presented here.

An indication of the energy efficiency changes in iron and steel production of the processes in a number of selected countries is given in Figure 5-2[141] (adapted from Phylipsen, 2000). This figure includes the energy use from the reducing agent. The figure

---

[141] Since specific energy consumption depends on sector structure, cross-country comparisons cannot be made based solely on trends in the absolute value of the energy efficiency indicator for each individual country. In the methodology used, the actual energy efficiency levels (or rather SECs) are compared with a reference energy efficiency level (accompanying best practice SEC) at the given sector structure. This means that both the actual SEC and the reference SEC are similarly affected by changes in sector structure. The sectoral SEC is established by calculating a weighed average of the reference SECs of individual processes and/or products. The Energy efficiency index, as shown in Figure 5.2 is the result of dividing the current SEC (corrected for the structure of the sector) by the accompanying best practice SEC.

presents data at a national level (*i.e.* including all process routes) and therefore gives an indication of the efficiency of the iron and steel industry in the different countries. As can be seen from this figure, Brazil is relatively efficient and has a lower energy efficiency index than many OECD countries. The reforms in the Polish iron and steel sector are also visible, with an energy efficiency index of around 230 in 1991 and slightly more than 150 in 1998. Substantial improvements in the Indian energy efficiency index (EEI) are also noted between 1985 - 1995.

Figure 5-2

Energy efficiency index trends for iron and steel production in selected countries

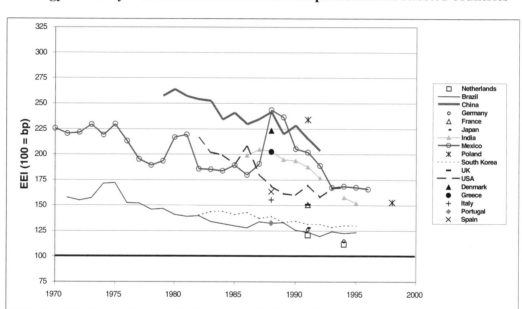

5.2.5   Case studies: India, Poland and Brazil

Three countries: India; Poland; and Brazil, were chosen for more in-depth study. These countries vary substantially in national circumstances and sectoral structure, thus providing an indication of some of the possible global variations in the sector. Moreover, data availability, though patchy, is relatively good (compared to other countries). India is representative of a large country with a large share OHF, a mixture of large ISPs, small EAFs, substantial production under the DR process and some advanced technology (Corex) production. Brazil has relatively low GHG intensities, largely due to the use of charcoal and hydro electricity. India and Brazil are also important players in global steel production. In contrast, Poland has significant over-capacity, is facing reductions in demand and has very old facilities. Each of these is reviewed in greater detail below.

The iron and steel sector in India

In India, three routes for iron and steel production are under operation:

- Integrated Steel Plants (ISPs), using blast furnace-open hearth (BF-OHF) or blast furnace/basic oxygen furnace (BF-BOF);
- Mini Steel Plants, scrap based Electric Arc Furnaces (scrap-EAF);
- Mini Steel Plants, sponge iron based Electric Arc Furnaces, iron from direct reduction (DRI-EAF). These can be either gas-based, or coal-based.

One or two Corex plants are currently being built.

There have been significant changes in the Indian iron and steel sector over the last few decades. Although the government owns 6 of the 7 large-scale integrated steel plants, there are many smaller-scale and privately owned steel plants in operation (estimated at 160 in 1998 (Kanjilal 1998) and 180 in 1999 (Sathaye and Gadgil). Demand is growing rapidly and the government's emphasis on increasing capacity is to expand and modernise existing facilities (rather than to build new ones).

Table 5-3 gives an overview of the number of plants, total capacity and production.

Table 5-3

Production and number of large-scale plants in the Indian iron and steel industry in 1995/96

Type	Production (Mt/y)	Number of plants
ISP	15.7	7
Scrap-EAF	1.5	N/A
DRI-EAF (gas)	2.2	4
DRI-EAF (coal)	1.8	12[1]

[1] Since 1995/96, another 4 coal based DRI-EAF plants have been installed and are now in operation

The current production is largely dominated by integrated steel plants. However, new capacity is mainly found in the EAF route, both from scrap and DRI. It can be expected that new capacity will be added over the next decades and, as EAFs require less investment capital (partly as they are mostly smaller units), these are expected to dominate the new construction. Therefore, the relative share of the EAF in production is expected to increase continuously.

For primary steel production, if current trends continue, the OHF will probably be completely phased out by 2005. An overview of the relative share of the steel production processes is given in Figure 5-3.

Figure 5-3

Relative amount of steel produced by the different process routes in India from 1982 to 1995

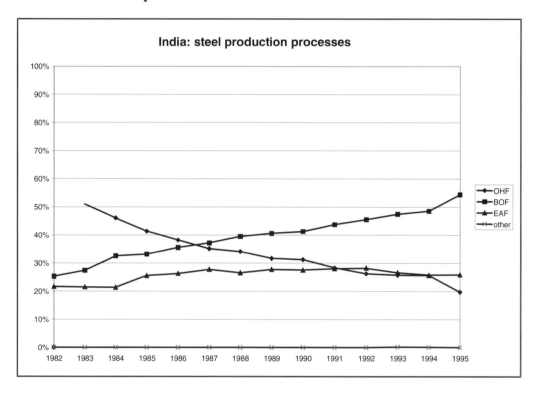

Annual data for energy use are available for ISPs from 1983 through 1995, as well as total energy consumption for all steel plants in 1994/95, including and excluding coke production, are provided in Figure 5-4. (Note: The fiscal year in India runs from March to April. Data for 1994/5 are plotted as 1994 data.) The increase in overall ISP energy consumption is expected to continue, in line with increasing steel demand, for the next several decades.

The Specific Energy Consumption can be calculated from the energy consumption data and production figures per process (Table 5-4). The CO_2 emission factors for each of the production processes are also calculated. Caution should be taken in any interpretation of these figures, as these estimates are based on averages for the entire sector and disaggregation may not be appropriate.

254

Figure 5-4

Energy consumption for steel plants in India (PJp)

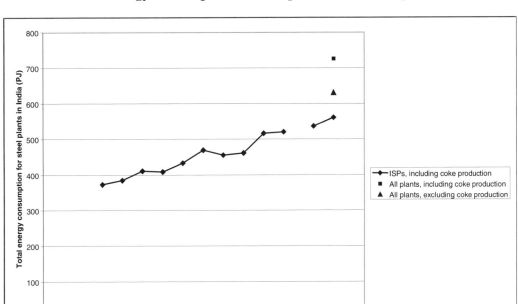

Table 5-4

**Specific energy consumption and CO_2 emission
factors for the different process routes in 1994/5, India**

Process routes	Specific Energy Consumption (GJ/tcs)	CO_2 emission factor (tCO$_2$/tcs)[1]
ISP	36.4	3.7
Scrap-EAF	18.8	1.4
DRI-EAF (gas)	25.3	1.55
DRI-EAF (coal)	35.6	3.37

Source: (Phylipsen, 2000) and own calculations (CO_2 emission factors)

[1] For the electricity emission factor, an average of 74 kg/GJp is used, based on fuel mix and an electricity generating efficiency of 30%.

255

Table 5-5 gives an overview of the different energy inputs in the Indian iron and steel sector. Data on fuel inputs for different process routes are not available.

Table 5-5

Fuel inputs in the Indian iron and steel sector (1994/5)

Solids (PJ)	Liquids (PJ)	Electricity (PJe)	Total Final (PJ)
620 (90%)	30 (4%)	41 (6%)	692 (100%)

Source: LBNL, 1999

The iron and steel sector in Brazil

In Brazil, three processes for iron and steel production are in operation:

- Integrated Steel Plants (ISPs), using blast furnace/basic oxygen furnace (BF-BOF);

- Mini Steel Plants, scrap based Electric Arc Furnaces (scrap-EAF);

- Mini Steel Plants, sponge iron based Electric Arc Furnaces, iron from direct reduction (DRI-EAF). These can be either gas-based, or coal-based.

The blast furnace/open hearth route is no longer used.

An overview of Brazilian production in each process through the various steel making routes is given in Figure 5-5. Between 1971 and 1995 steel production in Brazil has increased approximately 5-fold and the shares of the different production routes has changed significantly over this time. While in the early 1970s BF-OHF and BF-BOF produced approximately equal amounts of steel, rapid increases in BF-BOF production in the 1980s now means that it is by far the most dominant method. The open hearth furnace production route was totally phased out in Brazil in 1989. Steel produced via the EAF process has approximately tripled between 1971 and 1995. However, its share in total steel production has decreased slightly since the 1970s, from around 25% in 1978 to about 20% in 1993 and 1994 and 18% in 1995 (LBNL, 1999). With a production of 0.32 Mt in 1997, the contribution of DRI-EAF is relatively limited (LBNL, 1999).

Figure 5-5

Crude steel production in Brazil

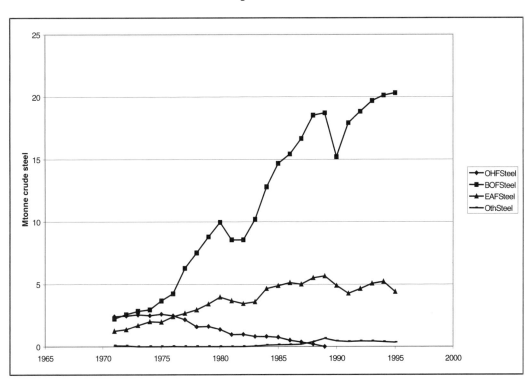

Source: LBNL, 1999

Figure 5-6 gives an overview of total energy consumption trends in the iron and steel sector in Brazil. Data on inputs for each of the process routes are not available.

An important characteristic of the Brazilian iron and steel industry is the large contribution of biomass (in the form of charcoal). Together with an electricity system that is largely based on hydro, the carbon intensity of iron and steel making in Brazil is therefore relatively low (Table 5-6), particularly when compared with either India or Poland, which are largely coal-based.

However, the low emissions intensity does not necessarily correlate to overall high efficiencies: due to the non-availability of SEC data on a plant or process route level, no conclusions on this issue can be drawn. As an indication, Table 5-7 gives an overview of the input of the different energy inputs in the Brazilian iron and steel sector. At a sectoral level, the SEC has decreased slightly since 1970, mainly due to the (autonomous) phase-out of the open hearth furnace, which accounted for approximately 40% of total production at that date (Figure 5-7).

Figure 5-6

Primary energy consumption in the Brazilian iron and steel industry

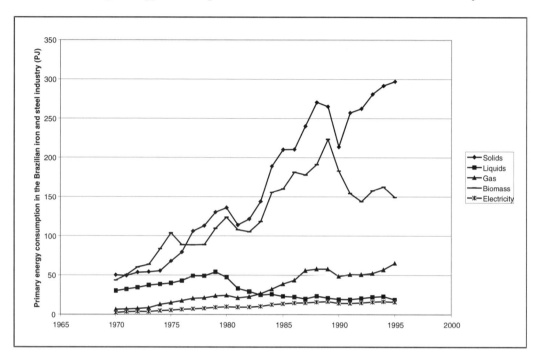

Source: LBNL, 1999

Table 5-6

**The specific energy consumption and carbon
intensity of the Brazilian iron and steel sector**

	Specific Energy Consumption (GJp/tcs)	CO_2 emission factor (tCO_2/tcs)
Entire sector	23	1.32

Source: Phylipsen, 2000

Figure 5-7

SEC development of the iron and steel sector in Brazil

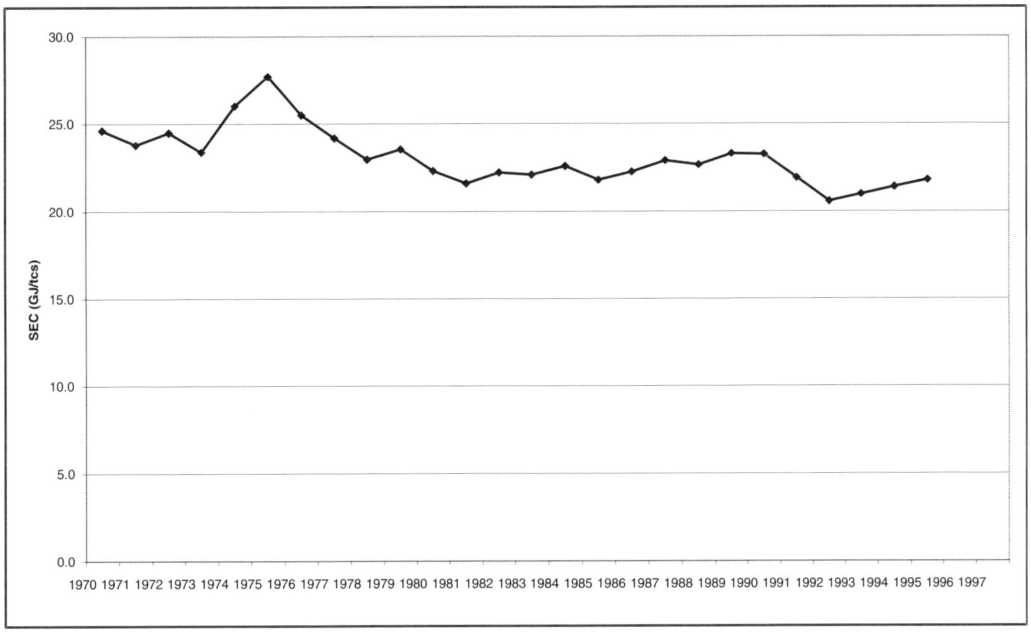

Source: LBNL, 1999

Table 5-7

Fuel inputs in the Brazilian iron and steel sector (1995)

Solids (PJ)	Liquids (PJ)	Gases (PJ)	Biomass (PJ)	Electricity (PJe)	Total Final (PJ)
297 (54%)	19 (3%)	65 (12%)	149 (27%)	16 (3%)	546 (100%)

Source: LBNL, 1999

The iron and steel sector in Poland

Data on steel production in Poland by type and energy consumption are available only between 1993 to 1999 (see Figure 5-8).

Much existing Polish steel technology is old: of the 25 steel mills in operation, 18 started production before the first world war (Prus 1998). However, restructuring in the steel sector is underway as part of Poland's EU accession programme. The consequent modernisation of the sector has meant an influx of capital and a resulting rapid and

259

substantial increase in the share of continuously cast steel (from 8% in 1992 to 70% in 1997 (Prus 1998). Significant changes have also occurred in the share of different process routes. BF-OHF accounted for 10% of total production in 1997, compared to 30% in 1990 and is set to fall further as all but two BF-OHF facilities have been earmarked for closure (Prus 1998).

Figure 5-8

Total production of crude steel in Poland (1999 data are provisional)

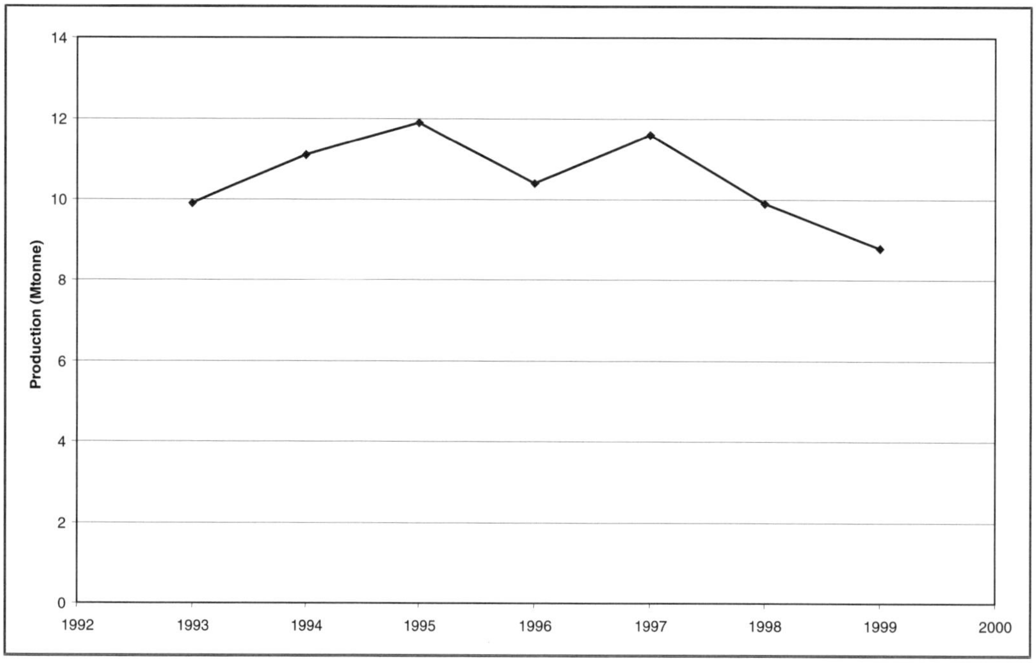

Source: IISI, 2000

The majority of steel production is in BF-BOF plants. In 1998, some sources indicate that 93% of the steel production was through a BOF and 7% through OHF (IISI, 2000). However, the Polish Energy Agency gives data on energy consumption for steel production by the EAF process, suggesting that this is used for at least some steel production. This inconsistency demonstrates that data availability is a problem.

Based on the data provided in (Worrell *et. al.*, 1997), in combination with the data on continuous casting as given in (IISI, 2000) the current SEC of the iron and steel sector in Poland is estimated at around 26 GJ/tonne. No data on plant level are available.

The CO_2 emission factor is estimated assuming that the fuel that is used for the production of steel is 100% coal. The emission factor is then comparable to the emission factor for ISPs in India, 3.6 ton CO_2/tcs (1998). From the IEA energy balances, the following division for the Polish iron and steel sector was derived (Table 5-8):

Table 5-8

Fuel inputs in the Polish iron and steel sector (1995)

Coal and derivatives	Natural gas	Renewables	Electricity	Heat	Other	Total
179.4	3.0	23.0	2.9	27.1	7.7	240.2
75%	10%	1%	11%	3%	1%	100%

Source: IEA, 1998

N.B. Energy use in coke ovens and blast furnace are not included in these figures.

5.2.6   Comparison of the case study countries

A number of similarities and differences emerge from the analysis of these three countries. The difference in SEC values between India and Brazil is mainly caused by the fact that no BF-OHF furnaces remain in operation in Brazil, whereas 20% of capacity in India is still through this route. Furthermore, the DR-EAF route is virtually absent in Brazil (relatively more scrap used as input for the EAFs, thereby significantly reducing the energy consumption compared to India.

Table 5-9

Comparing CO_2-intensities for the different process routes

Process routes	India		Brazil		Poland	
	SEC (GJ/tcs)	CO_2 emission factor (tCO$_2$/tcs)[1]	SEC (GJ/tcs)	CO_2 emission factor (tCO$_2$/tcs)	SEC (GJ/tcs)	CO_2 emission factor (tCO$_2$/tcs)
ISP	36.4	3.7	23[2]	1.32[2]	26	3.6
Scrap-EAF	18.8	1.4	n/a	n/a	n/a	n/a
DRI-EAF (gas)	25.3	1.6	n/a	n/a	n/a	n/a

Source: Phylipsen, 2000

The estimate for Poland is based on (Worrell *et. al.,* 1997) and extrapolated using an overview of installed equipment.

[1] For the electricity emission factor, we used an average for the entire sector of 74 kg/GJp.

[2] For the entire iron and steel sector

261

The difference in energy and CO_2-intensities for the case study countries is summarised in Table 5-9. It is seen that, while energy intensities vary significantly between countries, the variation in CO_2-intensities per GJ fuel input is even greater.

5.3 Baseline construction: environmental performance

Based on both the specific case studies and on the broader review of the sector provided above, it is possible to develop a set of recommendations regarding baseline construction for potential steel projects. Several types of multi-project baselines are developed and discussed here; the analysis also indicates the kind and extent of the data required.

5.3.1 Input data

Obtaining energy consumption data useful for standardised baseline construction in iron and steel production is difficult. Highly aggregated data is available and this can be used to give general indications about a country's iron and steel sector, including the extent of the sector's autonomous energy efficiency improvements. However, as this data is aggregated for all plant types, it does not indicate whether improvements are as a result of a change in production routes, product mix or increased efficiency.

Some information is available on observed best practice plants. The data in Table 5-10 ("best actually observed" column) represent estimates based on plants that are currently running and of which energy consumption data are known. Data in this table must be treated with caution - plants listed here may be operating more or less efficiently than indicated in this table. The Corex process is more efficient than the ISP route. Plants operate typically at 19 GJ/ton, which is very near the design value (CEC, 1999).

Data on global average energy use by production route is scarce. Data might be estimated by extrapolating from a few important producing countries for which information is available (although, based on existing literature, even this data is difficult to come across):

1. China, Japan, US and Germany for ISP;

2. China, Japan, US, Mexico and Italy for scrap-based EAF; and

3. Mexico, Venezuela, Iran and Saudi-Arabia for DRI (gas).

Country-specific data on SEC per production route is also patchy. In theory it should be possible, albeit time-consuming, to gather the data for individual plants. Alternatively, a plant inventory could be carried out and national energy intensity inferred from weighted average production. For Brazil, only data for the entire iron and steel sector are available. As indicated before, according to (IISI, 2000) Poland did not produce any steel via the EAF route in 1998. However, Gilecki (2000) gives energy (electricity) consumption data for EAF steel production in the same year, thus indicating differences in data that cannot easily be explained.

The estimated averages used in this study are given in the following table. They should be interpreted with care and would need international review before being fixed as the values used in establishing baselines. In the short term, the values as given in the following table can be used as first estimates.

Table 5-10

Comparing energy intensities of steel production in selected countries and processes (GJ/tcs)

Process	Best actually observed[a]	Mid-point SEC	India[d]	Brazil[d]	Poland
ISP	22	26[b]	36.4	23	26
Scrap-EAF	7.7	10[c]	18.8		
DRI-EAF (gas)	22	26[c]	25.3		
DRI-EAF (coal)	25	36	35.6		
Corex	19				

[a] SEC values represent the lowest SEC observed in a fully operational plant world wide in 1995-1996. *Source:* (De Beer *et. al.*, 1999)

[b] Estimate based on the values of China, US, Japan and Germany.

[c] Estimate based on the average of the upper and lower values achieved in practice as indicated in (De Beer *et. al.*, 1999). Because a large share of the production is in developing and OPEC countries, this is expected to be an underestimate.

[d] *Source:* Pyhlipsen (2000).

Emission baselines may also need to take into account improvements in energy efficiency that have occurred as part of BAU practices in the past. However, such a calculation requires country-specific data for at least two years and is therefore also difficult to obtain. Some indications for the case study countries are outlined in Table 5-11.

As indicated in section 5.2 and Figure 5-1, several different final products can be produced from the intermediate product, crude steel. These final products have different energy intensities (Table 5-12) and also different end uses. For example, cold-rolled products are needed for applications such as car bodies or the outside of refrigerators and their production entails an extra step. To determine total energy consumption in a cold rolling process, the values for hot and cold rolling should be summed.

Table 5-11

Indication of past autonomous efficiency improvements

	India	Brazil	Poland
Primary steel production	~0.5-1% per year[c]	~0% per year[b]	-0.6% per year[a]

[a] *Source:* Worrell *et. al.* (1997). This figure indicates an increase in Specific Energy Consumption in the period 1980-1991. Energy efficiency continued to improve between 1991-1995, but at a lower rate (Price *et. al.* 1999).
[b] Both Worrell *et. al.* (1997) and LBNL (1999), indicate only a very small change in efficiency in the Brazilian iron and steel sector in the period 1980-1995.
[c] Based on (SAIL, 1996) with indications over the period 1990-1995

Table 5-12

The differences between hot rolling and cold rolling with regard to energy intensity on a best practice basis.

	Fuel consumption (GJ/tonne shaped steel)	Electricity consumption (GJ/tonne shaped steel)
Hot rolling	1.53	0.35
Cold rolling	1.10	0.53

Moreover, the quality of coal and iron ore inputs used can influence the energy consumption of steel production. Using high sulphur and/or high ash content coal increases the Specific Energy Consumption of the steel manufacturing process. The quantitative relationship between coal quality and energy consumption is not exactly known, but for specific cases a rough estimate can be made. In general, a higher ash content in the coal, or a lower iron content in the ore, will lead to a higher energy consumption (Worrell, 2000).

Data problems

For all countries studied, acquiring the necessary input data was difficult. In general, national bureaux of statistics have been the main source of data. The data for India are more complete than those of the other countries studied (drawing on extensive research as described in Phylipsen, 2000 and fieldwork carried out in 1998/9 by the main author). Difficulties experienced are production data for electric arc furnaces and energy consumption data for electric arc furnaces. Data on the product mix from electric arc furnaces are also difficult to obtain at a national level. On the plant level, these data are available, so this information could be supplied for a refurbishment CDM project is under development.

264

For Brazil, data have been gathered within the INEDIS network[142]. However, the distinction between the different process routes is relatively difficult to obtain both for production data and energy input data. On a national level, the product mix and energy inputs are relatively well known for the iron and steel sector as a whole.

For Poland, the production data from (IISI, 2000) are not in agreement with the data for energy use as given by the Polish national energy agency (Gilecki, 2000). It is beyond the scope of this case study to determine the "real" values, so extrapolations have been used.

Data on crude steel production are also not always readily available. However, the values for developing the baselines could be determined with additional research. Similarly, there are problems with obtaining the data required for the adjustment of benchmarks for product differences: data are available, but additional research in the countries is required to assess its accuracy.

5.3.2   *Aggregation*

Based on data availability, comparability and sectoral variability, it is proposed that baselines be constructed on the basis of energy intensity in the manufacture a ton of crude steel at the international process routes level, *i.e.*:

1.   Integrated Steel Plants (ISPs);

2.   Scrap based Electric Arc Furnaces (scrap-EAF);

3.   Direct Reduced Iron (gas-based) Electric Arc Furnaces (DRI (gas)-EAF); and

4.   Direct Reduced Iron (coal-based) Electric Arc Furnaces (DRI (coal)-EAF).

No fuel separation is needed in categories 1 and 2 because in EAF the majority (more than 95%) of fuel used is electricity and in Integrated Steel Plants it is almost all coal. However for EAFs, it is important to examine the raw materials that used as iron-bearing materials (*i.e.* the proportion of scrap used) as these have a significant impact on the energy use.

It is not possible to aggregate baselines across process routes as they differ significantly in the amount of energy used to produce one ton of crude steel. Moreover, the different process routes use different feedstocks, energy inputs and produce and different products. Each of the different routes are used in most countries.

---

[142] The Inedis network (International Network for Energy Demand Analysis in the Industrial Sector) is an international network of specialists in the area of industrial energy efficiency. Data on industrial energy use and accompanying indicators are collected and stored in a database (LBNL, 1999).

The DRI-EAF (coal-based) process route could be considered as an inefficient variation on the Integrated Steel Plants concept, implying that GHG emission reduction projects from coal-based DRI-EAF should not be credited at all. Therefore, this process route is excluded in the remainder of the report.

Since the technologies used for iron and steel production are internationally uniform, it is not necessary to distinguish between geographical regions for technical reasons and standardised baselines for different process routes may therefore be set up at an international (global) level. This level of disaggregation is also in line with the recommendations of other studies on the suitability of multi-project baselines, *e.g.* that recommend using global, disaggregated benchmarks for commodities that are traded internationally and products and feed stocks that are heterogeneous (Lazarus *et. al.*, 1999),. However, the energy consumption of the same technology in different places can differ substantially, reflecting the age of equipment, quality of raw material inputs, the degree of integration of the process and the level of implementation of energy efficient technologies.

It may be necessary to adjust for the specific characteristics of an individual plant or product mix within a process route. For example, Phylipsen *et al* (1998), recommend correcting for the amount of hot-rolled and cold-rolled steel produced.

In theory, standards could also be established at a higher degree of disaggregation. Thus, for example, it would be possible to set standards for the different process steps within each process route, *e.g.* the energy used in a blast furnace. However, such a disaggregation is not recommended as process integration is then not rewarded as an option for emission reduction.

Setting baselines with still greater disaggregation (*e.g.* at the level of individual technology components such as motors and pumps) would be extremely data intensive. Moreover, it would be difficult to assess the emission reductions from projects using this level of disaggregation, because it would require an assumption regarding individual component use (*e.g.* how long. an individual motor runs[143].

Differences in SEC for the same technology operating in different places are generally caused by differences in operation and maintenance, or the age of the technology. Other causes can be the quality of coal and iron ore, which differs between countries.

---

[143] Note that motors and lighting from such industries as iron and steel must be excluded from a general "motor project" if there also is a iron and steel project to avoid double counting.

5.3.3 *Proposed baselines*

As with baselines set in other sectors, ideal emissions baselines in the iron and steel sectors should meet the following criteria (Ellis and Bosi, 1999):

- Be environmentally credible (to exclude projects that are not environmentally additional);
- Be transparent and verifiable by a third party;
- Be simple and inexpensive to draw up (low transaction costs/low costs for baseline development);
- Provide a reasonable level of crediting certainty for investors; and
- Have a potentially large volume of projects.

The variation in these criteria influences the number of projects that will be generated through JI and CDM. For the suitability of the baselines that will be described in the following pages, the potential large volume of projects is an important criterion.

Any baseline approach involves a trade-off between the criterion of environmental credibility and generating a potential large volume of projects. The baselines proposed in the following sections will first be described and then scored against these criteria.

Much of the following analysis mainly focuses on existing plants. New plants usually operate at a Specific Energy Consumption that is approximately equal to the world wide best practice and the SEC of worldwide best practice is thus considered the most suitable standardised baseline for new plants. This is particularly true as a number of plants in developing countries have been built and operated at a SEC that is at the world-wide best practice. However, exceptions do exist: for example, in the United States where it is not considered economically viable to build new plants with the lowest specific energy consumption due to low energy prices, lower efficiency plants are still being constructed. Thus, a baseline that incorporated these new facilities into the average might yield higher crediting levels.

Corex$^©$ plants too operate at approximately equal efficiencies world-wide, with most plants that are installed operate at a specific energy consumption near the best practice value. Thus, the best practice value of 19 GJ/ton crude steel is proposed to be a suitable baseline, both for new and refurbishment Corex plants.

Benchmarking energy use

Emission baselines could also be developed based on standardised (or "benchmarked") energy performance of a plant. In such cases, country specific GHG emission factors would need to be applied to the standardised energy value to calculate the accompanying

GHG emissions reduction[144]. Separating the energy and GHG intensity of the process avoids the requirement to set default GHG intensity standards for electricity generation, significantly simplifying the baseline setting process.

Several possible baselines based on the concept of benchmarking can be generated, such as average, median or "better than average". Average and "better than average" benchmarks can also be thought of in terms of the stringency of a baseline. A standardised baseline based on the energy intensity of different steel production routes would be very stringent if based on world-wide best practice values, but much more lax if based on world-wide average performance. A baseline based on the "national average" performance could be more or less stringent than a world-wide average, depending on the country.

Benchmarking based on recent technology additions is another option and indeed, one that is recommended in other sectors. However, for new plants, this option seems to be essentially the same as benchmarking on the world-wide best practice level (see *e.g.* the latest new iron and steel plants in South Korea) and so is not considered separately.

Five different possibilities for a standardised energy baseline for each of the production routes are discussed below:

1) A baseline based on the best practice energy performance world-wide.

Assuming that the plant operating with the best practice energy performance world-wide indicates the level above which environmental additionality is guaranteed, a baseline can be set at this level. In practice, adjustments to this level will need to be made in order to account for the amount of steel that is hot-rolled and cold-rolled (see Table 5-12) and for the quality of the coal and ore used. In such a case, only projects using advanced technology would generate emission credits.

2) A baseline based on the world-wide average SEC per process route.

Using this value would lead to a relatively lax baseline as plants that are responsible for approximately half of total iron and steel production world-wide would qualify as CDM/JI projects if the baseline "test" were the only additionality criteria.

3) A baseline based on "better than average" performance

Such a baseline would be between the values of the world average and best practice performance baselines outlined above. It would therefore also result in an intermediate level of stringency and an intermediate level of project numbers. It could be drawn up at an arbitrary level, such as 90% of the "average" level.

---

[144] The determination of the country specific emission factors is dependent on the developments in the power sector of a country. The Electricity Case Study suggests how such baselines could be established.

4) A baseline based on benchmarking on the country average SEC per production route

This option would result in baselines differentiated by country, as well as by production route. This type of baseline is not consistent with aggregation purely at a production route level, but it would have the advantage of being able to take into account widely differing national circumstances. As for baselines based on a worldwide average, this type of baseline could be drawn up at different levels of stringency (*e.g.* country average, 10% better than average).

5) A "graduated crediting" baseline

This alternative allows a percentage of the reductions to be counted - with the amount varied according to the stringency of the benchmark used (see Figure 5-9). The values could be set to take into account both national performance and BAT performance. Such an approach is more stringent than one based on national average figures (because not all emission reductions would be credited at that level), but would allow a larger number of projects than a standard set at the BAT energy performance level.

Technology matrix

As for a multi-project baseline based on a standardised energy value for production process routes, there is no technical reason to distinguish between countries or regions for baselines drawn up using the technology matrix approach. A standardised energy consumption figure could be established for each piece of equipment in a "standard" plant for each of the production routes examined.

The basic principle is the same as for the benchmarking approach: compare the SEC of the standard technology with the alternative, lower GHG emission technology. The differences in SEC can then again be "translated" to GHG emissions using country specific emission factors.

The possible standard configurations can be determined in the following ways:

1. Based on the configuration of the world-wide best-practice plant: The technologies that are used in the plant performing with the lowest SEC in the world are taken as the reference technologies.

2. Based on inventory of all the technologies world-wide: An overview of all technologies world-wide is made and penetration figures for each of the options are collected. Then, the modal technology, *i.e.* the technology that is implemented most frequently, can be included in the configuration of the standard.

3. Based on the implementation of technologies in each country: Although this requires a higher level of disaggregation than that recommended in this report, it would enable national circumstances to be taken into account. However,

269

establishing a baseline would require data collection at a country level in order to establish the modal technology.

Figure 5-9

An illustration of the "graduated crediting" concept (*e.g.* for BF-BOF production)

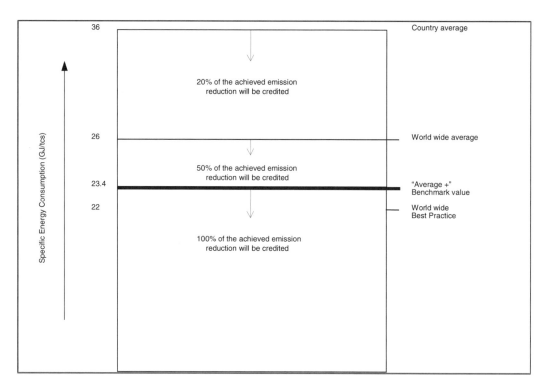

This is illustrated in Table 5-13. The estimated savings by adopting continuous casting in a plant using an ingot caster are 2 GJ/tcs (Price *et. al.*, 1999). A thin slab caster accounts for around an additional 0.4 GJ/tcs, derived from (De Beer *et. al.*, 1999). Because strip casting is an advanced technology, the savings are not exactly known. Additional savings compared to thin slab casting are indicated with X in Table 5-13. The data are the amount of GJ that will be saved per ton crude steel. The first number gives the amount of savings under a baseline based on world-wide best practice, the second is based on world-wide average, the third is based on country average.

For the iron and steel sector, these matrices would have to be developed for different steps, including the coke making process, the sinter plant, pelletisation, the oxygen plant, the iron making step, the steel making step, the casting process, the hot rolling mill and the cold rolling mill. Besides this, for the technologies that cannot be attributed to one of these processes, like heat recovery where the heat is used in another process step, another matrix would also need to be developed.

270

Developing a technology matrix may be difficult especially when technologies are included that do not cause a large step change difference in performance, such as heat exchangers, adjustable speed drives, high efficiency motors, *etc.* For these small technologies, it will be difficult to determine the accompanying change in specific energy consumption by examining plant-specific energy consumption data. In addition, the energy consumption of individual components (*e.g.* motors) is very much dependent on the amount of time they are used. To estimate the energy conservation and consequent GHG mitigation that is achieved by the implementation of energy efficient components, this amount of time also has to be estimated, as in a technology matrix no direct measurements are included. The effect of implementation of these smaller kind of technologies as a JI/CDM project is therefore almost impossible to monitor.

An example of the technology matrix approach for integrated steel plants

In the manufacture of flat products, a choice exists between ingot casting, continuous casting, thin slab casting and strip casting. Any of these routes would result in equivalent products being produced, but the energy used to produce these products would be different. Ingot casting is the "traditional" technology, continuous casting the standard in more than 80% of the installed plants, thin slab casting can be considered as best practice and strip casting as future technology.

Using the first technology matrix option, the standard "benchmark" technology would be thin slab casting (even though this technology is installed in not more than 3 or 4 plants). No GHG emissions will be credited when a continuous caster or an ingot caster is (partially) replaced by a thin slab caster. Strip casting will be credited, for the difference between thin slab and strip casting, but this is a future technology.

Using the second technology matrix option, the standard would be continuous casting. Replacing either an ingot caster or a continuous caster by a thin slab caster generates GHG emission credits for the difference between a thin slab caster and a continuous caster.

Under the third option, the ingot caster will be the standard. Installation of a continuous caster would be credited at the difference of continuous casting and ingot casting and the installation of a thin slab caster will be credited at the difference between thin slab and ingot casting.

Table 5-13

**A technology matrix for the casting process
in an integrated steel plant that produces flat products**

		Currently installed technology					
		Ingot caster	Continuous caster	Thin slab caster	Strip caster	*Etc.*	*Etc.*
Technology to be implemented in the JI/CDM project	Ingot caster						
	Continuous caster	0/0/2					
	Thin slab caster	0/0.4/2.4	0/0.4/2.4				
	Strip caster	X/X+0.4/X+2.4	X/X+0.4/X+2.4	X/X+0.4/X+2.4			
	Etc.						

5.3.4 Other issues: Fixed versus revisable baselines and timelines

The previous section outlined possible ways of standardising the starting point of baselines for potential iron and steel JI/CDM projects. If the value of the baseline remains constant for each year that the project receives credits, the baseline is fixed and static. However, given that the energy efficiency of iron and steel production has increased in many countries and that technology developments can make new investments highly energy-efficient, it may be more appropriate to assume some sort of autonomous energy efficiency improvement (*e.g.* 1% per year). This type of baseline, fixed at the start of a project's life, but dynamic over that life, would increase the environmental additionality of the baseline by reducing the likelihood of it creating non-additional credits. Alternatively, baselines could be revised periodically, *e.g.* once every 5 years, in order to take into account technological development.

Regarding the length of time over which a project can generate emission credits (*i.e.* the emission timeline), this analysis recommends using the average economic lifetime of technologies as the most important indicator. These differ from one technology to another. A rule of thumb is that electro-mechanical equipment (*e.g.* pumps and motors) have a lifetime of 10-15 years and buildings and large installations 25-30 years. (Daniels *et. al.*, 1998) give 20 years for buildings and large installations, 15 years for electro-mechanical equipment, 40 years for the coke ovens and 30 years for sinter and pellet production.

The problem with determining crediting lifetimes for JI/CDM projects in the iron and steel industry is that it is very difficult to give good estimates, because it is very rare that an entire facility is replaced. It is much more common for a plant to undergo major revisions during its lifetime without ever being completely replaced. It is therefore difficult to determine when a piece of equipment is at the end of its lifetime. This also implies that the age of the current stock can not be considered to be a useful indicator for determining the additionality of a proposed CDM/JI project.

The practice of refurbishing different parts of the iron and steel production route at different times also means that improvements in a plant's SEC is likely to be steady and incremental rather than large step changes. Applying an autonomous efficiency improvement into account when developing a baseline for an iron and steel project is therefore recommended, as this effectively includes technology development into the baseline. It is advised to use a fixed improvement rate (based on world-wide average efficiency improvement) and check the thus derived generic baseline every 5 years to see if the SEC development still conforms to expectations.

5.3.5 Scoring the baselines

It is useful to consider the criteria discussed above to evaluate the advantages and disadvantages of the baseline methods.

Table 5-14 indicates that the environmental additionality of different baseline approaches and assumptions can differ substantially, sometimes even within a single approach. For example, using a country average energy benchmark for Brazil would lead to a stringent baseline because iron and steel production in Brazil is relatively efficient. The risk of any projects under such a baseline not being additional is small. However, using a baseline drawn up using the same methodology (*i.e.* country average) for India would lead to a lax baseline because India has an old and relatively inefficient iron and steel sector.

The costs of setting up the different baselines can also differ substantially. A baseline predicated on a smaller number of data points, such as "best practice" data, will be cheaper and easier to set up than a baseline drawn up using a larger number of data points, such as the world average for a particular production route. Similarly, the "graduated crediting" approach, essentially drawn up using both country average and world wide average baselines will be more expensive than either of these baselines singly. The costs of baselines drawn up using a technology matrix approach are generally higher than those drawn up using a benchmarking approach, because one JI/CDM project could involve installing many different technologies. The mitigation effect of such a project would therefore need to be assessed by summing the individual effect of each technology change.

The transparency and verifiability of the different potential baselines also varies with different baseline approaches and assumptions, although to a smaller degree than the other criteria examined. Any standardised and documented baseline should be relatively transparent. However, the calculations of a more complex baseline (such as one based on

273

"graduated crediting" are likely to be more difficult to follow than those of a simpler baseline, such as that based on best practice performance.

Table 5-14 also gives a rough indication of the numbers of projects likely to qualify for credits under different baseline assumptions. This is assessed in more detail in the following section.

5.4 Baseline construction: potential volume of projects

The potential volume of refurbishment projects under each of the proposed baselines is estimated for each of the process routes in the countries under consideration (Table 5-15). These are general indications and have not been adjusted for the effect of product mix on energy consumption. The actual potential may therefore differ from the estimations overleaf.

In the context of project volumes, it is also useful to draw a distinction between new plants and retrofits. Given the magnitude of investment needed for new plants and the potentially long life of iron and steel plants, retrofit is more common than greenfield additions, especially when integrated steel plants are considered. New plants that have recently been built, in general show a specific energy consumption is of the same order of magnitude as in best practice plants - allowing the best practice standard to serve as the baseline. The high degree of variability in existing plants requires a more complex baseline structure for this group - leading to the distinction between greenfield and refurbishment plants.

The potential volume for GHG emissions reduction in new plants is difficult to determine, because estimates of capacity additions from new plants are difficult to make and have large uncertainties. As a first indication, it could be expected that the specific energy consumption of new plants in 10 years would be up to 2 GJ/tcs lower than the current world-wide best practice SEC for integrated steel plants and DRI-EAF plants, but less for scrap based EAF plants.

Table 5-14

Scoring the proposed baselines for the iron and steel sector against the criteria

Criteria	Benchmarking[1]					Technology matrix[2]		
	World-wide best practice	World-wide average	World-wide average with AEEI	Country average	Graduated crediting	World-wide best practice	World-wide mode	Country mode
Environmental Additionality[3]	++	- to +[5]	-- to +	-- to ++[6]	- to +	++	++[5]	-- to ++[6]
Potential volume of projects	--	+	+	0 to ++[7]	0 to +	--	+	0 to ++[7]
Transparency and verifiability	++	++	++	+	-/+	++	+	+
Costs to draw up the baseline system[4]	++	+	+	+	+/-	-	--	-

[1] With regard to benchmarking, monitoring and measuring the JI/CDM project remains an important issue to determine the achieved CO_2 emission reduction. Benchmarking only gives an indication on the additionality of projects.

[2] Using the technology matrix approach, the GHG emission that is credited is fixed and is thus not a real representation of the GHG emission achieved. The monitoring requirements are lower than in the project based or the benchmarking case, due to standardisation on technology level.

[3] Environmental additionality is defined as the credibility of the achieved emissions in projects being truly additional, which, of course, does not equal the environmental effect that is the result of the implemented projects.

[4] ++ means low costs, -- means high cost.

[5] Because world wide averages are used in the benchmarking baseline and modal technologies are used in the case of a technology matrix, the environmental additionality in the technology matrix is expected to be slightly better guaranteed in the latter case.

[6] If a country is relatively inefficient (in the case of benchmarking) or relatively old technologies are installed (in the case of a technology matrix) the environmental additionality is low. This is generally the case. If a country has efficient new, technologies (*e.g.* South Korea), the environmental additionality is large.

[7] If a country is relatively inefficient (in the case of benchmarking) or relatively old technologies are installed (in the case of a technology matrix) the potential volume of projects is large. If a country has efficient new, technologies (*e.g.* South Korea), the potential volume of projects is small.

It is very data and time intensive to calculate the potential volume of projects using the technology matrix. A simple estimate of the total volume can be made if it is assumed that the standard configuration of technologies is represented by the accompanying SEC values. Under this assumption, the SEC of the standard configuration defined by the world modal technologies would be equivalent to the world average SEC. Of course, in such a case, the total potential volume of projects would then be the same for technology matrix as for benchmarking using the world average. However, inasmuch as the data requirements for a technology matrix are more extensive, it can also be assumed that fewer projects would be undertaken - as the sheer difficulty of this approach would increased transaction costs and reduce project volumes. Such an assumption might apply to any technology matrix approach versus a benchmark approach of comparable stringency. In the subsequent analysis, only benchmark approaches are therefore considered.

The potential volume of projects that can be undertaken with benchmarking baselines is provided for India in Table 5-15. The data are derived as follows:

- It is assumed that plants that operate at a SEC that is less than 10% higher than the benchmark would be suitable for CO_2 emission reduction measures. This number of plants is indicated in the first column of the table.

- For each plant, the potential volume of projects is calculated by subtracting the Best Practice value from the benchmark value, or the SEC of the plant (whichever is lower) and then multiplying the result by the process route specific CO_2 emission indicator.

- The total volume (*i.e.* the sum of the first two steps for the country) is given in the third column.

It should be noted that the result is likely to be an over-estimate of potential volumes as, in practice, plants would not be expected in any single retrofit, to reach best practice performance levels. For Brazil and Poland, comprehensive plant data are not available. However, potential project numbers will be largest using the world-wide average, but likely to be no more than 6 for Brazil and 5 for Poland. Phylipsen (2000) calculated a reference Best Practice SEC for the Brazilian situation (*i.e.* 20% EAF and 36% cold-rolled), *i.e.* 18.7 GJ/ton. This value is used as the best practice world wide value.

Whereas the country average SEC in India is above the world-wide average SEC, this is not the case for Brazil and Poland. This does not imply that a benchmark on a world-wide average is not stringent enough for Brazil or Poland, but only that the plants in Brazil and Poland are already more efficient than Indian plants on average.

Table 5-15

Potential volume of refurbishment projects in the iron and steel plants in India

Baseline approach	Number of plants near the benchmark value	Potential volume of projects in selected plants (Mt CO_2)	Potential volume of projects in all plants (Mt CO_2)
Integrated Steel Plants			
World-wide Best practice (22 GJ/tcs)	0	~0	~0
World-wide average (26 GJ/tcs)	2	3	6
Country average	4	16	20
Scrap-EAF			
World-wide Best practice (7.7 GJ/tcs)[1]	0	~0	~0
World-wide average (10 GJ/tcs)	N/a	N/a	0.3
Country average	N/a	N/a	1
DRI-EAF (gas)			
World-wide Best practice (7.7 GJ/tcs)[1]	0	~0	~0
World-wide average (10 GJ/tcs)	N/a	N/a	0.5
Country average	N/a	N/a	0.5

* Graduated crediting would result in greater potential project numbers than baselines based on worldwide best practice, but lower potential project numbers than baselines based on world-wide average or country averages.

From Table 5-15 it becomes clear that there is a tradeoff between environmental additionality and the potential volume of projects. That automatically generates the question if it is possible to generate a larger potential volume of projects, while not losing on the additionality criteria. The "graduated crediting" approach outlined in section 5.3 and Figure 5-9 could be one way of achieving a satisfactory tradeoff - although, as discussed above, it imposes potentially significant data requirements and costs.

5.5   Conclusions and recommendations

There are a number of potential energy-related JI/CDM project types in the iron and steel sector. These include:

- increasing the energy efficiency of steel production (*e.g.* by installing more efficient equipment, implementing good housekeeping measures);

- changing the manufacturing process (*e.g.* by installing new equipment like thin slab casters); or

- changing the input fuel for direct reduction (*e.g.* from coal to gas).

It is possible to define multi-project baselines in the iron and steel sector. The component of these baselines that could be standardised is that of the energy consumption of different process routes per ton of crude steel output. Further adjustments would need to be made to take into account the different energy intensity of different iron and steel products. Adjustments may also need to be made to take into account the quality of fuel and ore inputs used. A standardised "translation" of these energy values to GHG equivalents is not practical given the variability in fuels used in iron and steel production between countries and the fuel mix of central electricity production. CH_4 and N_2O emissions are almost absent in the production of iron and steel and thus need not be included in the baseline.

Internationally standardised baselines for iron and steel projects based on energy intensities could be aggregated to the level of different process routes, *i.e.*:

1. Integrated Steel Plants;

2. Scrap based Electric Arc Furnaces;

3. Direct reduced iron (gas based) Electric Arc Furnaces;

4. Direct reduced iron (coal based) Electric Arc Furnaces.

As the direct reduced iron (coal based) route is as an inefficient and outdated process, it is recommended that projects using this process should not be considered eligible for JI/CDM status. Energy intensities could be used for projects worldwide. However, some corrections may need to be made to account for country specific circumstances, *i.e.* coal and iron ore quality and product mix, *i.e.* the fraction of cold-rolled steel *versus* hot-rolled steel.

In general data availability at the level of aggregation needed to develop baselines is limited in international publications. Thus, for example, while the analysis of India reviewed in this case study shows that the necessary data are available, even this information would require additional verification and are not sufficiently comprehensive to fully develop country specific sectoral baselines. Reviewing national data also yields conflicting information: this is the case in the Polish case study. Establishing robust baselines in these countries will require additional data to be collected bottom-up (in the country and compared with international statistics.

Two types of baselines have been evaluated in this report, *i.e.* benchmarking and technology matrix. They both have advantages and disadvantages.

Neither approach is not inherently better than the other with respect to environmental credibility: both could provide stringent or lax baselines, depending on the assumptions used. Moreover, the environmental additionality, or not, of a single baseline assumption can vary substantially depending on national circumstances. For example, using a baseline derived from country average data would lead to a lax baseline for India, but a stringent baseline for Brazil.

Overall, it is recommended that baselines be set using a standardised energy value for an individual iron and steel process route. Such a benchmarking-type system is easier to develop than a system based on the technology matrix. Moreover, the data requirements for the latter are large and the inclusion of technologies that do not cause step change difference in performance is expected to be very data intensive and very difficult to develop.

It is also recommended that separate baselines be developed for greenfield and refurbishment projects. For greenfield projects (new capacity), a benchmark based on the world-wide best practice energy intensities for different production routes is the most suitable, as it reflects recent capacity additions under BAU conditions, including in both developed and developing countries (*e.g.* in India and South Korea). Indeed some of the most advanced iron and steel production technology (*e.g.* the Corex process) is already in place or is planned in developing countries.

For refurbishment of existing plants, a benchmark based on a "better than world-wide average" is considered to be a good trade-off between environmental credibility and the potential volume of projects. However, determining what is "better than average" is likely to be an arbitrary decision, particularly given the lack of data on plant performances.

Given the improvements in energy efficiency noted over the past two decades, an autonomous energy efficiency improvement should be factored into a standardised emission baseline (for both greenfield and refurbishment plants). This baseline is likely to need evaluating every 5 years to check if the SEC development conforms to previous expectations.

Another method to increase the potential volume of projects while still preserving the environmental credibility is to allow credits for projects that improve currently operating plants to below the national average energy intensity, even if the performance of such plants does not achieve the "better than average" baseline. This type of baseline is more stringent than one based on national average performance (because not all emission reductions would be credited at that level), but would encourage more projects than projects judged against baselines drawn up using BAT energy performance.

It is difficult to give general rules regarding the standardisation of emission timelines for JI/CDM projects in the iron and steel sector, mainly because the average lifetime of the industrial technology used is very difficult to determine. The current age of the stock is therefore not considered to be a useful indicator for determining the additionality of CDM/JI projects.

5.6   References

De Beer, J., J. Harnisch, M. Kerssemeeckers, 1999. *Greenhouse Gas Emissions from Iron and Steel Production*, Ecofys, The Netherlands.

CEC, 1999. Integrated Pollution Prevention and Control (IPPC). *Best available techniques reference document on the production of iron and steel*, European Commission, Directorate-General Joint Research Centre, Seville, Spain.

Daniels, B.W. and H.C. Moll, 1998. *The base metal industry: Technological descriptions of processes and production routes; status quo and prospects.* Center for Energy and Environmental Studies, Research Paper no 92, University of Groningen, Groningen, The Netherlands.

Ellis, J. and M. Bosi, 1999. *Options for Project Emission Baselines.* OECD and IEA information paper, Paris.

Gilecki, 2000. Personal communication with Ryszanol Gilecki, Agencja Rynku Energii S.A., Warsaw, Poland, on 14 March 2000.

Lawrence Berkeley National Laboratory, 1999. *International Network on Energy Demand in the Industrial Sector (INEDIS) Database.* Berkeley, CA: LBNL.

IISI, 1992. *Steel Statistical Yearbook 1992.* International Iron and Steel Institute, Brussels, Belgium.

IISI, 1998. *Energy use in the steel industry*, IISI, Committee on Energy, Brussels, Belgium

IISI, 1999. *World Steel in Figures Online, 1998.* Statistics published on the Internet (www.worldsteel.org), International Iron and Steel Institute, Brussels, Belgium.

IISI, 2000. *World Steel in Figures Online, 1999.* Statistics published on the Internet (www.worldsteel.org), International Iron and Steel Institute, Brussels, Belgium.

Kanjilal, Ashoke, 1998, *India Iron and Steel Plant Equipment,* US Foreign Commercial Service and US Department of State (www.tradeport.org/ts/countries/india/isa/isar0051.html)

Lazarus, M, S. Kartha, M. Ruth, S. Bernow, C. Dunmire, 1999. *Evaluation of Benchmarking as an Approach for Establishing Clean Development Baselines*, Tellus Institute, Boston, Stockholm Environmental Institute, Boston.

Olivier, J.G.J., A.F. Bouwman, C.W.M. van der Maas, J.J.M. Berdowski, C. Veldt, J.P.J. Bloos, A.J.H. Visschedijk and J.L. Zandveld (1996), *Description of EDGAR Version 2.0: A set of global emission inventories of greenhouse gases and ozone depletion substances for all anthropogenic and most natural sources on a per country basis and on 1°x1° grid*, RIVM, Bilthoven, The Netherlands.

Phylipsen, D., 2000. *International comparisons and national commitments,* PhD Thesis. Dept of Science, Technology and Society, Utrecht University, Utrecht, The Netherlands.

Price, L., D. Phylipsen, E. Worrell, 1999. *Energy Use and Carbon Dioxide Emissions in the Steel Sector in Key Developing Countries: Preliminary Sector Analysis*, Lawrence Berkeley National Laboratory, Berkeley.

Prus, Aleksandra, 1998, *Poland: Steel Industry*, US and Foreign Commercial Service and US Department of State (www.tradeport.org/ts/countries/poland/isa/isar0019.html)

Puhl, 1998. *Status of Research on Project Baselines under the FCCC and the Kyoto Protocol*, OECD Environment Directorate, Paris.

Sathaye, Jayant and Ashok Gadgil, LBL 1999, *Role of Development Banks in Promoting Industrial Energy Efficiency* (www.lbl.gov)

Steel Authority of India (SAIL), 1996. *Statistics for Iron & Steel Industry in India*, New Delhi: Steel Authority of India Ltd.

WEC, 1995. Energy Efficiency Improvement Utilizing High Technology - An Assessment of Energy Use in Industry and Buildings, World Energy Council, London.

Worrell, E., L. Price, N. Martin, J. Farla and R. Schaeffer, 1997. Energy intensity in the iron and steel industry: a comparison of physical and economic indicators, in: Energy Policy, V 25, Nos 7-9, pp 727-744.

Worrell, E., 2000. Personal communication with Dr E. Worrell, Lawrence Berkeley National Lab, Berkeley, CA, USA.

GLOSSARY

additive (or extender)	material(s) added to clinker to make cement
AEEI	autonomous energy efficiency improvement
AIJ	activities implemented jointly
AIXG	Annex I Experts Group on the United Nations Framework Convention on Climate Change (UNFCCC)
audit-based programmes	Programmes that rely on the systematic collection of data on building and energy system performance characteristics at the customer site. The goal of these programmes is typically to identify and quantify energy efficiency improvement opportunities in combination with an implementation plan.
baseload	The minimum amount of electric power delivered or required over a given period of time at a steady rate.
BAU	business as usual
bench tests	Tests of equipment performance characteristics conducted in a controlled environment such as a laboratory or manufacturer's test facility.
BF	blast furnace
blast furnace slag	One of the common additives used in cement. It is the by-product of iron and steel manufacture and grinding this additive for use in cement is energy intensive.
BOF	basic oxygen furnace
CDM	Clean Development Mechanism (project-based mechanism introduced in Article 12 of the Kyoto Protocol)
CFL	compact fluorescent lamp
CH_4	Methane
CHP	Combined heat and power. A plant that is designed to produce both heat and electricity

cli	Clinker
clinker	The key component of cement and the most GHG-intensive.
CO	coke oven
CO_2	carbon dioxide
combined cycle	An electric generating technology in which electricity is produced from otherwise lost waste heat exiting from one or more gas (combustion) turbines. This process increases the efficiency of the electric generating unit.
conversion efficiency	Efficiency at which a thermal power plant converts input fossil fuel (*i.e.* coal, gas, or oil) into electricity.
crediting lifetime	Length of time (in years) during which a project can generate emission credits.
demand-side management (DSM)	Utility programmes designed to control, limit or alter Energy consumption by the end user. DSM objectives may include energy conservation, load management, fuel substitution and load building.
diversity factor	The ratio of the peak demand of a population of energy-consuming equipment to the sum of the non-coincident peak demands of the individual equipment.
DR	direct reduction
DRI	direct reduced iron
dry process	A process whereby the raw materials for cement production are ground and then mixed (as a dry powder).
EAF	electric arc furnace
EEI	energy efficiency index
EIT	countries with economies in transition
EJ	exajoule (= 10^{18} Joule)
emission credits	Unit used for the measurement (*e.g.* in tonnes of CO_2-equivalent), transfer and acquisition of emission reductions associated with JI and CDM projects.
end-use indices (EUI)	The ratio of the energy use of a building, system or end-use over a given time period to a commonly recognised index of size or capacity. Examples include lighting energy use per square foot of floor area and motor energy use per unit of production output.

environmental credibility	Quality of a baseline with respect to realistically reflecting the emission level that would likely occur without the JI or CDM project(s).
environmental effectiveness	Extent to which the project-based mechanisms result in maximum emission reductions and maximum participation through JI and CDM projects, thereby contributing to achieving the objectives of the Kyoto Protocol.
EU or EU15	The 15 members states of the EU.
fluorescent lamps	A discharge lamp whereby a phosphor coating transforms ultraviolet light into visible light. Fluorescent lamps require a ballast that controls the starting and operation of the lamp.
free riding	A situation whereby a project generates emission credits, even though it is believed that the same project would have gone ahead, even in the absence of JI or CDM. The emission reductions claimed by the project would thus not really be "additional". Free riding therefore affects the number of projects obtaining credits under JI and CDM.
gaming	Actions or assumptions taken by the project developer and/or project host that would artificially inflate the baseline and therefore the emission reductions. Gaming therefore affects the amount of emission credits claimed by a JI or CDM project.
GHG	greenhouse gas
GJ	gigajoule (= 10^9 Joule)
greenfield projects	New projects (as opposed to existing plants that are refurbished)
grid	The layout of an electrical distribution system.
GWh	gigawatt hour, *i.e.* 10^9 Wh.
GWP	global warming potential
hp	horsepower
HPS	High pressure sodium lamps.
HVAC	Mechanical heating, ventilating and air-conditioning of buildings.
IEA	International Energy Agency

incandescent lamps	A lamp that produces visible light by heating a filament to incandescence by an electric current.
ISP	integrated steel plant
JI	Joint implementation (project-based mechanism introduced in article 6 of the Kyoto Protocol).
kWh$_e$	kilowatt hours of electricity use
leakage	Leakage occurs if actual emission reductions (or sink enhancements) from a CDM or JI project lead to increases in emissions (or sink decreasing) elsewhere.
load curve	A plot of the demand placed on an energy system during an hour, day, year or other specified time period.
load factor	Number of hours in a year during which a power plant is generating electricity.
market segment	A segment of a customer or end-user market identified by common demographic, firmographic or energy use characteristics. Examples include the single-family detached home segment in the residential sector; and the office building segment in the commercial sector.
MJ	megajoule (= 10^6 Joule)
Mt	million metric tons
mtoe	million tons of oil equivalent
multi-project baselines	Emission baselines (also referred to as "benchmarks" or "activity standards" in the literature) that can be applied to a number of similar projects, *e.g.* to all electricity generation CDM or JI projects in the same country.
nameplate data	Data provided by equipment manufacturers that identify the make, model and performance characteristics of the equipment. These data are published in the manufacturer's product literature and key data elements are affixed to the equipment on the nameplate. Often the equipment nameplate itself does not provide sufficient information for energy analysis.
N$_2$O	nitrous oxide
OECD	Organisation for Economic Co-operation and Development
off-peak load	The demand that occurs during the time period when the load is not at or near the maximum demand.

Order Form

OECD CENTRES

Please send your order by mail, fax, or by e-mail to your nearest OECD Centre. You can also order through the online service: www.oecd.org/bookshop

OECD BONN OFFICE

c/o DVG mbh (OECD)
Birkenmaarstrasse 8
D-53340 Meckenheim, Germany
Tel: (+49-2225) 926 166
Fax: (+49-2225) 926 169
E-mail: oecd@dvg.dsb.net
Internet: www.oecd.org/bonn

OECD MEXICO CENTRE

Edificio INFOTEC
Av. Presidente Mazarik 526
Colonia: Polanco
C.P. 11560 - Mexico D.F.
Tel: (+52-5) 281 12 09
Fax: (+52-5) 280 04 80
E-mail: mexico.contact@oecd.org
Internet: www.rtn.net.mx/ocde

OECD TOKYO CENTRE

Landic Akasaka Building
2-3-4 Akasaka, Minato-ku
Tokyo 107-0052, Japan
Tel: (+81-3) 3586 2016
Fax: (+81-3) 3584 7929
E-mail: center@oecdtokyo.org
Internet: www.oecdtokyo.org

OECD WASHINGTON CENTER

2001 L Street NW, Suite 650
Washington, D.C., 20036-4922, US
Tel: (+1-202) 785-6323
Toll-free number for orders:
(+1-800) 456-6323
Fax: (+1-202) 785-0350
E-mail: washington.contact@oecd.org
Internet: www.oecdwash.org

I would like to order the following publications

PUBLICATIONS	ISBN	QTY	PRICE*	TOTAL
☐ Emission Baselines: Estimating the Unknown	92-64-18543-7		$100	
☐ Energy Technology and Climate Change – A Call to Action	92-64-18563-1		$75	
☐ Dealing with Climate Change	92-64-18560-7		$100	
☐ Energy Labels and Standards	92-64-17691-8		$100	
☐ World Energy Outlook 2000	92-64-18513-5		$150	
☐ CO_2 Emissions from Fuel Combustion 1971-1998	92-64-08506-8		$150	
☐ Ancillary Benefits and Costs of Greenhouse Gas Mitigation: Proceedings of an Expert Workshop	92-64-18542-9		FF480	
☐ National Climate Policies and the Kyoto Protocol	92-64-17114-2		FF120	
☐ Action Against Climate Change	92-64-17113-4		FF120	
☐ Towards Sustainable Development	92-64-16080-9		FF155	

*Postage and packing fees will be added to each order.

DELIVERY DETAILS

Name _____ Organisation _____

Address _____

Country _____ Postcode _____

Telephone _____ Fax _____

PAYMENT DETAILS

☐ I enclose a cheque payable to IEA Publications for the sum of $ _____

☐ I enclose a cheque payable to OECD Publications for the sum of FF _____

☐ Please debit my credit card (tick choice).   ☐ Access/Mastercard ☐ Diners ☐ VISA ☐ AMEX

Card no: └─┴─┴─┴─┴─┴─┴─┴─┴─┴─┴─┴─┴─┴─┴─┴─┘

Expiry date: └─┴─┴─┴─┴─┘

Signature:

DISTRIBUTORS FOR OECD PUBLICATIONS
DISTRIBUTEURS DES PUBLICATIONS DE L'OCDE

GERIA-ALGÉRIE
mpagnie Algérienne de
Documentation et de Conseil
ADOC)
MIL cité
la n°25 Dely Ibrahim, Alger
/Fax: 213 2 36 57 18

RGENTINA-ARGENTINE
cina del Libro Internacional
. Cordoba 1877
20 Buenos Aires
/Fax: (54-1) 815-8156
mail: olilibro@satlink.com

STRALIA-AUSTRALIE
A. Information Services
. Whitehorse Road, P.O.B 163
cham, Victoria 3132
, (03) 9210.7777
.: (03) 9210.7788
ail: service@dadirect.com.au
rnet: www.dadirect.com.au

STRIA-AUTRICHE
old & Co.
ben 31, Wien 1
(0222) 533.50.14
.: (0222) 512.47.31.29

LGIUM-BELGIQUE
n De Lannoy
nue du Roi, Koningslaan 202
0 Bruxelles
, (02) 538.51.69
: (02) 538.08.41
ail: jean.de.lannoy@infoboard.be
rnet: www.jean-de-lannoy.be

n De Lannoy
e des Chevaliers, Riddersstraat 4
0 Bruxelles

NADA
ouf Publishing Company Ltd.
9 Canotek Road,
awa ONT K1J 9J3
(613) 745.2665
: (613) 745.7660
ail: order.dept@renoufbooks.com
rnet: www.renoufbooks.com

res:
1 1/2 Sparks Street,
ttawa ONT K1P 5R1
el. (613) 238.8985
ax: (613) 238.6041

2 Adelaide Street West,
oronto ONT M5H 3B8
el. (416) 363.3171
ax: (416) 363.5963

Éditions La Liberté Inc.
0 Chemin Sainte-Foy,
te-Foy PQ G1X 3V6
Fax: (418) 658.3763
ail: liberte@mediom.qc.ca

eral Publications Inc.
University Avenue, Suite 701
onto, ONT M5H 3B8
(416) 860.1611
: (416) 860.1608
ail: fedpubs@fedpubs.com
rnet: www.fedpubs.com

Publications Gouvernementales
5 Université
ntréal QC H3B 3A7
(514) 954.1633
: (514) 954.1635
ail: pubgouv@inforamp.net

For electronic publications only:
Ivation DataSystems Inc.
265 Carling Avenue, Suite 502
Ottawa ONT K1S 2E1
Tel. (613) 563.3993 Ext. 235
Fax: (613) 563.7233
E-mail: jec@ivation.com

CHINA-CHINE
China National Publications Import
    and Export Corporation (CNPIEC)
Serials Department
16 Gongti East Road
Chaoyang District
Beijing, 100020
Tel. (10) 6506-3070
Fax: (10) 6506-3101
E-mail: cnpiec@public3.bta.net.cn
Homepage: http://www.cnpiegc.com

Swindon Book Company, Ltd.
Astoria Bldg. 3/F
34 Ashley Road, Tsimshatsui
Kowloon, Hong Kong
Tel. 852-2376-2062
Fax: 852-2376-0685
E-mail: swindon@netvigator.com

CZECH REPUBLIC-
RÉPUBLIQUE TCHÈQUE
USIS - Publications Service
Havelkova 22, 130 00 Praha 3
Tel. (02) 2423.0907
Fax: (02) 2422.9433
E-mail: pospisilovaj@usiscr.cz
Internet: www.nis.cz

DENMARK-DANEMARK
Munksgaard Book and
    Subscription Service
35, Nørre Søgade, P.O. Box 2148
1016 København K
Tel. (33) 12.85.70
Fax: (33) 12.93.87
E-mail: subscription.service
    @mail.munksgaard.dk
Internet: www.munksgaard.dk

J. H. Schultz Information A/S
Herstedvang 12
26 20 Alberslund
Tel. 43 63 23 00
Fax: 43 63 19 69
E-mail: schultz@schultz.dk
Internet: www.schultz.dk

EGYPT-ÉGYPTE
The Middle East Observer
41Sherif Street, Cairo
Tel/Fax: (2) 393.9732
E-mail: fouda@soficom.com.eg

FINLAND-FINLANDE
StockmannAkateeminen Kirjakauppa
Keskuskatu 1, P.O. Box 128
00100 Helsinki
Tel. (358) 9 121 4418
Fax: (358) 9 121 4435
E-mail: akajournals@stockmann.fi
Internet: www.akateeminen.com

FRANCE
OECD
Mail Orders 2, rue André-Pascal
75775 Paris Cedex 16
Fax: 33 (0)1.49.10.42.76
Enquiries: Tel. 33 (0) 1 45 24 81 22
Fax: 33 (0) 1 45 24 19 50
E-mail: sales@oecd.org
Online Ordering:
www.oecd.org/bookshop
Internet:www.oecd.org

Dawson
B.P. 40, 91121 Palaiseau Cedex
Tel. 01.69.10.47.00
Fax : 01.64.54.83.26

Documentation Française
29, quai Voltaire, 75007 Paris
Tel. 01.40.15.70.00

Edernet
Maison Detchartenia
Rue de Kiroleta
64480 Ustaritz
Tel. 05 59 93 03 04
Fax : 05 59 93 16 06
E-mail: bharriague@wannadoo.fr

Gibert Jeune (Droit-Économie)
6, place Saint Michel, 75006 Paris
Tel. 01.43.25.91.19

Librairie du Commerce International
10, avenue d'Iéna, 75016 Paris
Tel. 01.40.73.34.60

Librairie Dunod
Université Paris Dauphine
Place du Maréchal de Lattre de
Tassigny
75016 Paris
Tel. 01.44.05.40.13

Librairie Lavoisier
11, rue Lavoisier, 75008 Paris
Tel. 01.42.65.39.95

Librairie de l'Université
12a, rue Nazareth
13100 Aix en Provence
Tel. 04.42.26.18.08
E-mail: liuniv@aix.pacwan.net

Documentation Française
165, rue Garibaldi, 69003 Lyon
Tel. 04.78.63.23.02

Librairie Sauramps
Le Triangle
34967 Montpellier Cedex 2
Tel. 04.67.06.78.78
Fax : 04.67.58.27.69

A la Sorbonne Actual
23, rue de l'Hôtel des Postes
06000 Nice
Tel. 04.93.13.77.77
Fax : 04.93.80.75.69

GERMANY-ALLEMAGNE
OECD Bonn Centre
August Bebel Allee 6
53175 Bonn
Tel. (0228) 959.12.15
Fax: (0228) 959.12.18
E-mail: bonn.contact@oecd.org
Internet: www.oecd.org/bonn

GREECE-GRÈCE
Librairie Kauffmann
Stadiou 28, 105 64 Athens
Tel. (01) 32.55.320
Fax: (01) 32.30.320

HUNGARY-HONGRIE
Euro Info Service
Margitsziget, Európa Ház
1138 Budapest
Tel. (1) 111.60.61
Fax: (1) 302.50.35
E-mail: euroinfo@mail.matav.hu
Internet: www.euroinfo.hu

ICELAND-ISLANDE
Mál og Menning
Laugavegi 18, Pósthólf 392
121 Reykjavik
Tel. (1) 552.4240
Fax: (1) 562.3523
E-mail: mm@centrum.is

INDIA-INDE
Oxford Book and Stationery Co.
Scindia House, New Delhi 110001
Tel. (11) 331.5896/5308
Fax: (11) 332.26.39
E-mail: oxford.publ@axcess.net.in

17 Park Street, Calcutta 700016
Tel. 240832

INDONESIA-INDONÉSIE
PDII-LIPI
P.O. Box 4298, Jakarta 12042,
Tel.: 62-21-573-3465
Fax: 62-21-573-3467
E-mail: PDII-info@pdii.lipi.go.id
Internet: http://www.pdii.lipi.go.id

IRELAND-IRLANDE
Government Supplies Agency
    Publications
4/5 Harcourt Road, Dublin 2
Tel. 661.31.11
Fax: 475.27.60

ISRAEL-ISRAËL
Praedicta
5 Shatner Street, P.O. Box 34030
Jerusalem 91430
Tel. (2) 652.84.90/1/2
Fax: (2) 652.84.93

R.O.Y. International
P.O. Box 13056, Tel Aviv 61130
Tel. (3) 64 99 469
Fax: (3)64 86 039
E-mail: royil@netvision.net.il

Palestinian Authority & Middle East:
INDEX Information Services
P.O.B. 19502, Jerusalem
Tel. (2) 627.16.34
Fax: (2) 627.12.19

ITALY-ITALIE
Libreria Commissionaria Sansoni
Via Duca di Calabria, 1/1
50125 Firenze
Tel. (055) 64831
Fax: (055) 641257
E-mail: licosa@ftbcc.it

Libreria Commissionaria Sansoni
Via Bartolini 29, 20155 Milano
Tel. (02) 36.50.83

Editrice e Libreria Herder
Piazza Montecitorio 120
00186 Roma
Tel. (06) 67 94 628
Fax: (06)67 84 751

Libreria Hoepli
Via Hoepli 5, 20121 Milano
Tel. (02) 86.54.46
Fax: (02) 805.28.86

Libreria Scientifica
Dott. Lucio de Biasio "A.E.I.O.U."
Via Coronelli, 6, 20146 Milano
Tel. (02) 48.95.45.52
Fax: (02) 48.95.45.48

JAPAN-JAPON
OECD Tokyo Centre
Landic Akasaka Building
2-3-4 Akasaka, Minato-ku
Tokyo 107-0052
Tel. (81.3) 3586.2016
Fax: (81.3) 3584.7929
E-mail: center@oectokyo.org
Internet: www.oecdtokyo.org

DISTRIBUTORS FOR OECD PUBLICATIONS
DISTRIBUTEURS DES PUBLICATIONS DE L'OCDE

KOREA-CORÉE
Kyobo Book Centre Co. Ltd.
P.O. Box 1658, Kwanghwamoon
Seoul
Tel. 82-2-397-3479
Fax: 82-2-735-0030
E-mail: JMS@kyobobook.co.kr

MALAYSIA-MALAYSIE
University of Malaya Co-operative
    Bookshop Ltd.
University of Malaya
P.O. Box 1127, Jalan Pantai Baru
59700 Kuala Lumpur
Tel. 60-3-756-5000/756-5425
Fax: 60-3-755-4424

MALTA-MALTE
Miller Distributors Ltd.
Miller House
Tarxien Road, Airport Way, Luqa
Tel. 66.44.88
Fax: 67.67.99
E-mail: gwirth@usa.net

MEXICO-MEXIQUE
OECD Mexico Centre
Edificio INFOTEC
Av. San Fernando no. 37
Col. Toriello Guerra
Tlalpan C.P. 14050, Mexico D.F.
Tel. (525) 528 10 38
Fax : (525) 606 13 07
E-mail: mexico.contact@oecd.org
Internet: rtn.net.mx/ocde/

MOROCCO-MAROC
Librairie Internationale
70, rue T'ssoule, B.P. 302, Rabat
Tel. 212 7 75 01 83
Fax: 212 7 75 86 61

NETHERLANDS-PAYS-BAS
SDU Uitgeversexterne Fondsen
Postbus 20014, 2500
EA's-Gravenhage
Voor bestelligen:
Tel. (070) 37.89.880
Fax: (070) 37.89.773
Internet: www.sdu.nl

De Lindeboom Internationale
    Publikaties b.v.
P.O. Box 202, 7480 AE
Haaksgergen
Tel. (31) 053.574.000
Fax: (31) 053.572.9296
Internet:
    home.worldonline.nl/~lindeboo
E-mail: lindeboo@worldonline.nl

Subscription Agency:
SWETS & ZEITLINGER BV
Heereweg 347B, P.O. Box 830
2160 SZ Lisse
Tel. 252.435.111
Fax: 252.415.888
E-mail: infoho@swets.nl
Internet: www.swets.nl

NEW ZEALAND-
NOUVLELLE-ZÉLANDE
GP Legislation Services
P.O. Box 12418, Thorndon
Wellington
Tel. (04) 496.5655
Fax: (04) 496.5698
Integrated Economic Services Ltd.
P.O. Box 3627, Wellington
Tel: (04) 499.1148
Fax: (04) 499.1972
E-mail: oasis@clear.net.nz
Homepage:
    www.oasisbooks.co.nz

NORWAY-NORVÈGE
Swets Norge AS
Ostensjoveien 18, P.O. Box 6512
Etterstad
0606 Oslo
Tel. (22) 97.45.00
Fax: (22) 97.45.45
E-mail: nicagen@swets.nl

PAKISTAN
Mirza Book Agency
65 Shahrah Quaid-E-Azam
Lahore 54000
Tel. (42) 723.17.30
Fax: (42) 576.37.14

PHILIPPINES
National Book Store Inc.
Anvil Publishing Inc.
3F, Rudgen II Building
No. 17, Shaw Blvd., Pasig City
Metro Manila 1600
Tel. 63-2-633-6136
Fax : 63-2-631-3766
E-mail: anvil@fc.emc.com.ph
    Pubdept@anvil.com.ph

POLAND-POLOGNE
Ars Polona
Krakowskie Prezdmiéscle 7
00-950 Warszawa
Tel. (22) 826.47.60
Fax : (22) 826.86.73
E-mail:
arspolona@arspolona.com.pl

PORTUGAL
Livraria Portugal
Rua do Carmo 70-74, Apart. 2681,
1200 Lisboa
Tel. (01) 347.49.82/5
Fax: (01) 347.02.64

SINGAPORE-SINGAPOUR
Hemisphere Publication Services
Golden Wheel Building, #04-03
41, Kallang Pudding Road
Singapore 349316
Tel. 65-741-5166
Fax: 65-742-9356
E-mail: ashgate@asianconnect.com
Homepage: http://www.ashgate.com

SLOVENIA-SLOVÉNIE
Gospodarski Vestnik Publishing
    Group
Dunajska cesta 5, 1000 Ljubljana
Tel. (61) 133.03.54
Fax: (61) 133.91.28
E-mail: repansekj@gvestnik.si
Internct: www.gvestnık.si

SPAIN-ESPAGNE
Mundi-Prensa Libros S.A.
Castello 37, Apartado 1223
28001 Madrid
Tel.914 36 37 00
Fax: 915 75 39 98
E-mail: libreria@mundiprensa.es
Internet: www.mundiprensa.com

Mundi-Prensa Barcelona
Consell de Cent No. 391
08009 Barcelona
Tel. (93) 488.34.92
Fax: (93) 487.76.59
E-mail: barcelona@mundiprensa.es

Libreria de la Generalitat
Rambla dels Estudis,118
08002 Barcelona
(Suscripciones) Tel. (93) 318.80.12
(Publicaciones) Tel. (93) 302.67.23
Fax: (93) 412.18.54

SWEDEN-SUÈDE
Akadembokhandeln
P.O. Box 301 61
104 25 Stockholm
Tel. (08) 728.25.00
Fax: (08) 31.30.44
E-mail:
    info@city.akademibokhandeln.se
Internet:
www.akademibokhandeln.se

For electronic publications only:
STATISTICS SWEDEN
Informationsservice
115 81 Stockholm
Tel. 8 783 5066
Fax: 8 783 4045
Internet: www.scb.se
E-mail: scb@scb.se

SWITZERLAND-SUISSE
ADECO
Chemin du Lacuez 41
1807 Blonay
Tel. (021) 943 26 73
Fax: (021) 943 36 95
E-mail: mvandier@worldcom.ch

Librairie Payot S.A.
4, place Pépinet, CP 3212
1002 Lausanne
Tel. (021) 341.32.29
Fax: (021) 341.32.35
E-mail: payotlivre@bluewin.ch

Dynapresse Marketing S.A.
38 avenue Vibert, 1227 Carouge
Tel. (022) 308.07.70
Fax: (022) 308.08.59
E-mail: dynapresse.abonnements
@dynapresse.ch

See also:
OECD Bonn Centre
August Bebel Allee 6
53175 Bonn
Tel. (0228) 959.12.15
Fax: (0228) 959.12.18
E-mail: bonn.contact@oecd.org
Internet: www.oecd.org/bonn

TAIWAN
Engineering Book Co. Ltd.
2F, No. 13, Chung Yuan E. Road
Hsin Chuang, Taipei Hsien
Tel. (886-2) 2279 7182
Fax: (886-2) 2277-6183

THAILAND-THÄILANDE
Suksit Siam Co., Ltd.
113, 115 Fuang Nakhon Rd.
Opp. Wat Rajbopith
Bangkok 10200
Tel. 66-2-225-9531/2
Fax: 66-2-225-9540,222-5188

TRINIDAD & TOBAGO,
CARIBBEAN
TRINITÉ ET TOBAGO,
CARAÏBES
Systematics Studies Limited
St. Augustine Shopping Centre
Eastern Main Road, Saint Augustine
Tel. (868) 645-8466
Fax: (868) 645-8467
E-mail: tobe@trinidad.net

TUNISIA-TUNISIE
Grande Librairie Spécialisée
Fendri Ali
Avenue Haffouz
Imm El-Intilaka Bloc B 1
Sfax 3000
Tel. (216-4) 296 855
Fax: (216-4) 298.270

TURKEY-TURQUIE
Dünya Infotel
"Globus'' Dünya Basinevi
100 Yil Mahallesi
34440, Bagcilar Istanbul
Tel. (90-212) 629.08.08 Ext. 247
Fax: (90-212) 629.46.89
E-mail: infotel@dunya-gazete.com
Internet:
www.dunya.com/infotel.html

UNITED KINGDOM-
ROYAUME-UNI
The Stationery Office Ltd.
49 High Holborn
London WC1V 6HB
Branches at: Belfast, Birmingham
Bristol, Edinburgh, Manchester

The Stationery Office Ltd.
Postal orders only:
    P.O. Box 276, , London SW8 5I
General enquiries:
    Tel. (0171) 873 0011
Fax: (0171) 873 8463
Internet: www.theso.co.uk

For electronic publications only:
Data Beuro
19 The Thinnings
Flitwick Beds MK45 1DY
Tel. (01525) 752.689
Fax: (01525) 752.690
E-mail: sales@databeuro.com
Internet: www.databeuro.com

UNITED STATES-
ÉTATS-UNIS
OECD Washington Center
2001 L Street N.W., Suite 650
Washington, D.C. 20036-4922
Tel. (202) 785.6323
Toll free number for orders:
(800) 456-6323
Fax: (202) 785.0350
E-mail:
washington.contact@oecd.org
Internet: www.oecdwash.org

VIETNAM
Xunhasaba
32 Hai Ba Trung Street
Hanoi
Tel.: 84-4-825-2313
Fax: 84-4-825-2860

Subscriptions to OECD periodica
may also be placed through major
subscription agencies.

Orders can be sent to our distribute
in your country, or one of the five
OECD Centres: Bonn, Mexico, Pa
Tokyo or Washington.

Orders and inquiries from countrie
where distributors have not yet bee
appointed should be sent to:
OECD Publications
2, rue André-Pascal,
75775 Paris Cedex 16, France.

OECD PUBLICATIONS
2, rue André-Pascal,
75775 Paris CEDEX 16
PRINTED IN FRANCE
(97 2000 13 1P)
ISBN 92-64-18543-7
No. 51513